MISSIONARY LIFE
AND WORK

MISSIONARY LIFE AND WORK

*A Discussion of Principles and Practices
of Missions*

By
HAROLD R. COOK

MOODY PRESS
CHICAGO

Library of Congress Catalog Card Number: 59-11469

Copyright ©, 1959, by
THE MOODY BIBLE INSTITUTE
OF CHICAGO

Ninth Printing, 1974

ISBN: 0-8024-5425-9

Printed in the United States of America

To
ADDISON AND MARY
whose consistent Christian living
and fellowship
have been a real help
and inspiration

PREFACE

THE SUBJECT OF THIS BOOK is broad—so broad that it is almost presumptuous for a single author to attempt to deal with it. It covers the broad range of missionary experience from the application to the mission society through the most common matters of life and work on the field to the period of furlough and its ministry.

Yet, presumptuous or not, there has long been a need for such a book. Teachers of Missions have asked for it. More than a dozen years ago I myself tried to persuade another experienced missionary and teacher to write it. The growing number of missionary candidates in our training schools has called for it. Dr. A. J. Brown's *The Foreign Missionary* is still useful but it does not fully meet our need today. And other books in the field are either limited in their scope or lack the touch of personal experience.

This book is intended specially for missionary candidates in training. They need to see something of the situation that will face them as they go abroad. They need to be aware of some of the problems. Many a new missionary has suffered a severe jolt when he has come face to face with a grim problem that he didn't even suspect existed in missionary life. It may be a problem in his own life, or in someone else's or in the work. But if he knows that such a problem may come he is in some degree prepared to meet it. It won't bowl him over when it comes.

The amount of space given to each subject does not indicate its relative importance. For example, there is an extended section on missionary correspondence. This stress seems necessary because so little has been written on the subject and it is one area in which there is a great need for improvement. On the other hand, the great amount of attention given to languages and language learning is fully justified by the importance of the subject. It is a basic matter in missionary service, yet it is also one in which we have often shown ourselves to be extremely weak.

The personal style of approach that especially characterizes the first part of the book is the one that I have used in my own classes in Moody Bible Institute. I have also tried to make the treatment as simple and practical as possible for the average missionary. There is a certain amount of theory involved, but in general the book, as a textbook, follows the usually accepted principles.

Just one further word. The instructions in this book will be useful to him whose heart is in the work. Missions is in the heart. Over and over in the book there is an emphasis on heart attitudes. It is entirely possible to know a great deal about methods and principles and still fail as a missionary. It is also possible to follow some methods that are not in themselves sound and to succeed in spite of it because the heart is right. But the really effective missionary will be concerned about both. He will make sure that he is really Christ's "sent one" at heart, and he will continually seek the best ways of carrying out his great task.

God bless you as you consider this task.

HAROLD R. COOK

Moody Bible Institute
Chicago, Illinois

CONTENTS

PART ONE

The Missionary Candidate and Probationer

PART TWO

The Missionary's Personal Life

PART THREE

Missionary Relationships

PART FOUR
The Missionary's Work

PART FIVE
Furlough

PART ONE

*The Missionary Candidate
and Probationer*

CHAPTER ONE

INTRODUCTION

THE MEETING WAS OVER. The speaker's fervent appeal was still ringing in the hearts of his listeners. One and another came forward to speak to him. Some had unanswered questions. Others merely wanted to tell him how they had been blessed by his talk.

One eager-eyed young man waited until the others had finished. Then he stepped forward. Earnestly he said to the missionary, "I wonder if you would mind telling me how I can get an application for your mission."

"An application?" queried the missionary. "Do you mean that you want to become a missionary?"

"Yes, I do," answered the young man quickly. "I believe the Lord wants me in His service on the mission field. But I wasn't sure until tonight just where I ought to serve. Your message answered my question. I would like to work with your mission."

"But what about preparation?" The missionary hesitated.

"Oh, that's all right!" laughed the young man. "I've been getting ready, even though I didn't know just where I was going. I expect to finish my course next June. But I'd like to make my application now, so I won't be delayed in getting out to the field."

"That's a good idea," said the missionary. "It does take quite awhile to process an application. But there's one thing I ought to mention. I don't suppose you have been in touch with our mission society before?"

"No," answered the young man slowly.

"Then they probably won't send you an application right away." The young man's face fell.

"You see, they like to learn a little bit about you first. It isn't like applying for a job when you apply for missionary service. You'll probably be giving your life to the work. At least you'll be spending some years in a place far away from here. And you'll have a great deal of responsibility. So they want to get acquainted with you and make sure you are well acquainted with them."

"But isn't that what the application is for?"

"Yes, partly. But sometimes the mission doesn't have to go through the whole procedure of a formal application to know how to advise a young person. All they need is a little preliminary information. For example, suppose they are not satisfied with your course of preparation. They may want you to take some additional studies that will prepare you better to fit into their program. But you may not want to take those studies. Maybe you don't think the service they have in mind is just what you wanted. Then you can turn to another society without the stigma of being formally rejected by the first one."

"It sounds reasonable. But really I don't think there will be any question. From what you said tonight, I'm sure that you folks are doing the sort of work the Lord has been preparing me for."

"I hope so. We certainly do need help. But I just wanted you to know that the mission will probably want you to fill out some preliminary papers first. After they look those over, if they're satisfied they'll send you the formal application blanks."

"I suppose that will take quite a bit of time, so it's a good thing I'm getting started early."

"Yes, it does take time. But this is too serious a matter to push through in a hurry. You are thinking of a life service, so you want to be sure, and so do we. That's why we usually encourage young people to get in touch with the mission as early as possible. It gives time to become acquainted and get problems straightened out. Some of our candidates are appointed even before they finish their schooling—usually during their final year."

"That sounds hopeful. But when they do send me the application blanks, would you mind telling me just what I should be ready for?"

"Not at all. But why don't you come to my room where we can talk things over a little more comfortably? The mission will probably send you full instructions, but sometimes it's good to talk ahead of time with someone who has been through it."

*   *   *

That is just what we want to do in these next chapters. The author does not claim personally to have gone through all the experiences discussed. It would take a number of missionary lives to do that. But from his own experiences, his observations in various fields, countless talks with missionaries and mission leaders, as well as prolonged study, he wants to talk over with you many of the principles and practical problems involved in *missionary life and work*.

CHAPTER TWO

MAKING APPLICATION

F IRST LET'S DISCUSS the matter of making application to the mission society. Elsewhere we have dealt with the qualifications and the kind of preparation you need to have.[1] It is understood that you have already been in touch with the board and are persuaded that it is the mission for you. So far as you know, they can make good use of your services. Their correspondence has been encouraging, so you decide to make formal application.

MOTIVATION

Just one thing before you fill out those final papers. We are going at this in a businesslike way, but sometimes the business angle tends to obscure the spiritual. Are you *sure* that your motives in seeking appointment are the right ones? Only you can tell, for no one else can look into your heart. You can give the right answers to the questions in the application, but what is your real reason for wanting to go out as a missionary? Is it the work that intrigues you, the life of the missionary, or the opportunity to do good? Do you feel that it is simply the highest form of Christian service? Are you more interested in the country or the people? Are you more concerned about their physical plight or their spiritual destitution? Do you merely *want* to go, or do you feel that you *must* go? In other words, are you going on your own initiative or is the Spirit of Christ really sending you? Are you more concerned about finding your own "place in life" or about doing what He wants you to do?

Don't be surprised that we come back to this matter of motivation. Of course you may have faced the issue when you first decided to become

[1] *An Introduction to the Study of Christian Missions.* Chicago. Moody Press, 1954.

16

a missionary. Perhaps you have faced it a number of times since then. But it is a question to which we cannot give too much serious attention. One of the greatest weaknesses in missionary work today is the lack of sufficient or proper motivation among some of the missionaries. If your motives are inadequate, you will either give up in the face of difficulties and discouragement, or you will carry out your duties in a perfunctory way. If your motives are improper, they will lead you in ways that may bring recognition or renown to yourself or to your organization but will not enhance the glory of your Lord and Saviour. We need men and women who know that God has sent them and who place His cause above every other interest. So be sure this matter is settled in your own heart.

PURPOSEFUL QUESTIONS

Now you have the application in your hands and you are ready to fill it out. What a lot of questions! They seem to go into many very personal matters. Some of them not only ask about you, but about your parents and grandparents! Are they all really necessary? What is the purpose of asking these things?

To understand the application you need to realize that it is more than a simple request for appointment. The questions are designed to give a word picture of the applicant. You see, the missionary is fully as important as the talents and training he may have. In fact, he is more important. He is never completely trained for all the work he will have to do. The question is: "Will he fit into the work in a useful way, and can he keep on growing in usefulness by adjusting to new situations, new problems and new tasks?" You may be well qualified for missionary service in general, but the mission wants you to know how you will fit into *its* fellowship and program. You may be qualified now for a specific task, but the mission knows that many of its most useful missionaries are not now doing the work they had in mind when they first went to the field. They adapted themselves to new tasks. Are you that sort?

So all those questions do have a purpose. They help the mission to picture *you*—not just the *surface you* but the *inner you*. They are aimed at certain features that the mission knows from experience are important. Therefore, completely honest answers are necessary and they give the most accurate picture. It is easy to see the mission's purpose in this question: "To what magazines do you regularly subscribe?" Or, "What books have you read during the past year, other than textbooks?" The answers reveal something of your interests. If you put down only those that you think would meet the approval of the mission, you give a false picture. Moreover, incomplete answers sometimes rouse the suspicion of the candidate secretary. They make him wonder if you are completely candid. Of course you do wish to "put your best foot forward," but it should be in the right way.

It is not always so easy to see the purpose behind other questions. Because of this, and because some of the questions are not very clearly worded at times, the candidate is puzzled to know how to answer. Many young people have brought me their papers asking help with questions. Occasionally I have had to say, "You had better write the mission; I am not sure just what they do want." This is the best procedure. Don't turn in the application with some questions unanswered. You will get a request to supply the missing information. Make sure you know what is wanted and then answer to the best of your ability.

REFERENCES

The mission will ask for references, including teachers, employers, pastor, etc. Where you have the liberty of selecting references, there is nothing wrong in giving those who are most sympathetic to you and your missionary purpose. That is what the mission usually expects. It is courteous for you to let your friends know that you have given their names. It is better still to ask their permission first. However, this is not necessary for business relationships or school authorities.

MEDICAL EXAMINATION

The report of a thorough medical examination usually accompanies the application. Sometimes the mission specifies the doctor, sometimes not. Both for your own sake and for the mission you should get as good an examination as possible. The careful family doctor may be all right. He knows your health history. But if he does not know the demands of missionary life and might slide over a number of items on the blank as not being important, probably it would be better to go to someone else. In some cases the mission will demand a final checkup by its own physician before you sail.

SUPPLEMENTARY INFORMATION

Obviously, for a mission to accept a candidate for missionary service merely on the basis of his written application and the replies of his references is risky. The picture the application gives is sketchy at best, the references usually give as favorable a report as they can. Missions use a variety of ways to supplement this information.

A simple way is to ask each one of the friends given as reference: "Will you give us the names and addresses of three other persons who know the candidate well?" In this way they may receive information from some who are not prejudiced in your favor. Often the mission has a representative interview you and report his impressions. Or, he may make inquiries about you. Sometimes you are expected to meet with a committee representing the mission. You even may be required to appear before the board itself. The purpose is to get to know you personally and draw firsthand conclusions. They will usually try to put you at ease. In fact, you seldom will be invited to meet with such a group unless they are already somewhat favorably disposed toward you.

Some missions have periodic candidate schools that they require their candidates to attend. They may ask candidates to spend a short time in the mission home. In either case, this is usually the last step before acceptance. It gives the mission an opportunity to get acquainted with the candidate in intimate contacts of day-by-day relationship. It helps them to see how he gets along with others. At the same time they can give the candidate instruction in the principles and practices of the mission and other helpful material.

In line with the modern trend toward the use of psychological tests, some missions have adapted them to missionary purposes. At least one mission has a psychiatrist on its staff who administers the tests and counsels candidates. All of this is an attempt to get an objective evaluation of the personality of the candidate and his aptitude for missionary work. There are definite limitations to the usefulness of such tests, as the psychologists themselves recognize, but in the hands of trained examiners they appear to be helpful.[2]

Some missions on occasion have used another test plan. Suppose, for

[2]See E. K. Higdon, *New Missionaries for New Days*. St. Louis, Bethany Press, 1956. Some missions, however, are now questioning the value of these tests. See Frank W. Price and Kenyon E. Moyer, *Mission Board Policies with Relation to Missionary Personnel*, New York, Missionary Research Library, July 25, 1958.

example, that you apply to the mission as soon as you finish your schooling. What do they really know about your ability to do missionary work? What can they find out? They can investigate your character and your talents. They can readily find out about your attainments in scholarship. They can evaluate your personality. They can learn something about your dedication to Christ and to His gospel. But how will you work out in an actual missionary situation?

You have spent most of your life in school. For some years you have even been away from your home church. Only on vacations have you visited it. During these years you could not take an active part in its work. Of course you attended church while you were in school. But transient students are more likely to be ministered to than to minister. You may have gone from church to church, choosing the one that offered the most interesting program on a particular Sunday.

In Bible school you are likely to have had some practical Christian work assignments. They do provide a certain amount of experience. But often they are not supervised, and they take only a few hours out of your busy student life. They do not involve the same sort of responsibility that full-time service would. A student pastorate is better. Yet only a limited number of missionary candidates have such experience.

So at times a mission asks certain candidates to spend a year or two in full-time church work or home mission work before going abroad. Or they ask teachers to get some experience in their profession, just as a doctor would have to take an internship. Missions do not want to send novices to the field. Untried workers, no matter what their schooling, are a risk.

Yet, except for professional and technical workers, missions have not shown much uniformity in making such requirement. The weakness is especially noticeable in many who are sent out for general evangelistic or church work. Some evangelistic missionaries have had little or no experience in either public or personal evangelism before going abroad. Many assigned to work with the church on the field, or to establish a church, know only the theories of the classroom and the little they have seen of its operations as members of a church at home.

A number of missions have welcomed the establishment of the program known as *Missionary Internship*.[3] It offers a well-organized plan in co-operation with churches of different denominations. The basic idea

[3]12735 Puritan Ave., Detroit, Mich.

is: The missionary candidate is assigned for seven months to work with a co-operating church under the supervision of the pastor. He is not simply a pastor's assistant. He is expected to do a job that otherwise would not get done. There is special emphasis on visitation and personal evangelism, which are so important in missionary work.

On its part, the church undertakes to support the candidate while he is with them. In addition, on one day of the week all candidates from one area meet to have fellowship and receive instruction and counsel. They share experiences, get a Bible lesson, and receive instruction in soul-winning and personality adjustment. Since the directors are men of considerable missionary experience, the program has proved very helpful. More and more missions are sending at least some candidates to get this experience.

DELAYS IN PROCESSING

If you are like most young people, you will probably become impatient before you finally receive word of your acceptance by the mission. It is true that processing an application often does seem to take a very long time. Delay is unavoidable. Usually a mission can take no definite action until all the papers are in. Many an impatient young candidate has written to the board to ask what has been done about his application, only to find that a friend has failed to send in the reference papers. He probably put them aside, and then forgot. This probably is one of the most common causes of delay.

There are other things, too. It must be remembered that much of the work of missions is carried on with the voluntary services of busy men. It is true of most of the members on many mission boards. If, as sometimes happens, members of the board, widely separated, have to review the papers of each applicant, that alone will take time. They may have to await a regular meeting of the board to make a formal decision. If some question is raised that calls for further investigation or correspondence, the decision may be delayed much longer. However, when planning a lifetime of service, you like to feel that your application has merited careful and prayerful consideration.

Then one day you receive the wonderful word that you have been accepted. You are no longer a candidate but *a missionary under appointment.*

CHAPTER THREE

APPOINTMENT AND PREPARATIONS
TO SAIL

APPOINTMENT BY THE MISSION BOARD is an important step. It fixes the direction in which one is going to move. Now you can plan with greater definiteness. Offers from friends to help provide outfit, passage and support can be accepted. When invited to speak in a meeting, you can let it be known you are under appointment to the mission field.

Appointment is only one step in getting to the field. There are many others to be taken. Sometimes they will come with breathtaking rapidity, especially if the need on the field is urgent and there are no hindrances. But sometimes they will seem to come with exasperating slowness, as when the mission says there must be full support pledged before sailing. You haven't the foggiest notion where it is all going to come from. There will be emergencies when you will need to act promptly and decisively. More often you will have to wait patiently on the Lord. If your trust is in Him and you are following His guidance, no move is made too soon or too late.

Of course you will want to know what step to take next. Some missions give fairly complete instructions. Some will take you in charge and do most things for you; others will leave most things to your initiative. They do not have the staff to help appointees as they would like. There are certain problems that will have to be met before sailing. In any case, if the mission helps to meet them, well and good. If not, you should know something about them yourself.

DEPUTATION WORK

First is the problem commonly called "deputation work." In simplest terms, it is the problem of making known to friends and to the Church in general the work to which you have been called, with a view to interesting them in it. Notice that I have not said, "to raise funds." That is included, but it isn't the whole thing. In fact you shouldn't even think of fund raising as the principal objective of deputation work. This is true, regardless of the mission from which you go.

Suppose that you are appointed by a mission that takes all the responsibility for raising your financial support. To some it might seem that then deputation work would not be needed. In a financial sense that may be true. (Usually the mission is glad to get what help it can.) But there is still need for deputation work. You may not need money, but missions cannot be run on money alone. The mission, and you personally, need the interest and the prayers of those people at home. Does intercessory prayer mean anything to you? Then how can you presume to do the Lord's work without it? May this not be the reason why so often a missionary settles down to a routine and perfunctory performance of his tasks? A missionary needs the consciousness that the church has sent him out, not just the board. He needs to know that Christian people at home are keenly interested in what he is doing, that they will give him the spiritual support without which he cannot succeed.

Your mission may not assume responsibility for raising your financial support. Most "faith" missions do not. There are denominational missions, too, that expect your support to be individually underwritten before you leave for the field. They will give help, but at least in part the missionary must raise his support. Then deputation work has increased importance. Without it you may not get to the field.

Here is a real danger: Your deputation ministry may become largely mercenary. You may become absorbed with the necessity for raising your support. You are likely to consider every appointment in the light of what it may produce. Your conversations with Christian people may gravitate toward money. The thought is with you morning, afternoon and evening. Yet, who can blame you? The lack of money may be the one thing that is delaying your departure for the field, so it becomes uppermost in your thoughts. At the same time you have an uncomfortable feeling that it should not be so.

There is only one satisfactory way to combat this danger. Get a sounder attitude toward deputation work in general. Look at this work as an avenue of ministry. Christians at home need to get a missionary vision. They need to be inspired by the example of young people who are willing to follow Christ to the limit. They need to get acquainted with missions and missionaries. Their interest in the missionary task of the Church needs to be aroused and sustained and directed. As a missionary appointee you can do something to help fill this need, for you are actually going out as a missionary. To some who meet you and hear you, you will become the embodiment of the missionary enterprise.

What about the money? "Your heavenly Father knoweth that ye have need of all these things." Then why should you take anxious thought for the supply of your needs? Didn't God call you to this service? Isn't He able to provide? Do you think you can live the life of faith on the mission field if you can't do it before you get there?

But how does God provide? In a multitude of ways. He often seems to delight in doing it in ways we could not foresee. The sources we count on often fail. Those from which we expect nothing may prove to be a mainstay. But generally we can say this: your support will come from churches or individuals, or both, who are either personally interested in you or are interested in the work you are going to do. They won't support what they don't know about. Neither will they support what they are not interested in. Under pressure they may occasionally make a donation. But the steady, dependable support that is needed in missions comes from those who are genuinely interested.

God is able to supply your needs miraculously. Once in awhile He does. He doesn't need a lot of avenues through which to send the necessary funds. One may be enough. But normally, for the good of the work and the blessing of the church, He uses more than one. So your job in this deputation work is to make friends. The more people you can interest, the more avenues God can use to supply the needs, and the more the church will be blessed. You won't be able to interest everybody. So don't worry if many times the people seem cold and indifferent. "In almost every congregation," a veteran missionary used to say, "there is someone to whom your message will appeal." Be yourself; be sincere; and show a real interest in others. Friendliness begets friends. But when it comes to financial help for yourself, honestly surrender that problem to the Lord.

In the light of what we have said, you can see some things that are wisely done in deputation work. There is the matter of your home church, for example. It may be that they will assume a part of your support simply because you are a member. But it doesn't always happen. And sometimes the part they are willing to take is very small. The reason may be that they really don't know you very well and so are not very much interested. What if you were reared in that church? In some churches the membership is constantly changing. You have been away to school for some years. It has been a long time since you were active in church affairs. The newer members don't know you. There is a new pastor who is unacquainted with you. Right here is where your deputation work needs to begin. Let them see you in the meetings. Get acquainted with the newcomers. Take an active part in church affairs. Be ready to substitute for a Sunday school teacher, to address the young people's group or to fill the pulpit if you are asked. The people need to know you to be interested in you.

How do you go about getting an entrance into other churches? There are various ways. Sometimes your mission can make such appointments for you. However, missionary appointees are not the most welcome speakers. They haven't been on the field yet, so they can't speak about the work from experience. They often have to content themselves with a brief word of testimony, a talk to a young people's group, or some other such opening. Or they may accompany the mission secretary or a missionary on furlough.

But there are some things you can do for yourself. Surely you made some friends while you were in school. Some of your Bible school or seminary friends may now be in the pastorate. They might welcome a visit from you and give you an opportunity to minister. The church may be small, and in an out-of-the-way place, but that may be to the good. Such churches don't often have a missionary speaker, so they are more likely to be interested and to continue their interest afterward than some of the large city churches. You come, too, as one who is already a friend of the pastor.

Then there are churches that you may have contacted in other ways. The problem is to let them know that you are available to minister, if they would like, and at the same time not sound presumptuous. It can be done tactfully, though. There are even some appointees who offer their services in places where they are not known at all. It takes a large measure of boldness, and there are proportionately not many who accept the offer. But if the appointee is a good speaker it may work out well and open the door to other places.

There are many other ways that an ingenious appointee may find of getting a hearing for his message. Sometimes at a conference he may make the acquaintance of pastors or leaders who, after they get to know him, will invite him to their churches. But in every case he should make it clear that he is sincerely interested in ministering, rather than being ministered to.

Just one word about the subject of your deputation message. If you are wise you will make the heart of it your personal testimony. That is, you will tell something about your own experience with Christ, your call to Christian service and to the mission field, the ways the Lord has led you and your expectations for the future. This is the thing that you know best. It is also the sort of thing that interests most people. People are interested in people. Your experiences may not be extraordinary, but people like to know that others have experiences similar to their own. Your dedication to the cause of Christ will inspire them. If they are young people, you may even be able by your testimony to challenge them to surrender their lives to Christ.

Now this doesn't mean that you are not to talk about anything else. Not at all. It simply means that your personal testimony should be the heart of your message. You may tell something about the work to which you are going. But of course the people will realize that you haven't been there, so you are not speaking from personal acquaintance. You may also want to give a Biblical content to your message. But if you simply preach a sermon, instead of interesting the people you will disappoint them. When they invite you as a missionary appointee, they expect your message to relate to your appointment as a missionary. Of course if you are asked for a series of messages the situation is changed. Then you will want to find out just what is desired. But for a single message your personal testimony is the most valuable thing you can give.

OUTFIT

As a missionary under appointment you will have a second major problem that is really a whole series of problems. This is the problem of your outfit. What, and how much, should you take to the field?

The answer to this question depends partly on the field to which you are going, partly on the work you are to do, and partly on yourself. There are a few fields where the conditions of living are enough similar to what we enjoy at home so that there is little reason to carry along much in the way of personal baggage. There are others so primitive that the missionary will need to take along much of what he is going to use, aside from food. For most fields the need will lie somewhere between these extremes. There are some jobs that call for very little in the way of special equipment. But others, such as medical work, require a great deal of equipment. And for most jobs there is some equipment not available on the field that will be of real help. Of course your personal preferences will always complicate the picture.

So what is said here has to do largely with principles which may be applied to specific cases. Many missionaries today are taking too much. Their outfits are too elaborate, too costly. Yet it is not altogether their fault. Their friends are eager for them to have everything that they need. And it is so much more exciting to give goods than money. So the missionary is likely to land on the field with several tons of equipment, not all of it really necessary.

What the new missionary may not realize at first is that the equipment that is supposed to make his work easier and more effective may be a great stumbling block. The missionary must be a wealthy man. Look at the goods he has! He has trunks and boxes and barrels without number. And what wonders he reveals when he opens one of those boxes! It doesn't matter that some of these "wonders" are commonplace in his own country. It doesn't matter that he really will be living without many of the conveniences that he enjoyed at home. The only thing that matters is that by their standards he is rich. He is richer than the wealthiest of their own people. How then can he understand them? How can he help with their problems? How can his gospel apply to their lives, unless it gives the key to the getting of those wonderful treasures he has?

It is easier to point out this problem than it is to solve it. And we shall not take the time right here to deal with it. Suffice it to say for the moment that an unnecessarily large outfit is a hindrance rather than a help. It sets you apart from the people you want to win. It excites their cupidity. It creates special problems of protection against theft. It ties you down to one place. (One missionary actually rebelled against moving to a new station because there would be no electricity to operate some of his equipment.) Yet where shall we draw the line? No one has yet come up with the perfect answer.

There is one basic principle. While it is too broad to help much, it may help some. "Take what you are reasonably sure you will need, and only those things that you definitely expect to use." As a new missionary you will have to depend on advice from those on the field. And they don't always agree. But don't take anything along just because "it might be useful sometime."

Your mission will often have a suggested outfit list. Almost always, though, it leaves much to your own discretion. If you are making up your own list, there are three questions that you will want to answer about each item:

1. Will it be needed, or *clearly* useful in my life and work on the field?

2. Is it worth the transportation and possible customs charge in addition to its original price?

3. Is it obtainable on the field at a comparatively reasonable price?

We might call these the tests of need, economy and availability. We cannot apply them perfectly. For example, it is often impossible to predict what the customs charges will be. However, they are likely to be higher than you think. Also, some friends will buy things for you who would not give you the money and allow you to use your own judgment. All you can do is accept their generosity with appreciation.

When it comes to purchasing the items for your outfit, you are in a privileged position as a missionary. Not only are there friends of missions who will see that you get a special price on some items, there are also organizations like Missionary Equipment Service[1] that are set up specially for your benefit. Always make inquiries before you buy. Whether the board makes you a grant for your outfit, or it comes from

[1]210 West Chestnut Street, Chicago 10, Illinois.

the gifts of interested Christian friends, it is the Lord's money that you are handling and you should handle it wisely.

Several years ago a missionary appointee was handed a gift from her supporting church to help with her outfit. Without consulting anyone she immediately went downtown and purchased an expensive wardrobe trunk at full retail price. Later she was short of money for some of the necessary parts of her outfit. The pastor said, "If only we had known that she wanted a trunk! There were lots of our members that had trunks stored away in their attics that they would have been glad to give!"

So get advice from your mission board and from missionaries and others who may be able to help you. But again, if some of your friends insist that they would rather give you goods than money, accept the gift gratefully and graciously, even though you might have been able to make a better buy yourself.

So far we haven't said anything about the individual items that might be found on a typical list. Actually there isn't much that would apply in every case. You will of course take clothing and other personal effects. The amount will depend on what you can get on the field. If you have difficulty in getting shoes to fit you, though, it might be well to take all that you will need for a term of service. And if you use glasses you ought to have an extra pair along in case one gets broken. It may take a long time to send them off for repairs.

Then you may need to take along the items essential to setting up housekeeping in another land, including kitchen equipment. But make careful inquiry before you take any electrical goods. Is electricity available? A.C. or D.C.? 32, 110 or 220 volts? 50 or 60 cycle? This is very important. And be sure to take an American flag, too. In some countries you are required to fly the flag of your country on certain specified occasions.

For your work you will also want the tools of your trade, whatever they are. If you are going to the humid tropics and there is risk of rust and mold, find out how to protect against it. Be sure to have adequate repairs and spare parts. And if you are thinking of taking a car, a truck, or any other motorized vehicle, check carefully with the field *before* you make the purchase. Too many missionaries have made such purchases first and then found out either that they couldn't get an import license or that the freight and customs charges would be greater than they could possibly pay. Sometimes, too, a car must have been used for a certain length of time before it can qualify for entrance as a used car.

One part of your equipment deserves special treatment. This is your library. Every missionary has books, and every missionary needs books in his work. The question is, how can he decide what books to take with him? One missionary was so impressed by the statement that he ought to "travel light" that he turned down the gift of an expensive set of commentaries and took along only a handful of books. He regretted it later. There are other people, however, who accumulate books as some accumulate bric-a-brac. They will need to do some weeding out. The general principle, as with other equipment, is that you ought to take with you all the books you are reasonably sure you will need, and only those that you expect to use. The number will vary widely, depending on the type of work you are going to do and your own personal liking for reading and study.

In addition to selection, there are two other major problems that you will face in connection with your library. One is the difficulties and expense of transportation, including the possibility of loss or damage in transit. With the tremendous increase of transportation facilities throughout the world, this matter of transportation is not nearly so important as it used to be. There are few places to which books may not be taken quite readily in as large numbers as you would care to take. Of course there is still the expense to think of. However, it may well be that a little extra invested in excess baggage for books at the beginning will pay valuable dividends later on in spiritual refreshing and mental stimulation, aside from the information they will give.

The second problem is that of adequate housing for your library on the field. This sounds laughable to some appointees with their tiny collections of books. All they need, they will say, is a couple of bookcases. But even one or two bookcases can be a problem in the primitive quarters in which some missionaries must live. And flimsy walls and leaky roofs are all too common. There are cockroaches, too, that seem to love the bindings of some books, and termites that drill neat round holes from cover to cover. Shellacking the covers may help protect them, especially if a little DDT is added to the shellac as some have suggested.

Most missionary appointees during their student days begin the accumulation of a library. This is the best way. Actually a library should be built book by book as we find those that interest and help us. The books of your library should be like friends. You have made their acquaintance and know more or less what to expect from them. So when the need arises you can turn to just the one that will be of most help. However, many students are also chronically short of funds to buy the books they might want. So before they go to the mission field, where there are no lending libraries, they often ask, "What books do I really need to take along with me?"

For the benefit of these a *minimum* library for the general missionary is suggested below. Books in the native tongues or in very specialized fields are not included. Nor should any missionary limit himself to this minimum if he can do better. But it may call to your attention some things that you would otherwise overlook, or help you to fill in a gap or two in your own library.

MINIMUM LIBRARY

1. *Bible* (English). Not only the Authorized Version but at least one of the more modern versions as well, as either the American Revised or the Revised Standard. If acquainted with the original languages, take your Greek New Testament and Hebrew Old Testament, together with the necessary lexicons and grammars.

2. *Concordance.* The unabridged Cruden's may be enough, though many prefer Strong's or Young's.

3. *Bible dictionary.* A good one-volume edition.

4. *Commentaries.* The absolute minimum is a one- or two-volume explanatory commentary. More extensive critical, devotional and homiletical commentaries may be needed for evangelists, translators and Bible teachers. Also commentaries on individual books may prove valuable. Personal judgment and preference enter in at this point. The basic question is: Do I need this book to help me understand the Scripture, so that I can more clearly explain it to the people?

5. *Biblical introduction.* A general handbook.

6. *Theology or doctrine.* Books taken will depend on denomination or preference, but everyone should have at least a good summary of Christian doctrine.

7. *Atlases.* A Bible atlas is needed. Also a small up-to-date world atlas is valuable.

8. *Devotional works.* Select according to taste. Do not omit them, however. They often bring spiritual refreshment and inspiration when it is most needed.

9. *Hymnbooks.* At least one good one for your own use.

10. *History.* At least a one-volume Church history. A history and survey of Christian missions is also valuable.

11. *Missionary principles. The Foreign Missionary,* by A. J. Brown, as a minimum. It is old but still remarkably valuable for basic principles.

12. *English language.* By all means take a good English dictionary and a grammar or handbook.

13. *Medical books.* Choose according to your ability to use them. By all means take the Red Cross textbooks on Home Nursing and First Aid, as well as a good book on hygiene (tropical hygiene for many fields). For the family select a book on infant and child care. After you are on the field, you will probably wish you had much more than this.

14. *Cookbook.* Take a good one, even though materials may not be available for many recipes.

15. *Miscellaneous recommendations.* No one list will fit everybody. The following additional suggestions, however, may be helpful:

    a. Biographies of missionaries and other Christian leaders.

    b. Studies of the country and people to whom you go.

    c. Sometimes an encyclopedia, for the wealth of practical information it contains.

    d. *Good* fiction for mental relaxation. (Too much of this may be harmful.)

    e. Books along the lines of personal interest.

Remember that the missionary has a many-sided ministry, and even his hobbies may be of value in that ministry.

One more word should be said about a missionary's outfit. This concerns packing and shipping. Packing so as to avoid excessive breakage calls for an experienced hand. Even in this country baggage often undergoes some fairly rough handling. And the slings that are used to lift goods and deposit them in the hold of a ship exert tremendous pressure on any package that happens to be in the center. Then sometimes baggage must be unloaded not on a pier but into lighters with a fairly heavy sea running. And it may have to be handled several times more before it reaches the mission station. So unless you have had considerable experience yourself, you would do well to get good help in packing. It will save you in the long run.

Before you start packing, find out what the customs requirements are. Often you will have to have an itemized list of every item in each container. It is good to have such a list anyway (though it means considerable work), in case any package goes astray.

Check the various ways of shipping your goods to the port of embarkation. Only a limited amount of personal baggage is usually permitted on a train ticket, and excess baggage is expensive. The cheapest way is usually by rail freight or truck line. However it is also the slowest; so you will need to allow plenty of time. Railway Express is very fast, making use of the fast passenger trains, but it is also expensive.

The free baggage allowance on ships is usually by weight. However, there are still some lines that allow a certain number of cubic feet, regardless of weight.

Consult your mission about the import regulations of the country to which you are going. While sometimes your baggage can go separately as unaccompanied baggage, there is at least one country that does not recognize such a category. It is possible, too, that you may not be allowed to bring in certain items as baggage. Get all the information you can.

Official Papers

There is a third problem you will have to face before you can leave for the field. This is the matter of the documents which you will be required to have. There was a time when missionaries didn't even need a passport. But today nearly every country requires a variety of documents before it will admit a foreigner to its shores. When you are tempted to complain about the requirements of other countries, just remember that the United States is probably the most difficult to enter of any country in the world.

Be sure that you find out *all* that may be required. Sometimes a travel agency or a carrier slips up on these things, and the traveler suffers. It is far better to have a paper or two that you don't need than to be held up for lack of one that you must have.

Your passport is essential. It is issued by your own government and shows that you are permitted to travel abroad with all the rights of a citizen of this country. It does not itself, however, assure you of entrance into any country. That is a matter for that country to decide. It sets up its own rules for the admission of foreigners. You can usually find out these rules from the consul of the country concerned in one of our major cities or at the port of embarkation. If you make application and meet the requirements, he will stamp and sign your passport authorizing you to proceed to his country. This authorization is called a "visa." There are times, however, when authorization must come directly from the country concerned to the consul before he will issue a visa. Because this takes time, you will want to start the process early.

Of the other documents required, the most common is the certificate of inoculation against certain diseases. There is now an international form in use with space to record vaccination against smallpox and inoculations against typhoid fever, yellow fever and Asiatic cholera. Vaccination within the past two years will almost certainly be required. Requirements as to the others differ from country to country. Sometimes a separate general certificate of good health is also required. A certificate of good conduct issued by the police department is also commonly asked for. And often you will have to accompany your application for a visa with several photographs of yourself. Since they are also needed for the passport, it is well to get a number of them at the same time.

There is one thing missionaries under appointment occasionally overlook. After you have been officially appointed, you are entitled to travel on railroads and bus lines at reduced rates, if you secure clergy certificates. Your local agent can usually give you the application form. Fill it out according to instructions and send it in with the fee for a book of certificates that will be valid for the calendar year. On railroads the reduction will be fifty per cent of the *first-class* one-way fare. You will need different certificates for the three major divisions of the country, however. Since the bus lines have only one fare, the reduction is twenty-five per cent, and only one certificate is needed for the whole country. There is at present no such arrangement with the air lines.

CHAPTER FOUR

THE PROBATIONER

MEANING OF THE TERM

A MISSIONARY IS A MISSIONARY, whether he is a new appointee just going to the field or a veteran of many years. But for practical purposes missionaries are often divided into three groups: probationers, junior missionaries and senior missionaries. There are differences from mission to mission; but the distinction is convenient for our purpose, because there are certain things facing the new recruit for the field that call for special treatment. He has not yet established himself as an effective missionary, so in a sense he is really a probationer.

THE TRIP TO THE FIELD

For some it may not seem necessary to give any advice about the trip to the field, for they have already traveled a great deal. But many a new missionary has traveled very little, even in his own country. The trip to the field will be an entirely new experience. It can also be a very enjoyable and profitable experience.

To nearly all fields you will go either by ship or by plane. In either case, though it may not be necessary to mention it, the price of the passage includes meals. If the mission needs you on the field in a hurry, they may want you to go by plane. But experienced missionaries will tell you that if you have a choice you will usually do well to go by ship. The reason is not alone because of cost. There are other things. The rapid transition from cold to hot climate by plane is sometimes hard. On the ship you make the transition more gradually. Then, too, the last few weeks of preparation for leaving, of meetings, farewells, packing, shipping, etc., may be quite hectic. You ought to have a brief respite before plunging into the new responsibilities on the field. An ocean voyage can be very restful and refreshing. And if your voyage is long and your ship calls at a number of ports, you will have a wonderful opportunity to see other people and places. The plane stops are too brief for this, and the airports too out of the way.

The larger missions usually arrange for the passage of their missionaries. But sometimes the missionary himself must do it. Remember that the shipping company holds you responsible for having the proper documents, and it may at the last minute refuse you passage if they are not in order. Any cancellation of passage must be made within a certain time limit, or you will have to pay. This applies to both ships and planes.

What is the proper thing to do on shipboard? You can get lots of advice on this subject, some good and some bad. The best thing to remember is this: If it is a passenger ship there are many people on it in just the same situation as you. This is their first voyage. So don't be afraid of being laughed at if you ask questions. You will usually find people glad to be of help. If you simply exercise ordinary courtesy and good taste, you will get by all right and probably have a good time.

Something should be said about Christian witnessing on board. Sometimes the captain will arrange for meetings, especially on Sunday. If he doesn't, it is perfectly in order for you to make a polite request for such a meeting. However, even more important than the formal meetings will be the informal contacts that you will be able to make with fellow travelers. On shipboard, after the first stiffness has worn off, it is usually easy to strike up a friendly conversation. If you are overly aggressive, people will soon begin to shy away from you, but if you are tactful and considerate they will welcome your company and even at times be quite ready to discuss spiritual issues.

This matter of being considerate of others needs special emphasis. Really it is only true Christianity in action. Our lives certainly ought to commend our gospel. We do not need to keep our message hidden, but a selfish disregard of the rights of other passengers is no part of the gospel. And neither is an ostentatious parade of religiousness. When missionaries fail in this matter, it is usually because a number of them are traveling together. It is then that they thoughtlessly monopolize some of the recreational facilities or cause needless irritation in other ways.

One of the worries of the traveler abroad is the thought of seasickness. Really, there's no use to worry. Seasickness is a distressing experience that comes to most people. But usually it isn't long before you get your "sea legs" and can enjoy the trip. There are some new drugs that have proved fairly effective in overcoming this "motionsickness." Ask your doctor about them. But most of the other recommendations that friends will give you, such as eating or not eating, have little value. It is true, though, that in good weather you will be more comfortable in the open air on deck than in a stuffy cabin.

Ordinarily the mission itself notifies those on the field of the impending arrival of a new missionary. In that way someone can be on hand to greet him, to see him through customs, and to take care of the details connected with his arrival. It can be a harrowing experience to arrive in a strange land among people whose language you can't understand and without the slightest idea of what to do next. It is hard enough for those who are used to traveling. It is much worse for a novice. So if your mission doesn't take care of the matter, be sure that those on the field receive notice enough ahead of time to make proper preparations. If you are going by ship, give the name of the ship as well as the date of arrival, since it may be delayed. They can then check the expected time of its arrival at that end. When traveling by plane be sure to give the flight number. And if you make any changes in your plans, be sure to send prompt notice so friends on the field won't look for you in vain.

There are generally two inspections you must pass in entering a country. One is that of the health authorities, sometimes called "quarantine." It calls for an examination of your inoculation certificates and is usually accompanied by an examination also of your passport with its visa and any other required papers. If everything is in order this may be a simple formality. If not, it may lead to considerable complications and at least a delay in your being cleared for entrance.

The second inspection is that of the customs authorities. They examine your baggage for any prohibited article and assess charges on any goods that are subject to duty. If you have a large amount of baggage this may not be done on the day of your arrival. Also it can be a rather trying experience because of the uncertainty of its outcome. Customs regulations are constantly changing. Also much depends on the attitude of the official who handles your case. You will have need of patience and an ample supply of good humor. A friendly spirit is a big help.

ATTITUDES AND ACTIONS ON ARRIVAL

As a new missionary just arrived on the field you will be quickly overwhelmed with a flood of new impressions and new experiences. They will come so fast that you will not have time to sort them out and analyze them. But at the same time that you are trying to take it all in, you yourself are making impressions on others. You may often be unaware that the people, even while you cannot speak their language, are busily reading your attitudes and interpreting your life. They form their judgments from what they see in you, the new arrival; and if their judgment is adverse at the beginning, you will have a hard time getting them to change it at a later date. First impressions have a remarkable durability. They can often make or break a ministry.

Fully as important as the impression you make on the people is the impression that you make on your fellow missionaries. They are the ones with whom you will have to serve. You are going to be a part of the team. They are already well disposed toward you. They want to like you. They hope you will make good and they are ready to help you. But they too will form some judgments about you from their earliest contacts with you. And if they don't feel that you will fit in, if they see in you things that are likely to disturb—they won't reprove you; they will treat you with every courtesy, but they won't give you that warmhearted confidence that lets you know that you are one with them and that you can count on all the help that they are able to give.

How can you create a good impression? It is not something you can work up artificially. It is largely a matter of attitudes. Our attitudes determine our actions. They even show in the expressions of our faces. People usually sense whether we like them. It doesn't take them long to find out if we feel ourselves superior to them. And if we are opinionated or inclined to be self-sufficient, they soon know it.

It is most important when you reach your field that you have a teachable spirit. It is true that you have already undergone a great deal of preparation for this work. You have been a learner for a number of years and now you would like to be a leader, a teacher of others. You may have had more formal education than some of those with whom you are to work—more, perhaps, than the one under whom you are to begin your service. Your training is more recent, and you may feel that the older missionaries are out of date—behind the times. You can show them how the work really should be carried on.

This attitude is not at all uncommon in new missionaries. But it is decidedly dangerous. The most humble of the veteran missionaries has knowledge which the new recruit needs. It is knowledge that he has gained in the school of experience. It may not be recorded in the textbooks but it has been worked out in real life. It is knowledge adapted to the situation that he is facing. If you, the new missionary, are teachable, this knowledge is yours for the asking. But if not, you may have to learn it in the harsh school of personal experience.

The older missionaries do not have all the answers. They know they haven't. You in time may be able to lead them to a solution to some of the problems. But you are in no position to do so until you have first learned what they have found out. It is good to think about the problems, and there is nothing wrong in drawing up theories as to how the problems might be solved. You may even want to write them out in detail for yourself. But when you first reach the field, put those ideas down at the bottom of your deepest trunk and leave them there to season. Meantime show a willingness to learn all that the older missionaries have to teach you. After a year or so it may be safe to take those ideas out and look them over. Some of them may still impress you as being valid. They may be worth trying, or at least discussing with others. But in most cases you will probably blush, as you read, at the immaturity of your thinking and the differences between your theorizing and the facing of actual conditions on the field.

So when you get to the field, put aside all your preconceived ideas and plans. Get your bearings thoroughly. Learn all that you can from the others. Ask questions, but not in an argumentative way. Then, when you are given the opportunity to help determine policies, you will be able to do so on the basis of a wealth of knowledge and experience—others' as well as your own.

Next to a teachable spirit I would put a willingness to serve wherever needed. There are too many young missionaries that go to the field with very definite ideas about what they should be called on to do. They resent being asked to do jobs that they consider menial or beneath their abilities and preparation. Men are ready to preach a sermon, but not to repair a door. Women will teach a children's class but shy away from washing the dishes.

There are many menial tasks to be done on the mission field. Sometimes a servant can be hired to do some of them. More often a missionary must perform them. So you must expect that you will be asked to do your part. In fact you may be asked to do more than your share since you are not yet able to enter fully into the more distinctly missionary end of things.

It is true that occasionally the older missionaries will take advantage of the newcomers. They feel that you aren't worth very much to the work at the beginning anyway, so why not give you the tedious chores that don't call for a knowledge of the language or the people, and free the older missionaries for more important work.

The trouble with this attitude is that it usually ends with you, the new missionary, spending so much time on the odd jobs that you don't get to learn the lessons you need in order to enter fully into the work. Your language lessons often are the first casualty. On the whole it is poor economy. Yet when you are inclined to complain and to become resentful, we would say: This is just one of those "light afflictions" that are temporary and that, if taken rightly, work in us the important grace of patience. It won't hurt you to suffer a bit of imposition. In fact, what you think is an imposition may not be such at all. The only thing that will hurt you and the work is to let resentment spring up and then to nourish it along. This is deadly. The most important part of the victorious life is the victory over self. Such a victory leads to real happiness.

Another word is in order for those who are ambitious to become pioneer missionaries. There is plenty of pioneering in missionary work today, but not much of it in a geographical sense. New ideas, new projects, new methods, new approaches to old problems are in constant demand. But before you are ready to pioneer in any sense, you need to learn the fundamentals. So in almost every case your first assignment will be to an already established work. This is only good judgment. The missionary with experience is the best one for the pioneer work. He knows the land and the people, or at least he has already dealt with somewhat similar situations. He knows the common pitfalls and how to avoid them. He knows what methods have proved successful before. His boldness is tempered by a discretion born of experience. It is not the work for a novice.

So be ready to serve your apprenticeship in an established work, and under supervision. Learn to take orders, if you have not already done so. Learn to co-operate in the carrying out of another's plans. Whatever the job that is given you, do it in such a way that you can be proud of the result. To be counted worthy to be entrusted with great affairs, you need to prove yourself faithful in the little things. Great missionaries do good work no matter where you put them. It is only the mediocre who need favorable circumstances in order to get along.

LEARNING THE LANGUAGE

Your first great task is to learn the language. This is basic. There are very few fields where you can carry on an effective missionary work in your own native tongue. You must learn to speak to others in their language. Unless you do, you can never really communicate the gospel to them. A message in an unknown tongue benefits nobody. Even a message in a language that is comprehended with difficulty is largely ineffective.

For example, you may have studied French in school. Then if you go and hear a message given in French, you may be able to grasp some of the facts that the speaker presents. You may gain a small amount of information, but the speaker will not move you to action. You spend all of your effort in trying to understand what he says. There is no time to think of the implications of his statements. It is the message in our own familiar tongue that stirs us to action. What we hear then are not just words whose meaning we have to puzzle out. We are scarcely conscious of the words. We are hearing ideas, ideas with overtones of feeling that stir up a response within us.

Language is the missionary's major tool. Whatever your special ministry on the field, you will have to use language in carrying it out. The preacher and teacher, of course, will have to have the greatest familiarity with it. But even the printer, the builder, the agriculturalist can hardly expect to get very far without it. There is a limit to what you can do with pantomime.

Everyone can learn a language. Some can learn with greater ease than others, but all can learn. This is particularly true in regard to the spoken language. The fact that some have failed does not mean that they were unable to learn. Failure almost always comes from one of two things: either from lack of interest and sustained effort, or from wrong methods. The first is the greater cause. Interest and persistent effort go together. You persist in the things that you are really interested in accomplishing. Your efforts drop when your interest lags.

Perhaps the thing that discourages you most is the realization after a time that you are unable to master the language in "ten easy lessons." Neither can anyone else. Language learning for almost everybody is a long and laborious process. When you hear of someone who has "picked up" a language in a few weeks, don't be deceived. What he has "picked up" is a few words and phrases like "hello," "good-by," "how are you?" "what does it cost?" etc., that help him to get by in a simple situation. Even so, the people often comprehend what they think he meant to say rather than what he actually did say. We do the same thing with foreigners who are just beginning to learn our language. Make up your mind that to learn to speak correctly as well as fluently, to express your thoughts so that people will think of them rather than the peculiar way you state them, you are going to have to give serious attention to the language over a long period of time. Don't give in to discouragement! Keep plugging!

There are comparatively few times when wrong methods may be blamed for a person's failure to learn the language. There are numerous methods of language teaching. Some are more effective than others. But there is none that is best for all people. Actually the teacher is more important than the method he may use. And if the student is really anxious to learn, he can often make good progress in spite of mediocre teaching. But now and then we find a student who seems unable to profit by any of the usual procedures. For example there is the man who memorized the grammar of a language but never seemed able to relate it to his actual attempts to speak. He did better when he forgot the grammar and followed the slower, more repetitious method of mimicking the people, the way little children learn.

Missions make various provisions for the language study of their missionaries. Much depends on the field to which you are going.

Sometimes language study in Europe is indicated. Those who go to the Belgian Congo will ordinarily have to take certain courses in Belgium. Since these courses are given in French, those who do not know French already will have to take it while there. The Brussels office of the Congo Protestant Council has performed an invaluable service for the missions in making the necessary arrangements. Missionaries proceeding to French Africa commonly spend a time in France or Switzerland learning French. In Portuguese Africa it is the government that requires that all missionaries must know the Portuguese language when they reach the field. So there is usually a period of study in Portugal itself. All these courses have the additional benefit that they acquaint the new missionary with the culture of the ruling power in the colony. This helps him to understand government policies and to deal with government officials. However, it is only the beginning of his language study, for he may still have to learn one or more tribal or trade languages in the area to which he is assigned.

Many times the missions have a special language school on the field. This happens most often where there is a single language that is widely spoken. If an individual mission is large enough, it may conduct such a school for its own missionaries. Otherwise the school is a joint project between several missions, or at least a school to which numerous missions send their missionaries. Such a school is the Spanish language school in San Jose, Costa Rica. It meets the needs of missionaries to any of the Spanish-American countries. The Presbyterian Mission provides the school building and the salary of the director and his wife, who have assumed this task as their missionary ministry. The students who come pay a small tuition fee, which covers the salaries of the Spanish-speaking instructors. The complete course is one year of three fifteen-week terms. There are four hours of classes every morning, five days a week. Classes are kept very small, allowing a maximum of personal attention. The students live in apartments or with families in the city and so are constantly in a Spanish-speaking environment.

Such schools have very real advantages. They have the benefit of experienced teachers; the courses are carefully planned; and the students do not have the distractions of being obliged to share in the responsibilities of missionary work while they are learning the language. When a student has completed the course, he does not have a complete mastery of the language, but he is usually ready to take a full share in the work on the field.

But schools cannot meet all the need. There are some languages not widely enough used to call for a school. The missionaries who need to learn a particular language may not average one per year. In such circumstances the work must be done in small classes as the need arises, or by private tutoring on the mission station. Such a situation is far from ideal, for the senior missionary in charge is already overburdened and has little time to devote to teaching the language. It is little wonder that often the language study gets badly neglected.

Of course it is not always another missionary who does the teaching. If native teachers can be hired, so much the better. It relieves the missionary in charge and assures greater regularity in the lessons. Since in many places, though, it is hard to find people who know how to teach their language to a foreigner, a combination is sometimes worked out. A missionary teaches the grammar of the language in terms that an English-speaking person can understand, while a national is engaged to teach such things as proper pronunciation, conversation, vocabulary, idioms, etc.

In any case we ought constantly to recognize that formal classes can only do part of the job. A real mastery of the language, such as the missionary ought to have, calls for continued learning long after language school days are over. Some missions very wisely have a prescribed course of study for their missionaries to pursue after language school. But whether they do or not, we need to realize that effectiveness of ministry is closely tied up with ability to use the language. One must keep on learning.

The methods used in teaching the language are pretty well determined by the school or teacher. The pupil has little to say. However, occasionally a pupil will take it upon himself to criticize his teacher for methods that he thinks are "old-fashioned" or inappropriate. Usually those with the least experience are the most vocal in their criticisms.

Perhaps the most common criticism is that which has to do with learning the grammar. More than one impatient student has complained, "Why do I have to learn grammar? Why can't I just learn to talk the way the children do? Actually the people themselves don't seem to know much about the grammar of their language, but they get along."

There is something to this argument. But I am not sure it is a something that would please the objector if he saw where it leads. It is entirely possible to learn a language the way a little child learns, which is largely by mimicry. But how many years do you want to spend at it? How long did it take you to learn to speak English correctly? And do you want to limit your conversation to childish prattle? Of course you are older now, which makes a difference. But that, too, has its handicaps. People won't be so patient with an adult's fumbling attempts as with a child's. The constant chatter of a child becomes irritating in an adult. And are you ready to stand the laughter that will accompany the humorous mistakes you make? Children are not easily embarrassed, so they go ahead in spite of mistakes.

It is true that the people themselves often do not know the grammar of their language. That is, they couldn't explain their grammatical system. But that doesn't mean that they don't observe grammatical rules. They do. Grammar is nothing but a description of the way a language is spoken. It is the pattern the people follow when they speak. To the language student it is what anatomy and physiology are to the medical student. When you make a mistake in the use of a word, people who don't know how to explain the pattern, the grammar, will simply say, "We don't say it that way." But their correction won't help you with any other words. You will have to learn every one separately unless, after awhile, you yourself begin to see a pattern emerging—that certain words, under certain conditions, act a certain way. Then you are getting into grammar. How much easier to learn the pattern and then apply it wherever it is called for than to work it out by countless mistakes in the trial and error method.

But grammar alone is not enough. It will help you to puzzle out the meaning of what is written. But until it becomes so much a part of you that you will apply it without conscious effort, you have not really learned the language. You haven't learned to talk until you cease to think of each separate word. What many people seem to fail to realize is that language is a matter of habits. You learn to express a thought in a certain way. You repeat it that way over and over until that form of words comes spontaneously to your lips whenever the thought calls for expression. This is what makes constant repetition so important in learning a language. Only frequent repetition can turn a deliberate act into a habit. Grammar is the skeleton, vocabulary provides the flesh to cover it, but only constant practice can make the language a living, working body.

Sometimes the criticism is made that the methods used on the field are not those of the college classroom. This is to be expected. In the homeland our students seldom hear the language except in the class or in the recordings of the language laboratory. The class period is not only the key to the whole program, it is the major part of it. On the field the class work is supplemented and reinforced by many other elements. The student hears the language constantly. He has frequent need to express himself in it. He is constantly receiving correction and instruction from other missionaries and from the nationals outside of the classroom. And when it comes to correctness, seventy per cent is scarcely a "passing" grade. Who could understand the talk of a person who is wrong in three words out of every ten that he uses?

While you may not have much to say about the methods used in the language classes, there are a number of things that you can do to make language learning more effective. The following are suggestions that the individual student can apply for himself. They will not guarantee efficient learning but they are a practical help.

1. *In learning the sounds of a language, use your eyes as well as your ears.* The ear can tell you only the impression that the sound makes on it. It doesn't tell you how the sound was produced. If you are going to imitate it you need to know how it was produced. While much of the production of the sound is not visible, there is more to be seen than most people realize. This is what makes it possible for deaf people to do what is commonly called "lip reading."

2. *Try to mimic your teacher, especially in phrasing, accent and tone.* The ability to mimic is a great asset to one who wishes to learn to speak another language. Instead of trying to figure things out, a step at a time, he tries to imitate in a single complex act all that he hears and sees his instructor do. This is especially valuable in phrasing. People don't talk by isolated words. In speaking freely we combine our words into groups or phrases. In each of these phrases the words tend to run into one

another and are scarcely distinguishable as separate words. Often a sound is dropped, as the "h" in the question, "Did he come?" which usually sounds like "Diddeecome?" with the accent on the last syllable. The mimic usually imitates the phrase because that is what he hears. And for the same reason he is likely to imitate the tone of voice. This is important in tonal languages. Even in languages that are not definitely tonal it is the easiest and best way to learn the patterns of intonation.

3. *Do your lessons aloud as much as possible.* It is true that we don't hear ourselves in the same way that others hear us. But this suggestion has other purposes than the simple achievement of a reasonably accurate pronunciation. When you do your lessons aloud, in a subject that calls for as much memorization as language does, you are aiding your memory. The visual memory alone, that is, the memory of words that we *see,* has a modest amount of retentiveness. If we add to this the audial memory, the memory of the same words as we *hear* them, our powers of retention are more than doubled. And if we add to this the motor memory, the memory of acts we have *performed* in uttering them, we have further multiplied our ability to remember. Besides, it is of no value to know what should be said, if we do not accustom ourselves actually to say it. And we can never really master the language until we get over the feeling of strangeness at hearing our own voice uttering such sounds.

4. *Practice what you have already learned on every possible occasion.* This is one of the secrets of the rapid learning of little children. They don't hesitate to repeat what they hear in every conceivable situation. A new word is like a new toy. By practice they find out what they can do with it and what they can't. And they don't worry about their laughable mistakes. That is part of the learning process. If you wait until you can speak faultlessly, you will never speak. It is the one who isn't afraid to talk, in spite of mistakes, who makes the most rapid progress.

5. *Listen attentively when others speak.* In this way you will catch on to some of the variations in the use of the language. Your grammar books won't contain everything. Your classes will not be able to provide you with all the information you will need. In the final analysis the language is what the people actually say. So listen while they talk— especially to those who are considered to be good speakers of the language.

6. Don't be afraid to reveal your ignorance by asking questions.
There is no disgrace in admitting that your knowledge is limited. Usually people are very glad to help you learn their language. Their answers to your questions are not always accurate. But as often as not that
is because they don't really understand your question. Let them help
you learn their language and you may find that they will have a friend-
lier feeling for you personally.

7. Get the notebook habit. Carry a small notebook in your pocket
or handbag. It will have more than one use. But in language study you
can use it to note down new words and phrases or new usages that you
hear. Some of these things you may not find in dictionaries or grammars. This is especially true where local usage differs from the standard form of the language. The notebook can be used, too, for questions
that you would like to find an answer for, from your teacher or from
someone else.

8. In a literary language, read extensively. That is, if the language
has a fair amount of literature in print, read as much of it as you can
find time for. Pick out the best and most representative works. Read
them without spending too much time looking up all the unfamiliar
words. If you look up every word you will get discouraged before you
go very far. Extensiveness of reading is more important here than full
comprehension. If it is a story you are reading, look up only enough
words to follow the trend of the thought. Gradually you will come to
see that certain words and expressions are used over and over. Even if
you don't look them up you will come to get a fair idea of their meaning from the different contexts in which you find them. And their constant repetition helps to fix them in your mind. Besides, unconsciously,
if you read extensively, you will be developing a feeling for the proper
forms of expression. You will be forming some ideas of good style in
writing. And the interest of what you are reading will carry you along
and encourage you to read further. It is much the same as in English.
Extensive reading almost always shows up in a better command of the
language.

9. A suggestion or two about the physical aspects of studying. Don't
sit too long at a time with your books. You will often find it difficult to
keep awake after awhile. Break up your extended periods of study into
shorter intervals. You will accomplish more. If you can't do anything

else, get up occasionally and walk around for a few minutes. Or vary your type of study to avoid monotony. Some people find that they can do well by studying while standing or walking about. Others have experienced that intensive study after the evening meal has a tendency to disturb their rest when they do get to bed.

10. *Tape recorders and record players are useful modern aids for language study.* They are also a part of the equipment of many missionaries today. The record player is only of use where the language is widespread and fairly well known so that records are available. The tape recorder, however, can be used anywhere. With it the missionary can record the speech of a native speaker and study it at his leisure. He can also record his own voice saying the same things and then compare the two. He can get as many repetitions as he wants without fear of tiring his informant. And he doesn't make the speaker distort his pronunciation by repeating too slowly. Even in language school it is sometimes recommended that the students bring tape recorders to help with their study.

OTHER STUDIES

The only formal study that nearly all missions require of their new missionaries is the language. Yet some missions have come to realize the importance of giving other instruction as well. Occasionally they give it in classes. More often they disseminate it informally through required readings or study, through conferences, or through the advice that older missionaries give by word of mouth. It may be that in the years to come other missions will realize what an important part this preparation on the field plays in the development of effective missionaries. We really need more than a "language committee" to direct the language study of the new missionary. We need a "new missionary committee" with responsibility for the on-the-field training of probationers. A full program that is well planned and carried out will yield great dividends.

Of course where the mission does not make provision for additional studies, you can still carry them out on your own initiative. It is not as easy nor as satisfactory, but it can be done. Here are a few studies you will find helpful.

1. *Mission policies and procedures.* Often the mission gives some of

this instruction to you before you leave for the field. Or it may provide you with a handbook or set of instructions with which you are expected to familiarize yourself. Still there are many details that you will probably have to learn from the other missionaries.

2. *Customs of the people.* Only occasionally does the new missionary get any planned instruction along this line. Mostly you will have to learn by observation, by asking questions or from the casual advice of older missionaries. It helps if you have had some instruction in anthropology beforehand. In any case you will find it well worth the time and effort to learn all you can in this area. Many a failure in missions can be traced to a failure to understand the people.

3. *Religions of the people and methods of dealing with them.* Even if you have had formal instruction in non-Christian religions, you soon learn the weakness of that instruction. The study of comparative religions in our schools is usually kept on a doctrinal level, comparing system with system. But often on the field you find that ordinary people are not familiar with the theoretical basis of their religion. In fact, many areas may have their own local deviations from what is considered the orthodox form of the religion. Also it is one thing for you to be acquainted with the teachings of a religious system and quite another to know how effectively to deal with the people who profess that faith. There is no substitute for experience in this matter, but careful study can help you avoid many of the worst pitfalls.

4. *How to live in the land.* Some missions offer "boot camp" or "jungle camp" training to help meet this need for those who are going to primitive areas. In most fields, however, it seems to be taken for granted that the missionary will be able to pick up such knowledge as he goes. For the most part you will have to depend again on the older missionaries. You may not even have a cookbook that will help you prepare the local products for food.

5. *Geography and history of the country.* Because of their traveling, the missionaries sometimes get to know the geography of a country better than most of the inhabitants. But not all of them get that knowledge. And in the matter of history, many of them are woefully ignorant of the background of the people among whom they labor. Unfortunately they sometimes give the impression that they think the history

of other people is not very important. Realizing this need, an association of missions in one country several years ago agreed to make it a requirement that all new missionaries coming to that field should get instruction in the history of the country. However, such a requirement is still not common.

6. *History of missionary and church work in the field.* Missionary work has its roots in the past. In some fields those roots go back a good many years. You cannot begin your work as if no one had ever labored before you in that region. Nearly always you are building to some extent on the foundations laid by other men. Yet all too often you have little knowledge of those foundations. You may even be unfamiliar with the history of your own mission, not to say the history of other missions in the same neighborhood. If each new missionary tries to make a fresh start, how can the work advance? And if you do not know what has been done before, how can you chart the course ahead? It is not always possible to get adequate instruction in this subject, but you will do well to inform yourself to the best of your ability.

STATION ASSIGNMENT

Sometimes at the end of your language school days, sometimes earlier, you get the word of your assignment to a regular post. Or perhaps you were already designated to that post before you left the homeland. The decision is usually not an arbitrary one. You may have been the subject of considerable discussion and prayer before it was made. Your qualifications have been reviewed. Any desire you may have expressed has been considered. But besides these things there are some pressing needs in the work that have to be cared for. And the ones in charge have to decide how well you might fit into the situation they have in mind for you.

The new missionary usually doesn't know some of the factors that enter into the decision. As a result there are times when you will feel dissatisfied with your assignment. You will not always get the appointment on which you have set your heart. Most missionaries are able to accept these disappointments with good grace. If such an experience should be yours, you would be able to accept it more easily if you understood the problems involved.

The mission prefers to put you where you desire to be. In fact, they may ask you your preference before they make the assignment. But obviously they can't satisfy everyone. There are vacancies that have to be filled. There are jobs to be done that are essential to the work. And often they don't have anyone who feels specially called to a critically needed ministry. So they have to appoint someone who can do the job, even though he might not have chosen it for himself. Perhaps you don't feel attracted to it simply because you are not familiar with it. If you will accept it as a God-given responsibility, you may find it a challenging ministry and a blessed one. A great deal depends on the attitude with which you take it up.

Not long ago some groups of missionaries in Africa were asked this question: How many of you are actually doing the work you expected to do when you came to Africa? On the average about half of them raised their hands. Does that mean that the other half were unhappy in their work? Not at all. Perhaps a few were. It may be that some were hoping for the day when they could be transferred to the work they wanted to do. But most of them had a different attitude. Since coming out to Africa their vision had broadened. They saw needs and avenues of service they had not dreamed of before. They were happy in the work to which they had been assigned. They weren't just making the best of the situation. Some had found that the unlooked-for appointment had put them right into the proper niche for their best service.

What many new missionaries fail to appreciate fully is the fact that their first work will most likely be in an established station under older missionaries. Many have the ambition to move out into "pioneer work." If they could only view the situation objectively they would realize that the new missionary is not the one to lead the move into new territory. He has the zeal and devotion, but he lacks the experience that is so necessary. And as for directing the work of a station, the new missionary needs to learn what is already being done before he is ready to introduce any innovations. Of course, do not always expect the newer recruits to follow the exact pattern established by their predecessors. This would lead to stagnation. But ideas are not necessarily good because they are new. And neither is the proponent of a new method entitled to be heard unless he can show how it is superior to the old. To do that he must be familiar with what is already being done.

The missionary's willingness to accept an assignment that is not to his liking is often a crucial test. It tells more about his ability to work together with others for the common good than all the recommendations from his friends. It demonstrates that mastery of one's own spirit that the Scripture says reveals greater strength than that of one who can conquer a city.

PART TWO

The Missionary's Personal Life

CHAPTER FIVE

PHYSICAL LIFE

B EFORE WE CAN DEAL with your work as a missionary on the field, we need to say a number of things about your life there. Some of these things might not require comment if you were living in a familiar environment and among people with a background similar to your own. But because you are in another land and among a different people, and especially because the effectiveness of your ministry will be so closely tied up with the example of your own life, you will need to give careful attention to these things.

We take up the physical life first, not because it is the most important but because it is the most obvious. Most missionaries are serving in circumstances quite different from those at home. That doesn't necessarily mean that they are worse. It simply means that the circumstances are different. So you will probably have to make a number of adjustments in your thinking and acting. Your very continuance in the work may depend on your ability to make these adjustments and to safeguard your health under new conditions.

MAINTENANCE OF GENERAL HEALTH

There is one basic principle that must be established at the beginning. It is a very scriptural principle. It is that *our bodies are the temple of the Holy Spirit and we should care for them as such.* Christ's call to you as a missionary is to *live* for Him—to *spend* your life, not to *waste* it. There is no merit in laying down one's life on the mission field when such a sacrifice is the result of negligence or carelessness. There is no excuse for deliberately violating sane principles of healthful living. But neither is there any excuse for pampering your body. And there is perhaps more danger of this today than there is of needless sacrifice. We have so accustomed ourselves to physical comforts and conveniences that we don't see how we can do without them, even when they are not actually necessary for good health. The only good safeguard is to have a proper attitude toward your body. You are to glorify God in your body as well as your spirit, which are His. This means that the body should neither be neglected nor pampered. Through it you perform your ministry unto God, so you must both keep it in good condition and also keep it in subjection.

Cleanliness is important. It is not simply a matter of appearances. It is a matter of health. Disease and dirt are close companions. Some of the people to whom you go may not be as aware of it as we are. But that merely doubles your responsibility. You must seek cleanliness for your own health and also to set an example for others. To some this may seem like a needless exhortation, for they are habitually clean. Would that all missionaries who got to the field were of this sort! But the fact is that many are not. They need to be warned ahead of time, so as to develop habits of cleanliness before beginning their service.

The missionary in many lands will have to exercise considerable care with his food and drink. There is often no water filtration and treatment plant, no department of public health to examine eating places and prohibit the sale of contaminated foods. Dysentery, typhoid fever, tuberculosis, worms, are a few of the diseases that can come to the missionary through his food and drink. Safeguarding oneself against such things takes time and constant attention, so it is no wonder that sometimes missionaries are tempted to disregard it all and "take their chances." They may not state it that way. They may say that they are going to trust in God; that they are on His work and that He will take care of them. But it amounts to the same thing. It is not usually an excess of piety but of carelessness—perhaps even of laziness—that leads them to such neglect. Not long ago two missionaries were invalided home from their field—the result of drinking contaminated water because other missionaries had ridiculed them about boiling it.

These simple rules will help avoid trouble: Eat raw only those foods that have an unbroken protective covering. The fairly common practice of using human excrement for fertilizer in some places makes it dangerous to use raw vegetables. Fruits, too, can easily be contaminated in the handling. Such things as bananas and oranges, however, are safe when the skin is unbroken. Otherwise cook the foods well. Meats, too, need to be thoroughly cooked.

Boil all drinking water and milk. Spring water and water from carefully tested wells may be safe. But water from a stream, no matter how clear it seems, is a definite risk, and many wells are contaminated by the proximity of an outhouse. Filters clarify water but do not purify it. Chemical treatment, such as chlorination, is sometimes a possibility. But boiling is the most commonly used and most widely available means of purification. The danger from fresh milk is that the animals themselves may be diseased or that it may be contaminated in the handling. In many places the milk is deliberately adulterated. So boiling, even though it changes the taste, is wise.

Sometimes in the tropics new missionaries fail to realize the dangers of eating foods left over from one meal to the next. Of course this is no problem when the missionary has a refrigerator, but not all missionaries are so well situated. In the absence of a refrigerator, the best plan is to prepare only as much as will be consumed in a single meal. Food poisoning is nothing to be taken lightly.

These rules apply, of course, to what you do in your own home. When you are visiting and are offered food or drink it is not always possible to know how safe an item is. Besides, there is always the possibility that you may offend your host if you don't partake of what is set before you. What then should you do?

No one answer will fit every case. A doctor in Japan was asked what one should do when offered raw fish. He replied, "I'm afraid I'd turn it down if I possibly could. Some areas have very serious types of worms which involve the liver. It's safer NOT to eat it." But you notice he qualified his statement with the words, "if I possibly could." There are times, especially among friends, when you can decline such food without fear of offending. If you can, do it. But there are other times when your host would not be so understanding. Then you will have to decide which is the greater risk, that of giving offense or that of contracting a disease. In some cases it may be best to eat and then trust that the Lord who allowed you to be placed in such a situation will protect you from any harmful consequences.

Of course there are sometimes other ways out. For example, there is the case of the missionary who was invited to partake of an intoxicating drink. He didn't want to do it, but he knew that to refuse might cause serious trouble. However, he hit upon a good expedient. He said, "In my country it is not permitted for a priest to drink such things." This satisfied the people for they could readily understand the idea of taboos for priests.

EXERCISE

Perhaps the missionary is not nearly in such danger of neglecting physical exercise as is the pastor in the homeland. The very circumstances of his life and work oblige him to engage in considerable physical activity. But there are still some missionaries whose life is comparatively sedentary, and others who really do not get the exercise that they need. The danger in this situation is one that not everyone readily recognizes. There is a close connection between physical health and spiritual vitality. The depression that sometimes comes upon the missionary can often be raised by a good game of tennis. Even a long walk can help. But of course in tropical climates no one should be so foolish as to engage in strenuous physical exercise during the heat of the day.

Since so many missionaries are in tropical lands, we should mention several precautions that ought to become habitual. Malaria, for example, is still a great threat in many places, in spite of the various new drugs available to combat it. Never allow stagnant water to stand near your house, nor underbrush of the kind that harbors mosquitoes. We know that mosquitoes transmit malaria, so our best course is a preventive one. We should remove their breeding places as far from us as possible.

Since it is not always possible to eliminate the breeding places, and mosquitoes can travel fairly long distances, there are two other possible precautions. Your house can possibly be screened against these unwelcome invaders, and an insecticide can be used to care for those that do slip in. At the very least you can take care to sleep with the protection of a mosquito net. It is not courage but foolhardiness to try to do without it. There are various types of good nets available, even for hammocks. But none is of value if there are ways for the mosquito to get inside, or your body comes in contact with the net so that the mosquito can sting you through it. Also when traveling in malarial districts, it is often advisable to take regular prophylactic doses of some antimalarial drug. The protection these drugs offer is quite variable, so get expert advice on their use.

We have already mentioned the danger of strenuous exercise in the tropics in the middle of the day. More than one missionary has suffered unnecessarily from heat prostration. You will do well to have a healthy respect for the power of the tropical sun.

Adaptation to Native Life

When a missionary goes to another country he becomes a stranger and a foreigner. There are a number of things that set him apart from the people of the land. Some are physical and some are spiritual. His appearance is different, his actions are different, his speech is different, and even his ways of thinking are different. This is not too much of a handicap for some kinds of work. For instance, we expect the diplomatic representative of another country to be a foreigner. Neither are we surprised or antagonized if a salesman for a product that is peculiar to another land is himself of foreign origin.

But these people are always regarded as outsiders. We will negotiate with them and perhaps buy from them. But their very foreignness creates a barrier against any closer relationship. Most of us, apart from a very few to whom anything foreign has an attraction all its own, are likely to treat them with reserve if not with actual suspicion. They are not of us, they don't understand us, and we in turn find it very difficult to understand them.

This attitude of course makes foreign missionary work very difficult. His religion is very close to a man's heart. He may at times be willing to discuss the outward manifestations of it, but the inner reality he will not reveal to any but his closest friends. We do not open our hearts to the examination of strangers and foreigners. And it is not the foreigner who will readily tempt us to try that which is new and unfamiliar.

It is strange that so many of us fail to realize just how much of a handicap our foreignness is. We seem to expect other people to take us at our own evaluation. We seem to think that they will naturally trust a missionary, no matter how confused his language and how peculiar his actions. Or else we feel there is something so inherently valuable in our ways that they will spontaneously recognize their superiority. At any rate there are many missionaries who never seem to make any serious attempt to overcome this handicap. They content themselves with getting just enough of the language to get by, and, within the limits of what is possible, they try to live a life nearly like what they would have in their home country.

This problem of adaptation to the life of the people is one that is constantly coming up in missionary circles. And you will find a great variety of points of view. Some go to one extreme, some to the other, but the great majority try to work out some sort of compromise between the two. For it is not an easy problem to solve. What we shall do here is simply to indicate some of the principles involved, with perhaps a brief treatment of the way some of them work out in practice.

Those who argue for the most complete adaptation to the life of the people among whom the missionary works reason in this way. We know that our foreignness is a great handicap to our work. Therefore we should remove that handicap as completely as possible. We should be like our Saviour who was "found in fashion as a man" in order that He might win men. We cannot get close to the people and win their confidence if they are constantly made aware of the fact that we are different from them. We must try to identify ourselves with them in every possible way, trying to be one with them in all their experiences. We must lay our lives alongside their lives in order to win them to Christ. This is true Christian love. It may mean physical sacrifice, but love that does not sacrifice is not true love.

This argument on the whole is very sound. Its one weakness is that it does not recognize that what is definitely desirable in theory may not be possible to work out in practice. For example we can follow the greatest of all missionaries, the Lord Jesus Christ, only up to a point. He did not become "like" man; he became Man. We cannot do this; we can only become more or less like the people to whom we go. The reality escapes us. In many cases even the likeness cannot be very close. Can a white American ever look like an African, or a Japanese, or a Papuan? Our racial features betray our foreignness in spite of everything we do to eliminate it. Remember the treatment we meted out to the Nisei Japanese on the Pacific coast during the Second World War. Many of them were American citizens who had never been in Japan; they shared our culture, spoke our language, even in some cases were

Christian in religion. Yet these things did not keep them from being treated as aliens—enemy aliens.

There are also other practical things to be considered in adaptation. Suppose you are an American. The people where you go will usually know it, though you try to keep it from being obvious. They may also know other Americans and know their standard of living. If the local level is quite low and you decide to adapt yourself to it, you may presume that the people will admire you for it. But in many cases you will be deceiving yourself. Instead of admiring they will despise you. Obviously you can't amount to much in your own country when you can't afford to live like other Americans. It will be useless to explain that you want to be like them; they will take it as evidence of a condescending spirit that is always irritating. Only a few will really understand.

In primitive regions, too, the attempts to live as the people do may jeopardize your health without any corresponding increase in the effectiveness of your ministry. No true missionary would hesitate to lay down his very life, if by paying that price he could accomplish his great purpose. But there is a difference between laying down one's life and throwing it away. Conditions of life are such among some peoples that the average life expectancy is less than the age of the missionary when he first goes out. Their high death rate is the natural result of the conditions in which they live.

Closely associated with this is the argument that the missionary should rightly set the example of a higher standard for the people. Of course it should be a standard that is not so high as to be completely unattainable. But really, who has the greatest influence on a people, the one who lowers his own standards to where he is just like the rest, or the one who holds up before them the example of a better life that they possibly can attain?

In the light of these things let us set down a principle: You should seek to identify yourself as closely as possible with the people you serve, so as to remove every possible hindrance from their attending to the gospel and following it. However, you should recognize that complete adaptation is neither possible nor always desirable. You must not attempt it in such a way as to forfeit health or respect. But on the other hand you must avoid self-indulgence.

In practice each field presents a different situation. The same possibilities of adaptation are not present everywhere. For example, complete adaptation is much more possible in parts of Latin America than it is in primitive areas of Africa. In Africa the white missionary is always recognizable as a foreigner. He cannot change his racial characteristics, nor does anyone expect him to try. He must be content to be different. This is also true in other areas where racial features are distinctive.

In matters of clothing, the missionary to Latin America would be in style in a suit or dress similar to those worn in North America. In parts of Africa, on the other hand, people wear little or no clothing. It is neither desirable nor expected that the missionary will imitate the people in this. They would have no respect for him if he did.

But what of those places, including parts of Africa, where the people are decently clothed, but their type of clothing is not what the missionary is accustomed to? Here is where there is a difference of opinion. In West Africa, for example, the missionaries on the whole seem to believe that they are so obviously foreign anyway that there would be no advantage in adopting native dress. There is even the possibility that the people might resent what they feel to be an insincere affectation.

In other places, however, missionaries have deliberately adopted native dress. This was true in inland China, where they were far less conspicuous, and consequently safer from being molested, if they dressed like the Chinese. It was a wise measure in days when foreigners were objects of curiosity and extreme suspicion in the interior. It would not be so necessary where foreigners are a common sight.

Perhaps we should say this in general: There are some places where clothing and personal adornment are simply a matter of preference. The only real reason for clinging to your American style is that you are used to it and would feel strange otherwise. For all practical purposes the other type would suit you just as well. Then to cling deliberately to the American style means that you are going to emphasize your foreignness wherever you go. Those who get to know you may overlook this, but every new acquaintance will first be struck by your strange appearance and it will create a barrier. How great this barrier becomes will depend largely on the personality of the missionary and the person with whom he is dealing.

Your customs and etiquette also proclaim your foreignness. How far should you adapt them to those of the people? The answer is quite clear: Just as far as you can without sacrificing any essential principle. Customs vary not only from country to country but from region to region, even where the language may be the same. In our own country we always admire those who "fit in" with the customs of the part of the country where they happen to be. They may be a bit awkward at it at first, but we appreciate those who make an attempt to conduct themselves like one of us. Of course this does not apply to what they may do in the privacy of their own homes. Most people are understanding in such matters.

Most missionaries do try to adapt in these things, although they may not be as observant or instructed as they should be in what is customary and proper. Only a few are as unwise as a young missionary in Latin America. In a land where it is considered impolite for a man even to receive a visitor in his home without wearing a coat, this missionary insisted on preaching in his shirt sleeves. He was as out of place as a man entering the pulpit in a T-shirt in our own country. But he refused to accept correction or to conform to the custom.

Where a Christian principle is involved, of course, there is no question of adaptation. There are many customs that are closely related to the religion of the people, and others that are either immoral in themselves or have immoral connotations. You will want to be sure of your ground; but once you are sure you should stand firm. You must not compromise your Christian witness.

There is a set of practical questions that have not yet been discussed. Should you live in the same houses as the people? Should you eat the same food? Should you have such things as refrigerators, electric lights, comfortable beds, etc.? Principles already enunciated will help you answer some of these questions, but not all. There is one criterion we have not yet mentioned.

Suppose we state this criterion in the form of a question: You want to adapt as much as possible to the life of the people; but what people? That is, what part of the population? Will you live like the richest or the poorest ? Like the ruler or like the subjects? Like the merchant or like the farmer? You see, while there are some societies where all the people live pretty much on the same level, there are many like our own where there are great differences. In fact, in some societies the dif-

ferences are greater than in American society. The rich are richer, and the
poor are poorer, and there is sometimes practically no middle class. If
you adapt to the life of one class you may be cutting yourself off from
an effective witness to the other.

It is this that makes these practical questions so difficult to answer.
There is no one answer that will apply equally to all situations. Veteran
missionaries from two different fields have argued over the question
of a missionary's owning a refrigerator. Their failure to understand one
another came from the fact that they faced two different situations.
The one field was tropical, so a refrigerator was far more needed than
in the other, which was in the temperate zone. In both fields most of
the people were poor, but in the tropical field refrigerators were common among the people. Anyone who could possibly scrape together
the price would get one. In the other field they were much less common, for people could more easily do without them. Only the wealthy
would have them. In the one field no one would think anything of the
missionary's owning a refrigerator. In the other it would set him apart
from most of the people.

THE MISSION COMPOUND

The mission compound has come in for a great deal of criticism in
recent years. The compound, as you may know, is an enclosure con-
taining one or more buildings for the residence of missionaries and their
households. It is really an Oriental institution, though in other fields,
as in Africa, many mission stations are similar in their arrangements.

In a sense the compound is a little mission colony. Into it the missionaries can, if they wish, retreat from the life that surrounds them.
They can make of the compound a little American island in the midst
of an alien society. Of course it is true that not only a compound but
any American home abroad is likely to partake of this character. But
when two or more families are brought together in a single place, the
tendency to such segregation is multiplied. Man is a social creature,
but if he can find adequate outlets for his social nature among those of
his own kind, he is less likely to seek it among others.

Missionaries are like others in this matter. A single missionary family
is not likely to lock itself up in the house. Not only for its ministry but
also for social purposes it is in constant touch with the people of the

land. It seeks them out in their homes, and in turn welcomes their visits to its own. It takes part in community affairs. It finds recreation together with others of the community. A missionary couple in Africa for their third term of service were stationed alone in an African town. When I visited them they said, "We are really enjoying this work; we have never felt so close to the people."

But put several missionary families together and you have a different situation. You may carry on the same amount of formal missionary work among the people. But visits with one another crowd out visits among the people. It is not a deliberate matter. You simply find it easier and more congenial to converse in your own language with people more like yourself. And when there is time for recreation, what could be more natural than to take it with the other missionaries? You don't choose to withdraw from the people. It isn't so positive as that. Even without sensing it you have simply allowed the attractions of fellowship with the other missionaries to absorb much of your time. And in consequence you become more and more alienated from the life of the people.

The mission compound in its worst aspect has been viewed as a symbol of colonialism. This is unfair to a great number of deeply earnest missionaries. Some of them may have a colonial outlook, but many do not. They have inherited the compounds from an earlier generation when they made better sense than they do today. But they haven't yet found out what to do about it. In some places the newer missionaries are distressed because the mission properties include homes that are far too grandiose for today's missionary families. But the family must live somewhere, and the buildings are not very suitable for other purposes. So the missionaries put up with a situation that is really not of their own choosing. How to correct the situation is hard to decide.

FOOD

The question of food is just as hard to solve. All missionaries make more or less use of local products, if only because they are likely to be cheaper. But to subsist entirely on a native diet may not always be possible. The people themselves may be undernourished because of lacks in their diet. They would welcome some additions and improvements. Usually if the missionary will eat what is set before him when he is a guest, the kind of food he puts on his own table will cause little criticism. However, if he appears to be fond of the favorite dishes of the people, it may give him a special place in their hearts. It always pleases us to have other people like what we like.

Adaptation is a problem each missionary has to work out for himself. This is true because the most important thing in the whole matter is the spirit in which it is done. Do you really love the people? Not do you love the impersonal thing we so often speak of as their "soul." Do you really love them as people? Does that love make you want to get close to them so that they will learn to trust you, and through you the Saviour that has sent you? If so, you are on the right track. You may make some mistakes. All of us do. But you are on far safer ground than the one who thinks that it is just a matter of following a set of rules and instructions. There are missionaries who have carefully followed the rules without ever winning the confidence of the people. There are others deeply loved by the people, and yet who never seem to get away from their foreign habits. It is the spirit that makes the difference.

A missionary to Japan writes: "Japanese people are incredibly sensitive to attitudes: an attitude of friendly equality evokes friendly cooperation, while an attitude of superiority or 'business' (no matter how well concealed) produces a response of cool reserve or formal polite non-co-operation, maddeningly frustrating to the foreigner."[1] With minor variations we might say the same thing of many other people. People generally are quite sensitive to our attitudes, or at least to what our attitudes seem to be.

REST AND RECREATION

We should not close this section on the missionary's physical life without saying something about rest and recreation. I like what a mission secretary wrote recently.[2] "One of the missionary's most besetting sins is that of falling into the error of living in a 'world of total work.' To make some leisure in our lives (at the risk of being misunderstood as less than wholly zealous) is not a concession to the weakness of the flesh, but indicates a true understanding of our spiritual needs, and of our creaturely status before God. How warped our lives must appear

[1] P. T. Like, in *Japan Harvest*, Winter, 1957.
[2] Victor Hayward, in *Congo Mission News*, July, 1957.

to Him, if we can never pause and enjoy Himself and His gifts for their own sake. We can take God more seriously if we take ourselves a little less seriously!"

Rest is important. Not only is it necessary to restore physical energy, it has a great deal to do with our spiritual vitality. The picture of Elijah under the juniper tree begging the Lord to let him die is the picture of a spiritually dejected missionary. But it is clear in the story that the big trouble was that Elijah was physically worn out. He needed rest and food.

Recreation is closely related to rest. The best rest is not always a complete cessation from all activity. It often means just a change to a different type of activity. That is why so many office workers like to set up a wood-working shop in their basement or garage. Financially it is usually unprofitable. But physically it offers good relaxation from a monotonous or sedentary job.

The principle we ought to follow as missionaries is this. We ought to get enough rest and recreation to maintain health and a fruitful ministry; but not so much as to favor laziness or detract from our ministry.

What does this mean in practice? It means getting "a good night's sleep" as regularly as possible. But it doesn't mean lying abed in the morning, when the sun is up and there is work to do. Don't get into the bad habit of staying up late at night and you won't have so much of a problem in getting up at a decent hour in the morning.

But many missionaries don't get the chance of staying in bed late. Activity starts too early in the morning, and they have obligations. However, in tropical lands there is often the "siesta." The siesta is not merely a custom in the tropics; it helps to maintain health. It is a brief period of rest after the noonday meal during the hottest part of the day, when strenuous activity is least advisable. But it can become the lazy man's trap. What begins as a short nap may extend to a sleep of several hours. Watch out for it.

One day in seven for rest is a good scriptural principle. But of course the missionary is sometimes busiest on Sunday, and circumstances make it difficult to set aside another day for rest. Preachers in this country often take Monday as a rest day, if they can. But they can more easily plan their schedules than can the missionary. He is not only on call at any time but the calls are more frequent. In spite of the difficulty, he should make a serious effort to get away from his work for a short time each week. Learn to work hard when it is time to work; but learn also to lay aside your cares from time to time so that you can return to the work with new vigor. And don't forget that the rest and recreation are necessary for the whole family and not just for the "man of the house." Often that little picnic that is such a delight to the husband means only extra work for his wife.

There is the matter of vacations, too. Usually the mission authorizes an annual vacation for its missionaries. Often it urges them to take it for the good of the work, and it may even help out by providing a vacation spot. But again there are problems. In any land vacation means extra expense. On the mission field in a remote station the missionary may find that the expense of getting out for a vacation is prohibitive. Or it may take so much time and energy for traveling that the benefits of the vacation are lost. Fortunately this is much less true today than it used to be, because of improved means of transportation. But it is still a factor.

Sometimes a missionary will go to another station for a vacation. Before doing such a thing, make sure that it is convenient for the others to have you. Don't make your vacation a hardship on other people. If they are in an isolated place where visitors seldom go, they may welcome your visit, especially if you are the sort of guest who fits into their program and lends a hand wherever it is needed. Don't even think of complete freedom from responsibilities in such a situation. It is out of the question.

CHAPTER SIX

SPIRITUAL LIFE

MOST PEOPLE IN THE HOMELANDS seem to take the missionary's spiritual life for granted. Whether they put him on a pedestal or look at him with highly critical eyes, they presume that he doesn't face the spiritual problems they do. Either he is so consecrated that he is above them, or else his nature is so different from that of ordinary people that he doesn't feel the same temptations.

This makes it quite a shock to the new missionary when he gets into the work and finds that the ones he works with do not live on some high, ethereal level. Forgetting that he is now one of them, he expects to find in them a perfection of Christian conduct and of spirituality that is sometimes woefully absent. He sees missionaries become depressed, lose their tempers, exhibit jealousy and ambition and even more unpleasant things. He may even get to think that it is only in *his* mission that such things happen. Surely in other missions they are all of higher spiritual caliber.

Let us face realities. It is true that missionaries as a class do tend to be more spiritually minded than other Christians. They would never become missionaries if they weren't. We might even say that they are more spiritually minded than most Christian workers at home. This is simply because it may call for a greater measure of consecration and self-denial to go into missionary service. It certainly isn't because of the circumstances of their life. These are certainly much more trying, with few of the encouragements that so often help us at home.

But missionaries are just ordinary Christian people with an extraordinary passion to extend the blessings of their faith to others. They usually have to prove the reality of their Christian faith and some maturity of Christian experience before their appointment. Some are

more advanced than others. Yet none is perfect. They are all subject
to temptation. And it should not surprise us if sometimes they yield to
the temptation.

The missionary faces three types of temptation. First, there are the
temptations that are common to all Christians. The missionary is not
immune to any of them. Some may affect him less than others but they
still come. Second, there are the temptations that come to those whose
responsibility it is to minister to others. These are temptations such as
the pastor experiences. And finally there are the temptations peculiar
to his situation as a foreign missionary.

To understand a missionary's temptations we need to understand his
situation. He is set down among a strange people, of strange language
and customs, uninvited and often unwanted. He is expected to present
his gospel by word and act in such a way that people will come to accept
it and trust the Saviour whom he represents. Those who believe, he
must shepherd and instruct and discipline, until such a time as there
may arise among themselves those who can carry on this work of spiritual leadership. Even then he is expected to continue his work of
counseling and inspiring the leaders and the church in general.

He probably serves under someone else—a superintendent or director. Yet he may be the only representative of the mission in his
particular area. So he is expected to use his own judgment in most matters that don't affect basic policies. For months at a time he may not see
another missionary, nor anyone from his own nation. There is no one
to report whether he is diligent or slothful. There may be no inspiring
conferences to attend, no radio messages to listen to, no one to minister
to his spiritual hunger. He must get his inspiration direct from God and
from the Word.

Of course this is not the situation of all the missionaries. Many of
them live in sizeable compounds with several other missionaries or missionary families. Then it is that we see the importance of knowing how
to live and work *together.* There are also missionaries who live and
work in headquarters or in the larger metropolitan areas. Some of them
have to spend much of their time in administration, office work, negoti-
ating with government officials, purchasing and shipping supplies, meeting new missionaries, entertaining visitors from the homeland, etc. It
is no wonder that they sometimes become despondent. They long for

the opportunity to engage in the more direct missionary work. Frankly, it seems to me that the missionary in the big city has more problems in keeping up his spiritual life than the one in the isolated outstation. Yet both have their problems.

Let us mention several specific temptations that face the foreign missionary. The first is born of self-satisfaction. In some places the missionary is spiritually far in advance of the people, or at least he feels that he is. Because of this he fails to realize his own need for spiritual growth. He may neglect the Bible except as he uses it in preparing messages for others. He prays in public regularly, but less and less in private. There are just too many demands on his time. And before long his spiritual level has dropped alarmingly.

Some missionaries are tempted to laziness. They are so largely on their own that it is easy to succumb. On the other hand there are some who are tempted in the opposite direction. They get so wrapped up in routine business and material affairs that they have little time or energy left for the things of the Spirit. Sometimes their very *busy-ness* is an attempt to avoid the more difficult work of a spiritual sort. But more often they become entangled in a whirl of activity before they realize it.

Then there is loneliness. For many missionaries this is one of the greatest trials. Especially is this true in the earlier years. Presumably unmarried missionaries would suffer from it more than others. Yet I am not sure that this is so. It is perfectly true that the married couple do have one another for fellowship and mutual consolation. Yet this very fact may sometimes cause them to make of their family a tight little social unit more or less isolated from the life that surrounds them. The single missionary, on the other hand, feels much more strongly the pull to become a part of that life. Maybe this in itself is just a reaction to lonesomeness. At any rate loneliness opens the door to many temptations that come to the missionary. When we are lonely we will do things that at other times we wouldn't even consider. This explains many of the abnormal love affairs that at times involve missionaries.

The problem of maintaining Christian ethics on the field also ought to be mentioned. In the midst of a corrupt society, with its strong downward pull, the missionary has to struggle to keep from being drawn into the same vortex of thinking, and even of acting. He sees that honesty, justice, sincerity, humilty and other Christian graces are very little regarded. He learns that the great American idea of the triumph of the "good guy" works out better in fiction than in the daily life he sees. When "everybody's doing it," isn't he being naïve to follow principles that nobody respects in practice?

This temptation manifests itself in a multitude of ways. And the issues are not always clearcut. Should the missionary sell the precious dollars he gets from home in the black market, knowing that the official exchange rate is very unrealistic and would mean a great loss? Should he follow the almost universal practice in some places of giving a "tip" to get a document or a signature that he needs? There are many such problems. Sometimes the answers seem clear at this end, but in another society they become quite confused. And even in more fundamental problems of morality the missionary may be tempted to let down his standards. It is in such a situation that the strength of his character is revealed, as it would never be revealed where Christian principles have a greater influence on society.

KEEPING UP THE SPIRITUAL LEVEL

How can a missionary keep up his spiritual level? Very much in the same ways in which he would do it at home. The major difference is that his situation is more difficult. The Christian minister in a so-called Christian country finds most of his fellowship among professing Christians. He seldom finds it necessary to oppose the trends of thinking and acting in his congregation. Perhaps in some cases he should; but usually he doesn't.

Contrast the situation of the missionary in a predominantly pagan land. A large part of his associations are with those who are not Christian. In fact, they may be determinedly opposed to Christianity. Instead of the congregation's helping to support his Christian life, it may be that their ideas of Christian living are largely determined by what they see in him. He often does not enjoy the fellowship and encouragement of other Christian ministers except at rare intervals. There are no inspiring conferences for him to attend, where his own spirit will be lifted up. So the ordinary means of grace become more critically important to him.

1. *Bible Study.* There is no substitute for the reading of the Word of God. The missionary uses it constantly, for he realizes that it is the

source of his message. His problem is that he is so constantly using it to get messages for others that he fails to seek in it a message for his own soul. He often finds little time just to read the Scriptures for his own spiritual nourishment and correction, or to meditate on what its teachings should mean to him. Instead of being the dreamy-eyed idealist that so many people picture him, the missionary most often becomes so occupied with a multitude of *activities* that he finds no time for dreaming. He becomes a Martha rather than a Mary. To keep up his spiritual level he must deliberately take time out to sit at the Master's feet.

2. *Prayer.* Prayer is of course fundamental. Seldom does the missionary neglect the more formal public prayers. Nor does he find it too difficult to keep up the prayer meetings with other missionaries. Family prayers, too, which sometimes include servants and visitors, are the usual thing. But none of these can be a satisfactory substitute for personal communion with God. There are times when an individual needs to be alone with God. There are things that we need to mention to Him when no one else is listening. There is a freedom to unburden one's self in private prayers that is not present in even the most intimate of family gatherings.

It is not at the beginning of our ministry, nor yet when we are facing serious problems, that we need to remind ourselves to pray. At those times we readily recognize the need. It is when we have settled down to a routine that we are in most danger. It is when things seem to be moving at a smooth pace and there is no special pressure to drive us to our knees that spiritual barrenness occurs. Yes, a missionary's life can sometimes become humdrum. He is not always facing crises, problems and important decisions. Neither is he always acutely frustrated or discouraged. Like any other workman, he develops routines for his work. And when the routine is well established, he becomes less and less conscious that the routine is only a framework through which the Spirit can operate. He then is in danger of neglecting the all-important spiritual core that makes the routine meaningful. The best way to avoid this danger is to have well-established habits of personal communion with God. We admit that prayers, too, can become a matter of routine. But if they are sincere, no matter how routinary, they keep us in contact with the source of spiritual power. The workman who reports his progress day by day opens the way for his employer to direct his efforts, and to stimulate, encourage and direct him in them.

Sometimes the question arises whether we should carry on Bible reading and prayers in the native tongue. Of course when others are present who do not know the missionary's language, it is only courtesy to read and pray in the language that all understand. There should be no remarks in another language unless they are immediately interpreted. But sometimes the missionary wonders about doing his own private devotional reading in the language of the people. Less often does he raise the question with regard to prayers.

The answer depends on two things; your objective and the degree of your familiarity with the language. To take the latter first, there are not many missionaries who are as familiar with the language of the people as they are with their own tongue. The things that they read do not as rapidly translate themselves into images and concepts in their own minds. The thoughts that they want to express do not spring to their lips spontaneously in words of the other language. In other words, a language which is not our own is always more or less of a barrier to the free flow of ideas. The size of that barrier depends on the measure of our familiarity with the other language.

Now let us turn to our objective. If it is simply to have communion with God through His Word and through prayer, we should unquestionably do it in our own language. This is the language that offers the minimum of interference with such communion. But if we are trying to do two things at once; that is, if we want to carry on a measure of communion with God and at the same time familiarize ourselves more with the language of the people and with the Scriptures in their language, then our answer may be different. The new missionary will find that his attention is so taken up with the words and forms of the language that there is very little spiritual communion. He would be wise to do his devotional reading in his own tongue, unless he can give far more time to his devotions than most. The missionary who is already familiar with the language may choose to do either. He should realize, however, that there is almost always a tendency to let linguistic questions intrude into the spiritual message.

3. *Reading Devotional Literature.* Besides Bible reading and prayer, the reading of devotional books helps to keep up the spiritual level.

Some missionaries have the custom of reading after lunch each day a brief portion of some book, preferably one of a devotional or inspirational nature. It takes only a few moments but provides food for later meditation, as there may be opportunity. It is not a substitute for Bible reading but an auxiliary to it.

4. *Meditation.* Meditation is almost a lost art to us Occidentals. We seem to feel that we must be ceaselessly active, or else that we must be spectators of the activities of others. If at some time we do attempt to meditate—we fall asleep! We tend to glorify our doers, our builders, our athletes, and we give comparatively little regard to our thinkers. We have the idea that the time employed in thinking, without any visible activity, is time lost. We are under constant pressure to "do something," even when we are not just sure what we ought to do.

This reveals itself also in our missionary work. The "programs" that we set up for ourselves and for those who work with us in the field are sometimes wonders of organized activity. They are exhausting to the missionary and exasperating to some of the long-suffering nationals. They "get results" of a sort. But whether they make a deep and abiding impression in the hearts and minds of the people may be somewhat of a question. And after all our main objective is to sway men's thinking. We want to win their hearts to the obedience of Christ. We want them to commit themselves to Him and to His cause.

The missionary when he goes to the field is not spiritually perfect. At the age at which he is sent out, the best we can say is that he is on the right road and that he has progressed far enough to be able to lead some others. We expect him to develop further, but we know that his development now will not enjoy the same guidance and help that he had before from pastors and teachers. It will result from his own initiative, from the experiences he has and the personal guidance of the Holy Spirit.

So he must learn to think, to meditate. It is not merely a matter of keeping up his spiritual level; he must also progress. Where life is concerned there is always either growth or stagnation. And growth demands exercise. Paul's advice to Timothy is very appropriate here: "Meditate upon these things; give thyself wholly to them; that thy profiting may appear to all" (I Tim. 4:15).

The reading of devotional works does help to stimulate meditation.

So also does the reading of the Scriptures, when we read them not per-
functorily but with discrimination. But we must not always depend on
these outside stimuli. There must be within us not only a capacity for
spiritual growth but also a desire for it. That desire itself will prod us
into making the disciplined effort that true meditation requires.

CHAPTER SEVEN

INTELLECTUAL LIFE

F ROM WHAT ALREADY HAS BEEN SAID, it is clear that the intellectual life and the spiritual life are rather closely related. Just as it is possible to decline spiritually on the mission field, so it is also possible to stagnate intellectually. There are several reasons for this.

REASONS FOR STAGNATION

First, the missionary is often isolated from the main currents of the life and thought of the church as well as of the world. This, however, is not nearly so common as it once was. Missionaries do have short-wave radios today, even in isolated stations. They can receive periodicals, as well as the latest books, with reasonable regularity. And fully as important, they have furloughs every few years when they are brought out again into the mainstream. The major problem is that the isolated missionary on the field must deliberately open the doors to intellectual stimulus, while in this country it faces him on every hand.

Much more important is the fact that a missionary may become so involved in routine or petty affairs that he has neither time nor energy to look further or deeper. Even an educator can become so overburdened with the details of administration and teaching that he fails to realize it when changed conditions call for a fundamental change of policy or curriculum. He is so busy keeping the machine running that he can't give a thought to designing and constructing a more efficient machine. This is one of the sources of friction between older missionaries and their younger colleagues. The older missionary merely wants help in carrying out the details of the pattern that was set long ago. The younger worker is inclined to question the pattern itself. We need both. We need the experience of the veteran to restrain the rashness of the neophyte; but we need the intellectual freshness of the younger man to stimulate us to re-examine our work.

Then there is a lack of libraries, ministerial associations, conferences, refresher courses, discussion groups and other such things that offer mental stimulus. Many missionaries are cut off from these things except on rare occasions. Their personal libraries are small, and new books are expensive. In such gatherings as they attend, they are more likely to be called on to minister than be ministered to.

There is a vast difference between fields, and even between stations in the same field. Yet many missionaries are dealing constantly with people whose entire conversation is on a low intellectual level. It is not that they are lacking in intelligence. Many of them are very keen. But their background has not prepared them to discuss much beyond the state of the weather, the crops, the family health, local gossip, and the plant and wildlife of the region. The missionary knows that it may make him seem proud and too high-minded, yet he will sometimes admit almost apologetically that he is hungry for a more intellectually stimulating conversation.

And then add to these conditions the fact that some people just don't have the intellectual curiosity and initiative to advance in spite of circumstances. A man like David Livingstone would never stagnate intellectually. In spite of the fact that his companions were usually primitive Africans, in spite of illness and weakness, his restless mind was always observing, always questioning. But not all missionaries are like that. And because they are not, it is easy to let the circumstances exercise their deadening influence on the mind.

KEEPING ALERT

Just how can a missionary make sure that he will keep mentally alert and continue to grow intellectually? Let me make a half dozen simple suggestions that should help. They all seem very simple, but they are nonetheless important.

First, be inquisitive. You never really stagnate until you cease to learn. And how much there is that is worth learning. Even among primitive people there is a great deal that is worth investigation. Of course you will want to follow your own lines of interest, but always have one or more subjects in mind about which you are eager to learn more. They don't have to have a clear relationship to your ministry. There is nothing wrong about a missionary's being interested in botany, as was Carey, or in geography, as was Livingstone, or in anthropology or zoology or a dozen other subjects.

Second, visit. You are not likely to stagnate while you are constantly giving out and taking in. As we have said before, there are many keen minds in other lands, even among illiterate people. But you will not find them if you shut yourself off in a corner. We won't say that all visitation is mentally stimulating. But it does keep you in touch with real life and with real problems. It is sometimes true of missionaries as it is of many ministers in our own land, that their preaching shows how little they really understand the people and their ways of thinking and acting.

Third, read. In reading you have one advantage over visiting. You yourself can choose your visitor and the subject for discussion. The trouble is that if you don't like the visitor's point of view you can shut him off without apology by simply closing the book; you don't have to face the issue. But good reading is stimulating. And it is not difficult today to get new books and magazines from home on almost any subject. The one necessary warning is this: if you love to read, be careful that your reading does not withdraw you from the society of living men.

Fourth, learn to meditate. We have already said something about this in connection with spiritual development. It takes meditation to give depth to your thinking. If there is any criticism of today's preachers that is more common than any other, it is the shallowness of their preaching, the "pompous pronouncement of pious platitudes." The preachers are not altogether to blame. We expect them to have a part in such a bewildering variety of activities that they don't have time for that unhurried meditation that would give depth to their message. To some extent the same situation prevails in the mission field. However, many a missionary labors in a more leisurely society than our own, and it is he himself who sets the pace of his activities.

Fifth, study. We hope you are not of those who think they have arrived, when once they have graduated from school. There is much yet to study. The language is one thing that you will need to continue studying long after language school days. You will also want to continue to study the Scriptures, if you don't want your ministry to become sterile. But it is often wise also to undertake a study that doesn't have a direct bearing on your missionary ministry. It should not detract from that ministry, of course. But the study of other things outside your own special field is good to keep you mentally alert. It is possible to take numerous courses of study by correspondence. These have the advantage of definite assignments, with corrections by experienced teachers. But it is also possible to set a course of study for one's self. In the absence of a library, it may be well to make it the study of one book. Or it may be simply a reading course in a certain subject. But it should be something definite to which you can turn from time to time as you have opportunity.

Lastly, have a hobby. Hobbies are only dangerous when they get out of proportion. When they are kept within bounds they offer a welcome change from the ordinary duties of life. They do good to the mind and spirit. But occasionally a hobby can get such a hold on a man that he pays more attention to it than to his main business. Then it may prove harmful. This usually happens when the man's regular occupation is distasteful to him. There is no limit to the variety of hobbies that are possible. A hobby is something that we do simply because we like to do it. It may have no other value for us, although it does sometimes happen that what started as a hobby developed into a useful enterprise.

CHAPTER EIGHT

ECONOMIC LIFE

SALARY OR SUPPORT

S OME MISSIONARIES are on a stated salary from the sending society. Others have a fluctuating income, depending on the amount that is sent to the society specified for them, or on their apportionment from what the mission has available for missionary support. But whatever the plan, the money that they receive as salary or support comes from the sending churches or from interested individuals. Seldom does a missionary have any independent means of support. Also it is only an occasional missionary on special service who is supported entirely or in part by a government, a school, or some other organization.

The normal procedure is for the church or individual to send gifts to the mission treasurer at home. Then at stated intervals, usually once a month, the treasurer will remit to the field. The ways of making the remittance are so varied that we shall mention only two of the more common ones here. Sometimes it is possible to deposit the money with a bank in this country, who will then authorize its agency in the other land by cable to make payment at the current rate of exchange. There may be times, however, when no such close banking connections are possible. Then it may be necessary to send a bank draft by mail that can be sold on the field to any bank or commercial house in accordance with local rules.

These matters of exchange rates and currency restrictions are quite complicated. The missionary of course must have his money exchanged into the currency of the country where he is. When currencies are stable and there are no restrictions, this may be a fairly simple matter. Banks or commercial houses in need of dollars to pay for imports will pay the missionary for what he has at the current buying rate for dollars. But today many currencies are fluctuating in value and many countries have imposed a variety of restrictions on monetary transactions. In the matter of exchange rates, let us look at two South American countries for example. The *boliviano* of Bolivia and the *bolivar* of Venezuela were at one time of about the same value, roughly twenty cents in American money. Today, however, an American dollar can be exchanged in Bolivia for more than nine thousand *bolivianos,* while in Venezuela it will get you only slightly over three *bolivares.* Venezuela's rate has been stable for a number of years, while Bolivia's has constantly been hitting new lows. In lands like Bolivia missionaries have often found it wise to hold onto their dollars until they need to exchange them, for next week they may be worth half again as much.

But in an attempt to stabilize their currencies, many countries, as we have said, have established currency restrictions. For example, when the missionary comes to sell his dollars, he may find that he is required by law to sell them through certain official channels. The government arbitrarily establishes the exchange rate, which is less than would be paid in an open market. Sometimes this leads to flourishing "black market" activities. But the missionary has conscientious scruples against dealing with the "black market" and so he suffers a loss in the exchange of his meager income.

When the remittance is sent to the field, it usually goes to a field treasurer, who is responsible to see that it is properly distributed. Where stations are widely scattered, this may involve a great deal of work. To one station he may be able to send money through a bank, to another through a business house, but to a third he may have to send cash by any means that he may find available.

We have described what is very common procedure. But there are innumerable variations. In addition there are always some individuals and organizations that send gifts direct to the field rather than through the mission treasurer. It may be because they think that sending direct is the most logical, or because they are afraid that the mission won't make sure that their gift reaches the hands of the missionary for whom they intended it.

Under most circumstances the missionary will do well to encourage his friends to channel their gifts through the mission office. Many a missionary can tell of letters received on the field with their contents pilfered. The mission usually has the safest way of transmitting funds. Personal checks are sometimes uncashable on the field, and in some places even bank drafts or money orders are difficult to handle. Moreover, for income tax purposes the giver will want an official receipt from the mission. The mission will usually transmit any gifts to the field without deduction for expenses.

But even so, there are still some who will persist in sending gifts direct to the field. Then there are several things that the missionary will be wise to do.

First, acknowledge any direct receipts at once. Even so, the donor will have to wait a long time before your receipt reaches him. Many times he fails to realize just how long it takes a letter to reach the field and get a reply. I have known a donor to write impatiently to inquire why a missionary did not acknowledge his gift even before the gift had time to reach the field.

Second, if the gift comes in the form of a check that has to be sent somewhere else to be cashed, make a careful record of it. Checks do get lost or stolen from the mails. Then it makes little difference that no one else can cash them but the person or bank to whom they are endorsed. The missionary will still suffer the loss unless he has a record to enable him to get them replaced.

Some missions require that their missionaries report regularly the moneys that they receive direct. Even where such receipts are not deducted from the allowance the mission gives, the information is needed so the mission can tell how its missionaries are faring. This is particularly true in the "faith" missions.

Not all missionaries are as businesslike as they should be in the handling of financial affairs. For this reason a word of warning may be in order. When money is received direct, but intended for some part of the work rather than for the missionary, take special care to see that it is held for that purpose. Handle it with the same conscientious care as if the treasurer had received it. Some people, without intention, find it all too easy to get mission funds confused with their own. Take care to be completely above reproach in such matters.

Perhaps we ought to say something about the manner of acknowledging gifts that are sent for your support. This applies whether the gifts reach you directly or through the mission treasurer. But it is of much more concern to those who serve under the "faith" missions than to others.

Even though the mission may already have issued a receipt for the donation, you ought to acknowledge it personally by mail. When you have to make a number of such acknowledgments month by month, however, it may become a problem. How many ways are there to say, "Thank you"? And just how effusive should you be in your expression of thanks?

The important thing is to say it. Don't put it off until you have time to write a ten-page letter. Just two words at the right time will be better than a whole page a month later. Say it with obvious sincerity and lack of affectation. If it was a special gift and you want to tell how timely it was, or tell how it is being used, very good. Or if it was an unusually large gift, or one that you know meant unusual sacrifice on the part of the giver, you will want to say a special word about it. A bare "thank you" is hardly enough. But in most cases a brief statement of appreciation is all that is expected. Remember that you are not receiving charity. You are the Lord's workman and worthy of your hire. The giver is the Lord's steward. If he is a true steward he gives because of the value of your services, not simply out of pity for your need.

Safekeeping of Funds

Keeping cash on hand is always a problem where there are no banks or safes. Yet this is a situation the missionary often faces. And thievery in some places is not only very common, it is also carried out with consummate adroitness. The problem would be a purely personal one if it were not for the fact that often the missionary has on hand funds belonging to the mission and to other individuals.

Two observations should be made at this point. One is to avoid all unnecessary display of funds. The missionary is often looked at as a wealthy man, and as such he is always likely to be robbed. But he greatly increases that likelihood if he lets it be known that he has considerable cash on hand.

The other thing is, use every reasonable precaution to safeguard the money in your hands. If you don't have a safe, a trunk with a good lock may serve. Above all things, don't leave money lying around on dressers, in teacups and in desk drawers, the way so many do in this country. If you have servants, you are merely putting temptation in their way. And since the missionary's house is so often open to a wide variety of visitors, you have only yourself to blame if money is missing.

PERSONAL EXPENDITURES

In some ways the missionary is in a more favorable situation than the pastor at home. The people who contribute to his support are not on hand to criticize how he spends his money. Not that he has much to spend, but it is often noticeable at home that churches paying the smallest salary are the most critical of any supposed extravagance on the part of the minister or his family.

The money you receive, whether as salary or as contributions for your support, is yours to use as you see fit. Of course you needn't expect to be free from criticism if you use it in ways that others think are unwise. But you will find that no good mission nor good mission executive will attempt to dictate your spending . The one thing you need to watch is that no lack of discretion on your part will work a hardship on someone else. On the mission field as well as at home there are some who are chronically getting into financial straits and have to have someone else bail them out. Yet the others receive the same allowance. And these improvident individuals are sometimes remiss in paying their share of expenses which are the common responsibility of a group of missionaries. They let others shoulder the whole burden. Take care not to be guilty in this.

Actually it is more important for the missionary to be foresighted in financial affairs than for the worker at home. Especially is this true of missionaries under the "faith" missions. The reason is that you are so much farther removed from the source of income.

The missionary under salary does know that his income will probably be the same month after month. However, even in normal times it may not arrive promptly on the first of the month. It may be delayed for any number of days. Mail service and even cable service is not perfect. Sometimes remittances are lost, go astray or get stolen. It may not be common, but even one such experience can be very distressing if payday always finds you down to your last cent. You may postpone the payment for some items of expense, but food usually calls for hard cash.

And there may not be funds available from which you can borrow until the remittance arrives.

Then there are the missionaries whose income fluctuates with the gifts of interested friends and churches. Their need for planning is even more acute. A large remittance this month may be followed by a very small one next month. The summer months at home are reflected by a diminished remittance to the field, while the Christmas giving is likely to reach you long after Christmas is past. Every remittance may be like a surprise package—you don't know what is in it until you open it. But it contains disappointments as well as joys.

Of course the best planning usually calls for a careful budget, one that you stick to. Most people don't like budgets because they tell us some unpleasant facts and they sometimes inhibit our spending. They reveal to us the inadequacies of our income to cover some things we would like to do. They tell us that if we make that purchase we are thinking about we are going to have to cut down on food, or clothing, or laundry, or some other expense. But budgets are very useful, and especially for the one who is not normally very careful about his expenditures. The very careful spender may perhaps get along without one, but the one who is more carefree needs the constant reminder that there are limits to his freedom.

A budget is a sort of prophecy based on past experience. Do you have any fixed expenses that you have to pay month by month? This would include such things as rents, installment payments, etc. (Yes, some missionaries today are buying things on the installment plan, just as others do.) Put these amounts down first. Then list the other regular expenses you are likely to have: food, clothing and other supplies, laundry and other services, travel expenses, including the upkeep of a vehicle if you have one, postage, etc. If the total is more than you are likely to have left after the fixed expenses are paid, you will have to do some cutting.

Don't fail to include in the budget items that are paid quarterly, semiannually or annually. An annual insurance premium can wreak havoc with a budget that hasn't made allowance for it by setting aside a monthly amount to pay it. And do allow a little something for the extras—those items that may not be altogether necessary but add a little spice to living. It may not be large, maybe just enough for a package of sweets, but never omit it altogether.

Of course your first budget won't be perfect. Be ready to make changes for the first few months in the light of your experience. Make it workable and make it work.

If you use it right, the budget will usually be a real help. It helps you to have money on hand to pay bills when they come due. It warns you at once when expenses begin to get out of control. It shows you where the fault lies when your expenses become larger than your income. It tells you how to cut expenses sensibly in time of need, instead of trying to make drastic cuts where it will do little good and may do harm. It is especially helpful to those whose income is irregular. Just as the better missions do, you can usually calculate about what your annual income will be. By dividing this into twelve parts, you can estimate about how much you will need to carry over from a good month to round out a lean one. Some missionaries have found that a budget has helped them to lay aside a small amount for emergencies, for furlough, or for the replacement of equipment that is wearing out.

Since we have mentioned the matter of insurance premiums, perhaps we ought to say a word about the missionary and insurance. We recognize that there are a few who have conscientious scruples against any insurance at all. They are not very many, and it is not our purpose here to enter into a discussion of their reasons. The fact is that the vast majority are not opposed, for insurance plays a large part in our modern life.

The day has passed when the missionary was considered an exceptionally poor risk for life insurance. Missionary mortality has been so reduced that a missionary's life expectancy is not much different from that of anyone else. Life insurance purchased in this country is valid wherever he goes, as long as he pays the premiums on time. But since the missionary is sometimes so far away that the premium notices are very slow in reaching him, it is well for him to arrange for payment in this country. Usually arrangements can be made to have the premium notice sent to the mission treasurer, giving him authorization to pay the amount from your allowance. On the field, though, you will want to be prepared for this deduction when it comes. If it comes out of an already small remittance, it may put you "on the spot."

Other types of insurance, such as accident and health insurance, are not so readily available for missionaries through commercial companies. One kind, however, seems to be increasing rather rapidly. This is automobile insurance, especially what we call liability insurance. It is usually purchased on the field. In one or two cases we have learned that the missionaries themselves formed a co-operative fund to cover damages to their own vehicles through accident. With careful management it has worked out very well.

TEMPTATIONS

We should not think that the missionary is immune to financial temptations or wrong attitudes toward money. Even though generally he is less susceptible than others to such things, he still feels their influence and may succumb to them. We say that he is less susceptible because of the very nature of his work. A minister or an evangelist may possibly gain more than a comfortable living from his work; a missionary never. The minister in this country serves a community where the general level of income is probably higher than his own and he sees his parishioners enjoy things that he cannot afford. The missionary, on the other hand, is generally in more comfortable circumstances than those he serves, even though his level of living is inferior to the usual American standard. So the missionary to begin with can scarcely be motivated by financial ambitions, nor does he face such constant provocations to jealousy.

But in common with most pastors, the missionary's salary is small. There are times when it is not adequate even for pressing needs. And almost always he faces problems in his work that apparently could be made easier if he had more money at his disposal. Then, too, when on furlough or in visiting the foreign colony abroad, he is made conscious of some of the things that he doesn't have. Can we blame him if at times of depression he feels a longing for a little more of this world's goods? It is not those who have the most who are most strongly tempted to a love of money.

How does such a weakness reveal itself in a missionary's life? In various ways. Occasionally it may lead to stinginess. But this is not usual. More commonly it expresses itself in complaints, hints, or indirect appeals for funds in the missionary's letters home. Or it shows up in his addresses and conversations when he is on furlough. We are not talking about straightforward appeals for funds for the work. These are perfectly all right unless, as with some of the "faith" missions, it is considered wrong to make such direct appeals to men for God's work. What we are talking about are the hints or indirect appeals, the dissimulation that some practice in the hope that they can get gifts without actually asking for them. Often they do produce gifts, but sometimes accompanied by a distaste for the missionary and the work he represents.

Try to keep free of any suspicion of such things. The temptation is strong, especially among those "faith" missionaries who are individually supported. But it is dangerous not only to the spirit of the missionary and the reputation of the mission he represents but to the work itself. Soon the missionary finds that he is paying more attention to the publicity values of the work he is doing than to the real need for it and the permanence of its result. He becomes more concerned about the impression his reports will make on the donors, and less about the abiding values. This is not a criticism of good publicity for an important job well done, which ought to be known and supported by Christian people. But it is a condemnation of an attitude, born of the love of money, that judges the worth of a ministry by the financial support it can attract. "Ye cannot serve God *and* mammon."

SELF-SUPPORT

In some ways what we have written above leads to the discussion of the possibility of self-support in missions. It is true that William Carey had the idea that missionaries could become self-supporting after a short time on the field. The London Missionary Society had the same idea and only gave it up after a number of years of experience. Other missions, too, have attempted the same thing. William Taylor's self-supporting missions were on a somewhat different basis. Yet they later had to be taken over by a regular missionary society.

One of the ideas that some young people have in thinking of self-support in missionary service is this: they can be paid an adequate salary by an impersonal company or government on the basis of merit and of work done. They will not be dependent on the generosity of Christians nor hampered by them in the kinds of work that they prefer to do. In other words, they want to feel independent in their work.

What they fail to realize is that independence is not always good. God wants us to be dependent—dependent primarily on Him, but also dependent on one another. "We are members one of another," says Paul (Eph. 4:25).

Now there are some very effective witnesses for Christ among businessmen, teachers and government employees overseas. We wish there were many more of these "nonprofessional" missionaries. They perform the duties of their job and also find time to do something in the way of missionary work. They are sometimes able to reach people whom the regular missionary could never reach. As auxiliaries to the missionary enterprise they are invaluable. But let no one think that they take the place of the regular missionary.

It is not our purpose here to go into the benefits and limitations of non-professional missionary service. What we are more concerned about is the missionary who, to continue his ministry or to augment his income, is considering the possibility of full or partial self-support.

First, he will soon find out that in most cases full self-support is a full-time job. That is, while he may have some spare time to give to missionary work, the best of his time and the most of it must be given to his employer's interests. He also lacks the freedom to go where he wants, when he wants, and to do what he wants. His employer's interests must come first.

Really, opportunities for adequate self-support are quite limited except in the employ of foreign companies. Then what missionary work you do may be coupled in the minds of the people with their exploitation, or supposed exploitation, on the part of "the company." No matter what you say, your missionary work must in some way, they believe, contribute to the interests of "the company."

As for partial self-support, it is usually discouraged by the missions for very good reasons. It is usually undertaken to try to augment an insufficient income from the home end. But it often aggravates the condition it is aimed to improve. When those who support the missionary learn that he has another source of income, they feel that their own responsibility is lessened. It doesn't matter that his additional income is small, and is only intended to fill in what is lacking. The tendency is for them to feel much less keenly their need to give.

Moreover, from the mission's point of view, to have its missionaries involved in commercial pursuits may jeopardize its standing. Among other things there is likely to arise a conflict of interests, with the missionary neglecting his primary work for the sake of that which helps provide his support. Or he may be too closely identified in the thinking of the people with business affairs. Or he may get entangled in legal affairs as a result of his business.

Of course these objections do not hold good for some kinds of occupation. They would not apply to part-time teaching, for example.

INCOME TAX

For many years, even after most people were paying an income tax in this country, the missionary gave it little thought. Either his income was too small, or he labored in a country where there was no such thing. But today other lands are also charging an income tax, and in this country the exemptions have not kept pace with the inflation. So nearly everyone is likely to find himself liable to the tax.

Some missionaries have objected to paying the tax abroad. Their chief argument seems to be that they do not receive anything from the wealth of the country but that instead they are contributing to it, that the money they receive consists of donations from another land and so should not be taxed as local income is. Whatever the merits of this claim, and there are arguments on both sides, and whatever other inequities there may be, the proper thing to do is for the missionary body as a whole to make an official representation to the government as a good citizen would. But if the decision goes against them, they should certainly "render unto Caesar the things that are Caesar's."

CHAPTER NINE

FAMILY LIFE

The Witness of the Christian Family

WHEN A MARRIED COUPLE goes out to the mission field, its witness to Christ and the Christian life is more than that of the two individuals. Something else has been added. It is their joint witness as a Christian family. Here is a place where one and one makes more than two.

In the Bible great stress is placed on the family unit. In the Old Testament we read, "As for me *and my house, we will serve the Lord*" (Joshua 24:15). And again in the New Testament it is, "Believe on the Lord Jesus Christ, and thou shalt be saved, *and thy house*" (Acts 16:31). This is thoroughly understandable in many societies to which the missionary goes, for family ties in those places are still very strong. So they are more impressed by the witness of the Christian family than by that of an individual.

In addition, we must consider the power of example. We often say that others should be able to "see Jesus in me." The missionary is expected to set an example of the Christian life. But what of Christian family life? Family life has problems that single individuals do not experience. This is one place where the Roman Catholic priest loses contact with his people. If he is true to his vows he knows nothing of fatherhood and of the normal responsibilities and the problems of the family. In a Roman Catholic country we have overheard people contrasting the Protestant missionary families to their own priests, to the definite disfavor of the latter.

The importance of this example of the Christian family can scarcely be overemphasized. It is a sort of silent preaching that often bears un-

94

expected fruit. We who labor in another land are often embarrassed by the lack of privacy such as we enjoy at home. We seem to be "living in a goldfish bowl." People even seem to be informed of things that happen in the supposed privacy of the family circle. Yet when family life centers about Christ, even common gossip becomes a means for spreading His gospel.

And of course, for those who accept the gospel and want to follow Christ, we set the pattern of Christian family life. At times we are surprised to see how one of the believers in his home mimics some detail that he has seen in ours. It is not always what we would have chosen to have him imitate, and it makes us conscious of how circumspectly we need to walk in every way.

The home usually means children. And their part in the ministry is an important one. How many times the missionary child has opened a door that would otherwise have remained tightly closed! How often the children have been the point of contact to reach the older people! Several years ago a missionary wrote from Africa:

> Sunday afternoon I took seven of the Christians out for village preaching along the Niamey road. Dave came along, so I sent him and the phonograph along with one evangelist to a rather large village. Every soul in the village came to see the "little white man" who could play the phonograph—and all heard the Gospel. . . . He is a wonderful asset in breaking down the barrier between these Africans and a strange white man.

Family vs. Ministry

The missionary faces the same problem as the pastor in the tug-of-war between his family and his ministry. And he has the same difficulty in solving the problem. Which has the prior claim? Which should have the preference when the two interests clash?

Rightly understood, there should be no basic conflict between the two. But often the missionary does have to make a choice between what he thinks are two opposing obligations. Shall he neglect the family obligation to fulfill the obligation to his ministry? Or shall he neglect the ministry to be faithful to his family? How shall he decide? Sometimes he reasons that the ministry is the more sacred obligation. At other times the family claims are the stronger.

With all due respect for those many worthy missionaries who may have acted differently, we would call attention to some very basic principles. They won't solve every problem, but they will help us to see the matter in a little clearer light than is sometimes the case.

First, in marrying you have voluntarily assumed certain obligations. Notice that we have used the word "voluntarily." You chose to get married. You may have married before you were called to the ministry, or it may have been afterward. But you exercised your free choice in preferring the married state to remaining celibate. And in choosing to get married you chose to assume the normal obligations of married life.

Look back to your marriage vows. Remember what you said at that time. You made those vows before God, and not only before men. Are they any less binding than your offer to give yourself for missionary service? Are they any less sacred? Are they annulled or amended, now that you are a missionary?

And just what are those obligations? They are not limited to the provision of food, clothing and shelter. The most commonly used expression in any form of the marriage vow is "to love and to cherish." When you promise this you are promising all the care and attention that you can give to the object of your love. Your obligation involves all the fellowship and the intimate relationships of the normal Christian home.

The pastor or missionary sometimes acts as if he thought he were in a separate class, exempted from these normal obligations. But nowhere in the Scriptures will he find support for such a view. He is no worse than the businessman who neglects his family for his business; but neither is he any better.

Several years ago a certain missionary magazine had a brief article on this subject with the simple title "Corban." The author could hardly have chosen a more appropriate title. In that one word taken from Mark 7:11 he reveals the heart of the whole matter. Because we have dedicated our whole time and energies to "the work," we are inclined to feel that that sacred dedication "excuses us from fulfilling the most sacred vow we ever made." The purpose of our dedication is so pious that few would dare to question it. But Christ Himself said, "Full well ye reject the commandment of God, that ye may keep your own tradition."

Second, marriage looks forward to parenthood and its obligations. It is true that children do restrict certain types of missionary activity. The missionary mother, in particular, is not so free to travel, to spend long hours in teaching, etc., as her unmarried sister. There is no getting around it; children do take time and call for a great deal of attention. Also, they need a settled home.

But as we have mentioned before, children do have also a ministry all their own. They open doors and hearts to the gospel, and they attract other children and, through them, their parents. Moreover, the missionary mother is nonetheless a missionary for being a mother. Her ministry may be different from that of the single woman, but it is fully as effective. In fact, what has never failed to amaze me, in more than one field, is the amount of missionary work accomplished by some of our most devoted missionary mothers. Perhaps it is because they have learned to make the most efficient use of their time; perhaps it is because they do without some of the primping and fussing; or perhaps it is just because they are so wholly and unselfishly dedicated both to the family and to the work. At any rate, hats off to them! They put many of the others to shame.

But sometimes these missionary wives and mothers face conflicts, too, in connection with "the work." This is especially true of those who went to the field single. They have had a period of independent ministry, teaching, nursing, evangelizing the women and children. Then they got married. The claims of a husband and a household have greatly reduced the time they can spend in "the work." And then the children have come. No one who has not experienced it can imagine the extent to which a little one "ties one down." And when there are several children, "How can you get anything else done?"

To the one who has already experienced an active ministry this change of status may bring real frustration. It would never do to admit it, but the wife may even feel a jealousy of her husband and the work he is free to do. She feels restless and dissatisfied. It is not surprising that some welcome the opportunity to turn the children over to nursemaids, so they can have a larger part in "the work." It is only later that they come to realize how much they have lost, when the children have grown away from them.

What is the answer? It is simply for the missionary wife and mother to get the right perspective of her job. When she got married she didn't just take another part-time job that she could sandwich in between her other responsibilities. Neither did she give up completely all connection with her former work. Fulfilling her role as a woman, she became a wife and a mother. She is no longer alone, no longer independent. "Thy desire shall be to thy husband," said God. Her orientation is changed. As a helpmate to her husband she finds joy in his successes, challenge in the opportunity of helping him to fulfill his ministry.

Her main job is now the family. Her other activities are subordinate to this. They are not completely omitted. She is no less a teacher or a nurse than she once was. It is simply that she has now assumed a greater ministry which has a prior claim. This is no new or strange doctrine. It is only what the Scripture itself teaches. And as we said before, it is amazing how much some missionary mothers are able to accomplish in addition to their family responsibilities, and with no neglect of the family. They have the right perspective of their ministry.

Like what we said about marriage obligations, parental obligations are far more than just material support and occasional discipline. Children are entitled to love, to counsel, to comfort, to affectionate interest in the things they do and the problems they have. They don't want us to be "pals" with them. We are too grown up for that. But they do want us to have a parent's concern for them.

I can never forget how, whenever we moved to a new house, my father always took time to rig up a swing for us boys. Nor can I forget how, when I got my first musical instrument, he bought an old cornet and sat down alongside me to teach me some lessons in music that my teacher never got across. A mandolin and a cornet make a horrible combination, but the accompaniment helped. For many years Dad worked seven days a week, so he didn't have much time to give us, but he gave what he could.

There are missionaries' children, too, who have fond recollections of their parents and of their parental care. Many of them are themselves in missionary service today—but not all. There are others whose memories are of being left continually in one home or another, while their parents went off "doing the Lord's work." Some can say that they have scarcely known their parents, at least not in an intimate way. Some, perhaps wrongly, have felt unwanted and neglected. And some have even become embittered. More than one missionary in his later years, including such a great missionary as David Livingstone, has regretted the neglect of his children. "They made me the keeper of the vineyards; but mine own vineyard have I not kept" (Song of Solomon 1:6).

Third, the Scripture gives us no ground to act otherwise. In Ephesians 5 the husband's relationship to the wife is compared to that of Christ to the Church. It is far closer than that of a shepherd to his flock, of a minister to his congregation. The last few verses of the chapter make it clear that in marriage it was God's intention that they should in truth become "one flesh." And as for the children, I Timothy 3 makes it clear that the one who wants to exercise care over the Lord's house must show that he is qualified by the care he takes of his own.

Does this, then, mean that the missionary must neglect his ministry for the family, whenever there is a conflict of interests? Not at all. Remember that we said there should be no basic conflict between the two. There may often be a conflict between *what we think* is our duty to the one and our duty to the other. But that is something quite different. It is not at all uncommon for us to confuse desire and duty. We even try to tell ourselves it is the fulfillment of a duty when we are really carrying out a secret desire. But just as often we mistakenly associate duty with sacrifice. We think duty is essentially unpleasant. We long to be with our families, but the Lord's work must be done; we must make the sacrifice. It doesn't make it any easier that sometimes the mission board has the same attitude. In its deep concern for the work it may fail to show the same concern for the workers. It may not realize that its most precious asset is its missionaries.

Let us look at the facts calmly and reasonably. Was it of God that you two became husband and wife and have established a family? If you answer, "Yes," that is fact number one. Did God also call you into His service and lead you to become a foreign missionary? Then that is fact number two. Now in the very nature of the case there are certain duties, certain obligations that pertain to both of these relationships. Some of them are stated clearly in the Word of God, some are just as clearly to be implied from what is stated, and others are not quite so definite. This is fact number three.

Put the three facts together. In each case you acknowledge that God is the author. He is responsible for your marriage, for your call to service, and for the obligations that pertain to both. Is God in conflict with Himself? Does He create a conflict between relationships that He has established?

But someone may say, "I was married before I became a Christian." And someone else may object, "I did not follow the Lord's leading in my marriage." In both cases they would say that God is not responsible for the marriage. But is He not responsible for the obligations that accompany marriage? And did He not send you into the work in the full knowledge that you already had those obligations? If a mission society sends out a missionary with a wife and child, it makes provision for the family within the framework of its plans. How much more so does God!

In the face of these facts, if there is any apparent conflict of duties, it *must be* because you misunderstand those duties. We said that some are stated clearly in the Word of God and that others are not so clear. It is in those that are not clear that we make our most serious mistakes. All too often we say, "I believe that God is calling me to . . ." although it may be in direct contradiction to a known duty. Christ condemned such an act as a plain violation of the Word of God (Mark 7:11).

So keep these principles in mind. You cannot evade one responsibility by assuming another, no matter how sacred it may seem. If you follow the Lord's leading you will have no real conflict of duties, though it may take serious effort to fulfill them all as you should. And if there is any apparent conflict, do what is *clearly* commanded first.

How does this work out in practice? Is it possible at all to be a missionary and to be entirely faithful to your family responsibilities? Don't you have to sacrifice some of your family life in order to carry out your ministry? Aren't we asking the impossible?

Please notice that we ourselves are not asking anything. The principles we have stated are according to the Scriptures. It is the Lord's demands that we need to satisfy. But we ought to realize that there are hundreds of ways of fulfilling the responsibilities He has given us. And many a missionary is faithfully carrying out those responsibilities in their fullness. All, however, are not doing it in the same way. There are differences of people and vast differences of situation that call for different kinds of action.

A husband, for example, is no less faithful to his responsibilities when he has to be separated from his wife to make an extended trip. He would be guilty, however, if he needlessly lengthened the trip, or multiplied his absences, or planned a trip for a time when he would be most needed at home. You see it all comes back to the matter of attitudes and basic principles. Does he really *want* to fulfill all his responsibilities, or is he trying to evade those that seem to him more onerous?

Parents are not evading a duty when, in an emergency, they find it necessary to let others care for their children. They are wrong, however, if they regularly turn the care of their children over to nursemaids, so that they are not even aware of what the children are doing, what they may be learning, nor what their problems really are. Again it is a matter of attitude. Are the children a burden to you or a joy? Do you really *want* to take the responsibility of rearing them, or do you wish someone else could do it and free you for "more important" work?

Missionaries will often disagree on the precise action to take in fulfilling their responsibilities. That is only to be expected. One prefers to keep his children at home and teach them; another thinks it wiser to send them away to school. Either may be right, so long as you are thinking primarily of the children and are not simply choosing the easier or more pleasant way for yourself.

Training of Children

This matter of child training is easily the most complex one that faces the missionary. There are many phases to it and it raises many problems.

Training does not begin when the child goes off to school. It begins right in the home. And it begins from the time the child is born. In fact these early home influences have more to do with his development than his later schooling.

This is why it so important for missionary parents to look after their own children. Children get their standards of values from those who are with them constantly and care for them. This is one of the reasons why in much of Latin America sexual immorality is so prevalent. Some would blame it on the extreme poverty of so many of the people and the miserable conditions in which they live. But the fact is that the men of the upper classes are often the worst offenders. From infancy they have been turned over to nursemaids, women often from the lowest levels of society who are willing to take such work for a pittance. We have often seen these nursemaids congregate in the public square with their tiny charges. What the children don't learn from their own nursemaid they are likely to learn from another, or from their common conversation. And the parents sometimes wonder, "Where did he pick up such words and such habits?"

The scriptural truth that "Evil communications corrupt good manners" (I Cor. 15:53) doesn't apply altogether to the nursemaids. In fact many of them may be very worthy individuals. It applies also to the children's playmates. Children learn a great deal from one another, sometimes more than they learn from their parents. This makes it important for the missionary to see and hear what his children are doing while at play. This is true whether they are playing with native children or with other missionary children. Not all missionary children are saints.

This doesn't mean that the missionary has to spend his time supervising their play. Not at all. A good parent, though, usually knows where his children are, and with whom. He checks up on them now and then, and keeps his eyes and ears open for anything that may be out of the way. Even more important, he has an interest in their affairs and enjoys their confidence, so that they themselves let him know what is going on. Or else he can tell from their conduct when something is wrong.

Sometimes a missionary asks what language should be used in the home, whether the language of the country or the missionary's native tongue. An older missionary gave us sound advice years ago, "Use your own language in the home. The children will pick up the local language. You can't keep them from it. But they will never learn the language of their parents unless they learn it from you."

The reason why many missionaries consider using the language of the country in their home is that they believe it will help them to learn it better. They want the practice. They believe, too, that it will help them identify themselves more closely with the people.

To some extent this is true. It is certainly true that when guests are present it is impolite to use a language that they don't understand. Use their language entirely if you can. But it is different in the intimacy of the family circle when visitors are not present. Then any possible benefits from using the native language are for the missionary alone, not for his children. Children easily become bilingual. They have no difficulty in learning both languages. But if their parents insist on the exclusive use of one language, when the family goes on furlough the children suffer. They are like foreigners in their own country.

Sooner or later parents face the problem of the children's schooling. They usually find that there are several possible solutions to the problem, none of them perfect. They have to pick the one that fits their situation the best. Only in a few cases do they have conditions roughly comparable to what the pastor in this country would enjoy. For example, there are numerous missionaries living in Tokyo, Japan. Some of the missionaries have gone together to establish a Christian school for their children. It is possible for the children to live at home with their parents and go to school each day, just as they would in this country. There are some problems in financing and staffing the school, but on the whole these missionaries are in a much better situation than most.

For those who do not live in a large center like Tokyo, or in a place where such a school is conducted, there are three possibilities on the field. One is to send the children to the local schools, if there are any. Another is to teach the children at home. A third is to send the children away to a boarding school conducted either by the mission or some other group.

With the local schools you have the advantage of keeping the children under home influences. This is a real gain. In some places it is definitely the thing to do. But there are many places where good schools are not available. The fact that they use the local language should not cause the missionary much concern. But he does need to be concerned about the kind of teaching and the associations his children will have. In addition we ought to mention another problem. We are used to the separation of church and state in this country. It is not only illegal but actually unthinkable in most places for a child to suffer discrimination in school because of his religion. It is not so in some other lands. Even in state schools there is discrimination. There are numerous pressures brought to bear to make the child conform to the faith of the majority group. Even when the teacher does not do so, the other children can make life miserable for the nonconformist.

Then there is the possibility of teaching the children at home. This is not so impossible as it might seem at first glance. It is not necessary for you to be an experienced teacher nor to plan your own curriculum. Neither is it necessary to occupy the whole day with the teaching. Missionaries, government employees and businessmen all over the world make use of the correspondence course of the Calvert School of Baltimore, Maryland. They begin with the preschool-age child and provide everything that is needed: textbooks, supplies and even instructions in how to teach the lesson. They provide also correction service. Children who are taught the Calvert course are often ahead of their grade when they come to the United States. This is not surprising when we realize that they get a great deal of personal attention that is not possible in our public school system. And because of this personal attention they don't need to spend nearly so long in the classroom to cover the same material. Many missionaries prefer this home teaching.

But it also has its problems. The time that is needed to teach one child may not be excessive. But what about those families that have a number of children, each one in a separate grade? When two or more families live close together, this problem can be minimized by co-operating in the teaching, but not all missionaries are so conveniently situated. Also, some feel that there is a lack of incentive when there are no other children to compete with in the class work, and the children have a need for the social contacts provided by group activities such as sports.

A third alternative is the mission school on the field. Missions in increasing numbers are carrying on such schools. Sometimes they are conducted by an individual mission for the benefit of its own children. At other times they are co-operative enterprises, either governed by the missions jointly or by an independent organization. Although there are some exceptions, the best are usually joint enterprises. The larger student body of such a joint work means more efficient use of the teaching staff and of the facilities available.

These schools present the parents with very few problems when the children can live at home. The situation then is quite similar to what it would be in the homeland. There is no loss of the home influences. Of course there is the matter of expense when the school has to be financed by fees paid for the students. But on the whole missionary parents could scarcely hope for any better arrangement. Yet the proportion who are in this situation is comparatively small. Those who labor in the main centers, or those who happen to be stationed where the school is located, are the ones who have this advantage.

A great many missionaries must send their children away to a boarding school. Whether conducted by the mission or by some independent organization, it provides facilities for students to live at the school as well as study there. Schools of this sort are playing an important role in the missionary enterprise. Some of them are remarkably well organized and operated. They merit a great deal more sympathetic help and encouragement than they are getting.

Yet missionary parents need to understand the situation better than some of them do, and they need to know some of the problems in such schools. Even the best boarding school involves the sacrifice of some home influences. This is unavoidable. No matter how hard they try, those in charge can never completely substitute for the parents. By the very nature of their task they are likely to be responsible for more children than any parent. And we cannot expect them to have such a complete and sympathetic understanding of each and every child as we would expect from the parents. This is especially true with regard to those children who are different from the average. And we need to realize, too, that some children adjust well to an institutional type of living, while others never get well adjusted. Different children from the same family will react quite differently to the same environment.

Then there is the problem of the supervisory and teaching personnel of the school. In times past it has all too often been the practice to assign to the school missionaries who did not work out well elsewhere. Perhaps they failed to get the language, or they proved ineffective in other types of work, and as a last resort they were assigned to the school for missionaries' children. It was a job that few missionaries really wanted, so there was a chronic shortage of staff. Anyone who could do "real missionary work" avoided such an appointment if he could. So some of those who entered the school work, even though they were qualified for the job, came with a sense of frustration that couldn't help affecting their work.

Fortunately there seems to be a change of attitude on the part of missions and even missionary candidates in recent years. We wish it would extend also to the thinking of more of the churches that support the missionary work. It is a realization that this is a special part of missionary service, and a very important one. It is "real missionary work" even when it doesn't have the halo of glamor that surrounds some of the other types of service. There have been missionary volunteers who have deliberately planned for this type of ministry. It is not surprising that some among them have been children of missionaries who have known the need at firsthand and have been challenged by it.

Yet we still do not have enough volunteers to meet the need. And there are still some who are not fully qualified, and many whose motivation for such a ministry is very weak. And the many good workers are often frustrated by the lack of sufficient help, sufficient funds, and sometimes sufficient sympathetic co-operation on the part of the parents or the missions.

The missionary parent should be particularly concerned about the house parents at the boarding school. They are the ones who take his place when the children are away at school. They are the ones who are responsible for the children for the greater part of the twenty-four hours. They have major responsibilities in character building, disciplining, comforting, encouraging, training in good manners and habits of neatness and cleanliness, etc.

One other problem should be mentioned, that of companionships. Even among the children of missionaries, not all are equally well behaved. Not all of them have learned discipline from their parents, and some whose parents did not exercise careful supervision have picked up various evil habits and practices. Their parents would be shocked if they knew of these things, but they are often unaware. Yet among children of the same age these things are likely to come out in their play or conversations.

It is true that this is a problem everywhere. There are just two things that make the situation different in a missionary boarding school. One is that when the children are living at home the parents are more aware of their children's companionships and the effect they are having on their lives. The other is that in a secular environment they are usually on guard against such things, while in a missionary school they are likely to presume that no such vigilance is needed.

There is one final problem with these boarding schools on the field. If the children are kept away from their home for very long periods, especially in the case of the younger children, the family ties are weakened. It is for this reason in part that some schools plan for at least two vacation periods during the year, when the children can go to their homes and enjoy the family relationships and influences once more. It is when this cannot be done, and especially when the school is so far away that only rarely can the parents expect to see their children, even during vacation, that the sense of estrangement becomes acute.

Of course there will always come a time when you will have to consider leaving the children in the homeland. This means a separation of not just a few months, or even of a year or so. It usually means several years at a time. So you will want to have some strong reasons for doing it. And the reasons are not lacking.

The major reason again has to do with education. You may be able to teach your children at home for some years. Or you may send them to one school or another on the field. But almost invariably there will come a time when they will have to stay in the homeland to complete their education. It may be before grammar school days are over. It is even more likely when the time for high school comes. If it can be postponed until the young people are ready for college, then it presents very little problem. Most young people under any circumstance will leave home to go to college. But the majority of missionary children are likely to be left at home before that time.

There is a second powerful reason for leaving children in the homeland. It has to do with morals. It is not nationalistic pride but a frank facing of reality when we state that moral standards in many lands are exceedingly low. They are low enough at home. But they are much worse in lands where Christian morality has not had as great an opportunity to make its influence felt. Of course the situation differs from place to place. Very often the missionary himself feels strongly the downward pull of his environment, and how much more the children, to whom this environment seems the most normal and familiar. Each case has to be decided on its own merits. The one thing necessary is that the missionary parent shall be alert to the danger.

There are some times when the parents feel it best to leave the children at home for this reason at a fairly early age. Usually, however, it is some time during the teens, most commonly the early teens. And they have the added reason that it is during the teens that love affairs are likely to spring up between the missionaries' children and some of the nationals, with all of the ensuing complications.

A third reason for leaving the children at home is not so commonly applied today as it once was: health conditions on the field. Yet though conditions are much improved in many places and there is more adequate medical help available and improved food supplies, there are still some times and places that give weight to this reason.

There is one alternative to leaving the children at home. It is an alternative that appeals to some missionaries but hardly ever to the mission society. It is that the parents stay at home with the children for several years. At times such an alternative is advisable. But obviously it makes a serious break in the missionary's service. It removes him from the work in which he has the most experience, at a time when his service is likely to be the most valuable, and obliges him to readjust to a different life and service at home. Then if he decides to return to the field after a few years, he finds that he has gotten out of touch, that a number of things have changed since he left, and that he must make another adjustment at a time of life when most of us find it hard to be adaptable. This alternative, too, is out of the question when there are a number of children in the family, unless the parents are willing to limit their missionary service only to their earlier years.

No doubt some will think of another alternative—something they have read that missionaries have done on occasion. That is, that the mother should stay at home with the children for a time, while the father continues his missionary service. It is true that there have been a few cases where this was done. In many more cases there has been a brief separation for as much as a year or two. But such a separation for an extended period can never be justified either on the basis of Christian principles or of sound missionary policy.

So, even though it means sacrifice and raises numerous problems, missionary children do stay at home when their parents return to the field. But where do they stay? And who looks after them?

There was a time when practically the only choice was the home of a relative or friend. But in more recent years we have seen the establishment of a number of homes and boarding schools to care for the children of missionaries. Many people, including not a few of the missionary parents themselves, seem to think that these institutions are the ideal answer to the problem. They take a great deal of the burden off the shoulders of the missionaries, the children are assured of Christian teaching and surroundings, the ones who operate the institutions do it as a Christian ministry, and the costs are usually low. There is no question that some of these homes and schools have had a useful ministry. But even the best of them could hardly be called the perfect answer to the problem. Let us look at two or three of their major weaknesses.

Common to all of them is the institutional atmosphere. Some of them have done a good job in eliminating much of this atmosphere. They really want the conditions to be as homelike as possible. Yet even the best cannot completely avoid it. And as we said concerning boarding schools on the field, many children easily adapt themselves to institutional life. They may not prefer it but they get along reasonably well in it. There are others, however, who never make a satisfactory adjustment. They are unhappy themselves and they are a constant worry to those who look after them. You see, these institutions are set up to care for the average youngster. The one who is "different" calls for special care and attention, which the school usually cannot give except at the expense of the others.

In addition to the institutional atmosphere, there is often a lack of normal social contacts for the children. This is especially true where home and school are combined. It is not so true where children live in the missionary home but attend the public schools. In the former case the children are sometimes so restricted in their contacts with the world outside the school and home that they don't know how to act when at last they leave its shelter. They are not prepared to face life and the free "give and take" that they encounter in their relations with people who make little or no profession of a vital Christianity.

A third weakness is rather difficult to pinpoint. It is the psychological effect that being in such a home has on many children. The children come to feel that they are different from normal children. They are not like the orphans in the orphan asylums, yet to some extent they often do get the feeling that they are objects of charity. This feeling is particularly strong if the home finds it necessary to appeal for donations to carry on its ministry.

There is one alternative to leaving the children in a home for missionaries' children. It is to arrange for them to live in a private home as a part of the family. Under suitable circumstances this can be the best plan. The children enjoy the atmosphere, the loving care of the home. Reasonably soon they get the feeling of "belonging." They attend the same schools with the other children of the community. They enjoy the normal social contacts of a member of the family. If in any sense they feel that they are the objects of charity, it is only the charity of the family that took them in, not charity of the impersonal, condescending sort.

The major problem is to find such suitable homes, and to find Christian people who are both able and willing to assume the responsibilities connected with caring for another's children. It ought to be a family with one or more other children of about the same age, if possible. By all means it should be a Christian family with ideals similar to those of the parents. It should be a family that the missionaries know well enough and trust enough to be willing to commit to its charge their most prized possession. It may sometimes be relatives—but usually not the grandparents. Grandparents find it too difficult to cope with the youngsters, or else they spoil them and exercise too little discipline.

When missionaries leave their children with a family, however, there is a price they must be ready to pay that is not calculated in dollars and cents. They must by all means give full authority and confidence to the foster parents. Have a clear understanding that they are to treat the child as their own. And make sure that the child knows it, too. There will always be discipline problems and you can't handle them from the field. It is possible at times to give some needed bits of counsel by letter, but to presume to give orders from far away, unless the foster parents ask for them, is foolish. When you are not on the scene you can't evaluate all the circumstances.

And be ready to suffer some loss of affection, especially on the part of younger children. They will learn to love those who actually care for them day by day. This is only natural. We know that tiny children completely forget their parents when they are separated from them for a time. Older children do not forget, but after a few years their memories get a bit hazy. When parents and children are reunited, it sometimes takes a little while to get adjusted to one another again, to get back to a place of really close confidence. You must rewin their affection. It is not easy to see your own children turn to others for advice and instructions when you are present. But it is part of the price of separation that must be paid. With patience you can regain a part of the price without in any way minimizing the affection that they give to those who took your place for a time.

Life of Unmarried Missionaries

Although most missionaries are married, there are many in various fields, especially young women, who carry on a ministry as unmarried missionaries. What about their home life?

1. *Living with a family.* A common arrangement in some places is for the single missionary, man or woman, to live with a family. Of course in those places where the people are likely to think that the single woman is a second wife, such an arrangement is very inadvisable. That problem does not come up with the single young man. But there are still places where the arrangement seems to work out satisfactorily. Then what principles should prevail?

In most cases, and particularly in the case of a younger missionary living with an older couple, the single missionary should be considered a part of the family as far as possible. Some of the dull ache of loneliness can be alleviated if the single missionary is made to feel that he "belongs." In reality, after a time the bonds of fellowship become almost as close as those of the natural family—that is, if their relationship is what it should be.

However, the single missionary would be wrong to take advantage of his privileges. There are some who forget that the head of the family is by right the head of the home. If you are to be a part of the family you must acknowledge his authority in those things that concern the running of the home. It is not for you to usurp that authority, nor to pursue your independent way as if the home were a hotel. If you want to make alterations outside of your own room, seek permission.

As a part of the family it is important for you to show a willingness to do your part of the work in keeping the home. You are not a boarder. The modest amount you pay into the household is usually calculated to cover only the actual out-of-pocket expenses in keeping you there. Your presence means extra work. Be sure that you bear your share. It helps if you are given a certain definite job as your responsibility. But in any case make it clear that you are ready to help.

And whatever you do, try to fit into the family program of meals, prayers, etc. There is nothing so irritating as to have someone habitually show up for meals after mealtime is past. And family prayers are an important means of tying the family together. Be there, and be there on time. Of course it is true that some families are not as orderly as others. But the one who is ready to fit in as much as possible is always appreciated. (Note: it is doubly irritating if one stays away from meals or overnight without giving word.)

2. *Living with other unmarried missionaries.* Most of the single men on the fields probably live with families or alone. Single women, however, often live in pairs or threesomes. When they are congenial, they provide fellowship for one another and a greater sense of security, both from physical danger and from wagging tongues.

No matter how congenial you are at the beginning, you do well to have a clear understanding about the division of housework, expenses, time for meals, etc. Don't wait until the problems arise. You can't arrive at a good arrangement in the heat of an argument. Don't take it for granted that each one will do what is right. The other may not agree with your understanding of what is right.

Some prefer to alternate the jobs, one doing the cooking for a week or a month, while the other cares for the housecleaning and vice versa. Others seem to prefer to divide the work on a permanent basis. And as for expenses, the only safety is in careful accounting. Otherwise you are bound to have misunderstandings and suspicions, even when they are not openly expressed. No one should ever have grounds for wondering whether you got the household money mixed up with your personal funds.

In the missionary work you do, try always to work in harmony. But harmony does not mean both playing the same note. The work of each one should complement that of the other rather than compete. When both want to be leaders in the same kind of work, there is bound to be friction. Either one must be content to follow, or both must have their separate ministries, which need not be independent but complementary to each other. For example, one may have the leadership of the women's work and the other the leadership of the children's work where they are stationed.

This latter arrangement is often the best. It means that you will not be together all the time. Some of the frictions that develop are the result of being together so constantly that minor irritations have a chance to be rubbed into open sores. Even if you do most things together, always plan to do some things separately. If for no other reason, it gives each one something to talk about that the other has not experienced.

Finally, keep always before you the Scripture admonition, "Preferring one another in love." Sincere praise for the other's accomplishments will do more to cure jealousy than any other antidote. You cannot rejoice with another over his blessings and dislike him at the same time. Misunderstandings are sure to arise. It is too much to hope that you will never be tempted to jealousy. There are times when little things that the other does, little obnoxious mannerisms perhaps, or little exhibitions of selfishness, will grate on your nerves. If you in your turn become self-centered and indulge in self-pity or resentment, the "little foxes" can "spoil the vines." But if you turn your view outward and follow this injunction from Scripture, it will smooth over many a rough spot.

PART THREE

Missionary Relationships

CHAPTER TEN

RELATION TO FELLOW MISSIONARIES

IN TALKING ABOUT UNMARRIED MISSIONARIES who live with others we touched on the major problem of missionary relationships. It is one of the most critical problems in missions and always has been. If it is given greater prominence in some of our missionary discussions today, it is largely because there are more missionaries in closer contact with each other and with the growing body of national leaders. It is not the opposition from outside that causes the most breakdowns in the missionary ranks; it is the dissensions within.

Surveys of the causes of missionary failures are exceedingly hard to make with any accuracy. Both the missionary and the mission society are understandably reticent in talking about the causes, even if they really know what they are. But one such recent survey, which seems to have been carefully conducted, places the blame for 59 per cent of failures on this matter of missionary relationships. That is, the missionaries concerned were unable to make a successful adjustment either to the authority of the mission, to their fellow missionaries, to the people among whom they labored, or in a number of cases between husband and wife.

In a discussion with mission leaders I once remarked at the high proportion of our problems that had to do with personnel. One disillusioned director remarked, "Is there one of our problems that doesn't have to do with personnel?" He was a bit extreme, of course, but his remark showed the prominence of such problems in missionary experience. If we could solve problems of this sort we could at least double the effectiveness of our work and possibly multiply it many times over.

117

FELLOW LABORERS, NOT COMPETITORS

In our secular life in the United States there is a great deal of competition. We say that "competition is the life of trade." And unquestionably competition has done a great deal to spur production, inventions, etc. It is prominent in sports, where each one tries to outdo the other. This is true even in team sports where a great deal is said about teamwork, about working together for the good of the team. Actually those who gain the coveted place on the team have had to compete for it, to show that they are better than their companions.

So it is not surprising that we carry this same spirit of competition to the mission field. Perhaps we didn't have to compete with others to gain our appointment to the mission. Yet once we are on that team we are ambitious to see it outshine others. Hence we are often hesitant about co-operating with others, for fear they will gain an advantage, and we allow the spirit of competition to affect our relations with our own team members. We compete with one another for appointments within the mission, for a greater share of personnel and funds for our particular work, for the friendship and esteem of the people, for recognition of one sort or another. We are not simply anxious to excel; we want to excel one another.

Competition can be very dangerous in missionary life and work. Especially is this true when the community is very small and the work to be done very great. The competitive spirit is generally quite the opposite of Paul's injunction to "Let nothing be done through strife or vainglory; but in lowliness of mind let each esteem other better than themselves" (Phil. 2:3, 4). If we were to heed this injunction it would probably remove one of the greatest sources of friction between missionaries. We need to remember that we are not in any sense competitors. The principle that should govern us always in our relationship with one another is that we are fellow laborers, belonging to the same family and working toward the same end.

VARIOUS COMMON DANGERS

1. *Petty annoyances.* There are some threats to missionary harmony that are always common to those who live and work together in constant and close contact. First, petty annoyances and irritations may come to

be magnified far out of measure. Under other circumstances these things usually would be overlooked. But a mannerism, that wouldn't bother you at all if you saw a person only occasionally, becomes unbearable when you have to be with him morning, afternoon and evening, every day of the week.

This is a common cause of friction between husband and wife. But in their case they deliberately chose one another as life partners. On the mission field missionaries are often assigned to work with those whom they would not have chosen. Presumably they do have the same objectives and some other things in common. Otherwise the situation would be more difficult. But even so they face some problems of adjustment.

You may think that you have had a similar problem with your roommate at school. He wasn't the roommate you would have chosen, and maybe he has shown some characteristics that you don't like. Yet you have learned to get along with him harmoniously.

That is good. Everyone who wants to go to the mission field ought to have the experience of getting along with a roommate. Those of you who have always had your own private room have missed out on a part of your training. Yet the situation is not entirely the same. If your roommate gets on your nerves you don't really have to see very much of him. There are plenty of other students with whom you can find the fellowship you desire. But on the mission field you two may be the only missionaries on the station or within a hundred miles of the station. There is no one else of your own nation or language or culture. So you must learn to get along with one another.

2. *Conflict of wills.* A second danger is found in the differences that are sure to arise between two strong-minded individuals. You are probably both used to leading, and maybe you haven't yet learned the self-restraint that co-operation always demands. Actually, one reason you were sent to the mission field was that you showed qualities of leadership and had a mind of your own. That is what missionary work demands. But it does make for tensions when two leaders have to work together.

We don't want to give the impression that when two work together one must be submissive while the other is dominant. This is not true. If it were, real co-operation on the basis of equality would be out of the question in any field of work. What we do mean is that the urge to assert oneself, when the other feels the same urge, is a source of potential difficulty *unless you have both learned self-discipline.* Real fellowship is impossible unless it is built on mutual respect.

3. *Jealousy.* We have already said something about our third source of danger: jealousy. People at home may think it strange that missionaries should be jealous of one another. Yet they themselves often suffer from the "green-eyed monster." It is foolish to think that missionaries are immune to temptation. They may be more successful in combating it than those at home, but the temptation is there just the same. And when they do succumb, the results are more disastrous, for they affect not only the individuals but the whole work.

Of what are missionaries jealous? Lots of things. There is the fellow who seems to get the language so much more easily than you do. Or the one who always seems to have such interesting adventures to talk about. Or the one whose house is so tastefully furnished and his family always so well dressed. There is the missionary to whom the people seem to turn spontaneously for advice, while they pass you by. There are some who seem to have five talents, while at times you wonder if you have even one. There are some whose names appear frequently in the mission publication, while yours is scarcely ever mentioned.

There is plenty to be jealous about if you look for it. And the trouble with jealousy is that it leads to resentment. We resent the fellow who, through no effort of his own, gets more attention than we do. Sometimes he is a very humble person, who is greatly embarrassed with the attention he is given. But we resent him. Or the other's fault may be only that he is willing to work harder, to put in more time than we on the job. So we resent his success. Yes, jealousy is a real danger in missionary relationships.

4. *Misunderstandings.* And then there are honest misunderstandings that cause a rift in fellowship. Sometimes they come because of wrong information, through lack of confidence or frankness with one another. Or they may result from the difference of our backgrounds, including differences of national or cultural background.

A brother and a sister in South America had had a disagreement. Shortly afterward the sister felt so bad about the matter that she decided to write a note to her brother to seek peace with him. Being a

Christian, she wanted to make some reference to the Scriptures, so she put down in the note "I John 3:1-2," the passage that begins, "Behold what manner of love the Father hath bestowed upon us . . ." But her penmanship was not of the best, or else the hyphen got omitted, for what the brother read was "I John 3:12." And when he turned to that passage he read with growing anger these words: "Not as Cain, who was of that wicked one, and slew his brother. And wherefore slew he him? Because his own works were evil, and his brother's righteous." No one could convince him that a mistake had been made. He was sure his sister meant the insult.

It is as easy for misinformation to spread on the mission field as it is at home. Perhaps it is easier, for often our information comes to us through the nationals. We do not mean to imply that they deliberately falsify, though that may happen. More often our lack of perfect understanding of their language makes us read wrong meanings into their statements. Or maybe one who has an elementary knowledge of English tries to tell us what a missionary said and gets it all wrong.

And as for differences of background, this source of misunderstandings is so prolific that some missions make it a policy not to put together people of different nationalities. All too often they fail to understand one another and so cannot work together in harmony. A Britisher, for example, may look at his American fellow worker as a "boor," while the American thinks the Britisher is a "prig." From their points of view, both of them may be right. But it doesn't lead to harmonious relations.

It may be that lack of confidence in one another or frankness in dealing with one another causes many more difficulties than any of the above. Sometime ago a certain mission faced serious division among its missionaries. As an interested outsider I received confidences from missionaries on both sides. The more I heard about the matter the more I regretted it. Both sides were in some measure right and in some measure wrong. But the overt act that had separated them from one another was not the underlying cause of the trouble. For a long time before, there had been an undercurrent of suspicion and lack of confidence. It was obvious to an outsider that the suspicions were poorly founded, but that made little difference in the case. No one had had the boldness to bring those suspicions out into the open for a frank discussion. So the suspicions grew, and soon most of the missionaries were obliged to take sides in a "cold war" that still had no clear reason for its existence.

5. *Older vs. younger missionaries.* Misunderstandings between older and younger missionaries have always been a source of difficulty in missions. Younger missionaries reach the field full of ideas and projects. They have all of the vigor and enthusiasm of youth. Now that their period of training is over, they are impatient to try their wings. And though they don't like to say it openly, they are quite sure in their own minds that they can do a better job than those who have preceded them. Their attitude is well expressed in a letter that a first-termer wrote to the magazine *Practical Anthropology:*

"I am a young missionary in my first term of service. I think I am a typical representative of the younger generation of missionaries in our mission and many others. I have been carefully screened by means of required physical and psychological tests from contemporaries who also sought to enter missionary service. I have been highly trained in my special field. In addition, I have taken courses in the theory, theology, and practice of missions. I have learned to be very critical of the methods of mission work practiced by those of the preceding generations. I have come to be very aware of the fact that the present situation in mission lands is crucial. I know that this new day of new problems demands that we adopt new approaches, adapt ourselves in different ways, or risk the probability of losing our opportunity . . .

"I have read many books and articles pointing up the fact that missions today are at the crossroads, especially here in Africa. We must today, as never before, have a sense of urgency about us, for the time left to us may not be long. We cannot afford to experiment. We cannot afford to make mistakes. It is now, or maybe never, to push forward, to get the native church on its feet, to make ourselves dispensable before the door is closed.

". . . It seems that these older missionaries have not received the same training that we have, have not read the same books that we have, are not as aware as we are of the need for drastic measures in these crucial times. In short, I am warned to look out for the older missionaries (and the younger ones who have become 'old' in outlook); they will oppose anything you suggest.

"What shall I do? . . ."

It is not often that we see a letter as frank and revealing as this one. The constant repetition of the personal pronoun "I," the naïve self-confidence of the writer, strike the reader at once. Is it possible for a Christian missionary to be so obsessed with his own importance? Remember, though, that he is a young man and cocksureness is a characteristic of young people. What is really more disturbing is the kind of teaching he seems to have received. It is true that blanket criticism of all that missionaries have done before, together with a glorification of many a new and half-baked theory of missionary work is in vogue. One of the most used words today in connection with missionary theory is "revolution." So it is no wonder that the products of our teaching reach the field with the obsession that it is their duty to bring about that revolution. And sometimes they only succeed in starting a revolution within the mission body that disrupts the work.

Young people are extremists. Things are either white or black; there are no grays. As they grow in maturity they learn to qualify their judgments. Another young missionary showed some of this maturity in answering the letter. He mentioned some attitudes that he and his wife had tried to cultivate:

"(a) That, after all, we are newcomers and no amount of theoretical training can take the place of long experience. We have much to learn; let's be learners until asked to lead.

"(b) All we ask is for a chance to prove ourselves—a chance to stand or fall on our own merits. We are voluntarily subject to those now in authority until such time as *others* may want to exalt us to a position of authority.

"(c) We are willing to sacrifice self-interest (no matter how strongly felt) for what those in authority feel is for the best interests of the mission.

"(d) We seek to improve the future of the work . . . rather than waste time and energy criticizing the present or past.

"(e) We let our actions do the major part of our speaking until we are asked to present our ideas also in words."

The conclusion of his answer is notable: "In short, we feel that the older generation can be gotten along with—indeed, must be gotten along with, even at the sacrifice of our less mature—though perhaps theoretically superior—ideas. We have always found them sympathetic to a well-thought-out idea, but tough, as they should be, on hare-brained proposals. Moreover, they are at least as concerned as we are that the work of the mission be continually improved and enabled to go forward more effectively."

We should not leave the matter here, though. The fault is not always on the part of the younger missionary. There are older missionaries who are quite set in their ways. Often, though, they are not quite so set as they appear. What happens is that the younger missionaries irritate them in one way or another, so they cling all the more obstinately to their former practices. It is strange how some of us, as we get older, find the ebullience of youth irritating. And it is hard for us to see, too, how those youngsters could have a worth-while idea that we haven't already considered. We have had years of experience but if that experience has taught us anything it should be that we still face many problems that are unsolved. We ourselves are not mature until we are ready to listen to anyone who may have a possible solution.

This problem of the relation of younger to older missionaries is one of long standing. A century ago Ludwig Krapf, the great East Africa pioneer, wrote: "Respect an old and experienced missionary, even although he should take little heed of your thoughts and suggestions as those of a novice. But do not accept unconditionally everything that he says or does, when either his sayings or his doings appear at variance with the revealed Word of God. If, at the commencement of his course, a young missionary can humble himself among others, good will come of him; but if, at starting, he insists on criticizing everything, and on having everything done according to his own fancy, he will bring ruin upon himself and the Mission together."[1]

6. *Criticism.* By far the most serious overt threat to missionary relationships, the greatest danger of all, is criticism of one another. It is a temptation that is so easy to fall into, and a habit so difficult to overcome. For it can readily become a habit. Some people become so accustomed to "picking other people to pieces" that they are genuinely unconscious of the amount of criticism that enters into their most casual conversations. For them to talk is to talk about people; and to talk

[1] J. L. Krapf, *Travels*, pp. 510-511.

about people is to talk about their shortcomings. It probably has no malicious intent, but its effect is still deadly.

Criticism is a poison. As such it should be used sparingly and with extreme care. It affects both the one who is criticized and the criticizer. We seldom realize just how much our criticism does to embitter our own spirits and poison our lives. Notice that the critic is not a happy person. How can he be? His spirit feeds too much on what is imperfect, disappointing, disillusioning. He is like a proofreader, who is so busy looking for misprints that he never gets the message of the book. In fact he doesn't dare get interested in the book, for if he does he may overlook a few omissions, transpositions, misplaced quotation marks and the like.

We are speaking here of criticism in its usual popular sense. Some people would call it destructive criticism, not realizing that all criticism is in a sense destructive. Fundamentally, criticism is passing judgment. The trouble is that most of our criticism is not sober judgment based on clear evidence. It is mostly petty faultfinding.

Some Ways of Meeting These Dangers

We have gone a long way toward meeting the dangers when we realize that they exist. But there are also certain definite things that we can do and attitudes that we can take in solving these problems.

It is always a great help when we can learn not to think of ourselves more highly than we ought to think. Paul gives us this advice, but how little we heed it. If we don't think too highly of ourselves, we may learn to appreciate others more.

Seek, too, for a greater confidence in the love and wisdom of the omnipotent God, even when He allows you to come into trying circumstances. This will enable you to rise above the circumstances. Many of us talk much about our faith in God when things are going reasonably well. But when they go badly we dare not blame Him, so we try to blame others. Is He supreme only when things are going well? Is He any less God when the trials come? Did He not know that you might find it hard to get along with some of the other missionaries, or with the mission society, or with the nationals? Did He really send you? Then may not this trial be clearly intended by Him to develop in you that patience, longsuffering, gentleness, love, etc., that you still lack? If the veteran missionary Paul, toward the end of his life, could write of not being perfect yet, how much less perfect are we! God is good to give us the trials that will develop our spirits if we will only learn the lessons they are intended to teach.

Christ Himself gave us another way to meet these dangers. One of His last lessons was an object lesson. He took a towel and went around as a servant washing His disciples' feet. This He did to set them an example, to show that they should be willing to serve rather than to be served. Imagine the Lord of the whole earth washing the feet of the man who was about to deny Him with oaths! He even *insisted* on doing it!

Christ added, "If ye know these things, happy are ye if ye do them." The lesson indeed is not easy to learn, but happy is the missionary who has learned it and put it into practice. And happy are the other missionaries who have to work with him.

Perhaps one of the best ways to learn that humility of which the Lord was speaking is this. Try rejoicing as sincerely as possible in the blessings, the honors that come to the other. Don't just give him a grudging word of congratulation. That is simply good manners. But don't be hypocritical about it either. Fight it out with yourself until you can go to the other in sincerity and say ,"I am really happy for you." Then show it.

One thing that will avoid much mistaken judgment and remove many occasions of criticism is a willingness to believe the best rather than the worst about the other. It is the practical application of I Corinthians 13: "Love believeth all things."

Not long ago a man went to another with a tale about a mutual acquaintance. The second man heard the tale and then blurted out, "I don't believe it! I know that fellow and I don't believe he would do such a thing!"

The first man indignantly exclaimed, "Do you mean to say you think I'm lying?"

"No," the other replied, "but I think you've got the wrong information."

The taleteller was not convinced, but he realized that he had better check on the facts before he repeated the tale to any others. Later he had to come back rather shamefacedly to admit that he was wrong. There had been a misunderstanding of the facts.

Why should we be more ready to believe evil reports than good about another? Especially when that other is one of our fellow workers? Sometimes the evil report may be right. But even our courts of law take it for granted that a man is innocent until he has clearly been proved guilty. Should we Christians be less considerate in our dealings with each other than the law courts are with us?

There is still one other way to avoid dangers arising in missionary relationships, especially those that crop up on a single station. That is to have regular consultation and prayer together. The two belong together. The missionaries on the station must be kept informed of what is going on if they are to work together. Secrecy generates suspicion. But information alone may only satisfy the curiosity. Likewise prayer alone may become quite aimless without information. Prayer brings the information into focus; it gives it meaning and purpose. Those who pray together are more ready to work together.

RELATIONSHIPS OF UNMARRIED MISSIONARIES

There are special problems in the relationships of single young people of opposite sexes in the mission field. In the United States those relationships are much freer than elsewhere in the world. And it is only natural that American young people should want to enjoy the same freedom wherever they go. The restrictions that other societies impose seem to them both irritating and unnecessary. Why shouldn't a young man walk down the street hand in hand with his fiancée? Why should a chaperon be present when he talks with her in the parlor? Why is it wrong to do a dozen other things that no one would ever frown at in his homeland?

The reason is very simple. He is not in his homeland. He is in another land with another culture. The question is not whether his thoughts and intentions are good. The question is, "What do these people think about his actions?" To keep a good name he has to keep from doing the things that offend them.

Of course it is possible for him to defy their etiquette. Sometimes other foreigners do it and get away with it. That is, there is no actual punishment involved, merely social disapproval. And if he is only a tourist, or a man whose success does not depend on his acceptance by the people, he may flout some of their customs with impunity. But obviously we are not talking about a missionary. His whole ministry depends on his acceptance by the people. They may perhaps overlook some minor infractions of the rules because, after all, he is a foreigner and foreigners have some strange customs. But who can tell when their amused tolerance will turn to active opposition?

After all, it is our conduct that commends our gospel. If our conduct in their eyes is lawless, then our gospel must likewise be destructive of good morals. If we don't want our gospel to be spoken against, we must be sure that they have no good reason to speak against us personally. There are some who think they are being persecuted for the sake of the gospel who are only reaping the results of their own unwise actions.

So if you go to the field unmarried, find out what your conduct should be toward those of the opposite sex. Then, regardless of your own feelings in the matter, conform to it. You will have no occasion to regret it.

CHAPTER ELEVEN

RELATION TO THOSE IN AUTHORITY IN THE MISSION

EVERY MISSION, regardless of its type of organization, must have
some who are in authority over others. Sometimes those in authority are appointed; sometimes they are elected. Some have broad
powers; others have powers that are more limited. The authority of
some is more or less permanent; others have temporary authority, or
authority for a single task until it is completed. But always there is the
problem of securing the obedience or co-operation of the other missionaries.

The insubordination of some missionaries on the field is a source of
real difficulty. In some missions it is a more acute problem than in
others, but they all face it. It is not a new problem but one that has
been common all through the history of missions. Yet perhaps the
problem is a bit more serious today than it used to be.

CAUSES OF INSUBORDINATION

Let no one be surprised that missionaries are guilty of insubordination. It is not simply that they are subject to the same temptations as
other Christians. There are special reasons why they are likely to be
more strongly tempted along these lines than others.

First there is the very character of the missionary. Those who choose
him for missionary service are usually quite insistent that he should
have initiative and aggressiveness. They expect him to be a leader.
But it is not always easy for a leader to follow the leadership of others.
In a meeting of missionaries where the subject of leadership came up,
one veteran missionary objected: "We need more followers; we've got

129

too many leaders already!" What he meant was that everybody expected to lead, and too few realized that for the sake of the work even those who are capable of leading must be ready to subordinate themselves to others. Those who are used to following have no difficulty. It is those who are accustomed to lead who have a hard time learning to be willingly subordinate.

Then there is the nature of the missionary's work. Not only is he put in a place of leadership, but for long periods of time there may be no one around to question that leadership. He is supposed to be responsible to a superintendent or to a field committee. But in practice he is largely on his own. Those who are supposed to supervise his work are seldom able to visit it and inspect it as they should. They have to depend largely on his own reports and any complaints that reach their ears. That is one reason why they try to be careful in choosing missionary candidates. They want someone who can be depended on to do a good work without close supervision. But a man who is used to acting most of the time on his own responsibility has difficulty in subordinating his will to that of others when the occasion demands.

We must remember also that some missions are weak in an organizational sense. There is very little centralized authority. Each missionary, at least after his probationary period, is more or less a free agent. This is especially true in cases where each missionary secures his own personal support. Since the mission does not support him, its control over him depends largely on his own willingness to co-operate. Under such conditions it is not strange that insubordination should arise. What is really remarkable is the considerable measure of willing subordination and co-operation that does exist.

Then, too, we need to realize that much insubordination involves relationships with a distant authority. Where the missionary work is widespread this can't be avoided. Superintendents often have to send instructions by letter or some other such means. But anyone who has ever had experience with the giving or receiving of written instructions knows some of the problems that can arise. They are as common in business as in missionary circles. "The home office doesn't understand our situation," complains a branch manager. And missionaries say the same thing about the authorities at headquarters. And sometimes they wonder, "Just what do these instructions mean? I can't quite figure them out." Or, "Why do they want me to change my plans? I don't mind doing it if it is important, but what's the reason?" There are many officials who can't seem to make their instructions clear and reasonable in writing. And there are missionaries who are equally inarticulate by mail and unintentionally cause offense, or who fail to explain a situation in enough detail. Many apparently deliberate offenses are really misunderstandings.

But we must still take into account that some young people do get to the field today who are self-willed and are not disposed to accept much control over their actions. Their attitude was clearly exemplified in a young man who asked for an interview one day. He wanted to inquire about mission boards. "I suppose," he said, "that I ought to go out with a mission board. Then after I have been on the field awhile and know the ropes I can become independent." When asked why he wanted to become independent he said, "A mission might tell me to do some things I don't want to do." Unfortunately this young man is not alone in such an attitude. Not all of them will state it so frankly, however, and so some of them do get past the board and cause problems on the field.

Manifestations of Insubordination

There are several ways in which this attitude of insubordination can express itself. Occasionally it leads to an open refusal to obey instructions. More often the instructions are simply disregarded, especially if the one who issued them is not at hand. And sometimes the one who doesn't want to conform can defeat the very purpose of the instructions by a grudging obedience just to the letter, or by willfully misinterpreting them. In extreme cases the insubordinate missionary withdraws from the mission and sets up his own work. Many so-called "independent" missionaries are people who find it very difficult to submit to any authority over them.

Necessary Action

Now we shouldn't give the impression that every order issued by a missionary in authority or by the mission board is always good and just and equitable. Far from it. And there are times when those who have authority exercise it arbitrarily, or they needlessly offend people by the way in which they give orders. There are occasions when missionaries who are normally co-operative find it necessary to express their disapproval of the decision of their superiors. There is nothing wrong in their doing so, provided they do it in the right way so as not to destroy authority itself.

Notice that we have mentioned missionaries "who are normally co-operative." This is the major problem. It is a problem of attitudes. It is for this reason that we mention the matter here. We want to see young people deliberately cultivate an attitude of willing co-operation for the good of the work, even when such co-operation may at times involve some personal sacrifice. Until you can put the good of the work ahead of any personal interest you are not ready to be a missionary of Christ. We have too many would-be missionaries who are piously inclined but don't know the meaning of the cross—the crucifixion of self for the salvation of others.

Such missionaries may not need a Bible verse to support their willingness to obey. Yet there is one that is so appropriate that we ought to mention it. It is Hebrews 13:17: "Obey them that have the rule over you, and submit yourselves: for they watch for your souls, as they that must give account. . . ." Is there any need for comment?

But the question still remains, "What should a missionary do when he thinks it is wrong to comply?" You can perhaps answer this question if you put to yourself several others.

Have you been asked to do something that you think is morally wrong? This is rather unlikely, but in such a case of course you can't obey. If you make your position clear, the other will usually respect your conscience even though he may disagree.

Does the one who gives the order have the right to do so according to mission organization and rules? Then you must respect his authority even when you are not convinced of his competence.

Does the order tell you to do something that you can rightfully be asked to do? Then what reason can you give for not obeying that won't sound like pure selfishness?

Do you think the order is not a wise one? That may be so, but who will have to give account for it? Your only obligation is to say so if you think it is unwise. But obey!

Do you have any way of appealing an order that you don't like?

Then make your appeal as humbly and graciously as possible, realizing that there may be some factors in the matter that you don't fully understand. Under no conditions should you carry the matter to your constituency at home through prayer letters and other means. It will only harm the work, if indeed it doesn't boomerang and damage your own reputation.

There may come a time when a missionary feels that he has no other recourse but to withdraw from the mission. It may be a major ethical issue that disturbs him, or a doctrinal issue, or it may be simply an accumulation of minor matters that indicate a trend. At any rate the missionary comes to the conclusion that it is impossible for him to work in harmony with the mission. The temptation is for him to justify himself before the world by publishing abroad the reasons for his deciding to withdraw. But if he is wise he will resist that temptation. There are always a few who will have to know his reasons. But attempts to broadcast an explanation usually do more harm than good. Even among his own friends they seldom enhance the reputation of the missionary, while the unfavorable publicity is sure to harm the work.

CHAPTER TWELVE

RELATION TO THOSE UNDER
YOUR ORDERS

E VEN BEFORE HE GOES to the field, the missionary needs to be prepared against the day when he will have to assume responsibility
for others. To wait until the time comes, and then expect to rise to the
need through natural talent is not good enough. Many have authority
thrust upon them without any great degree of natural talent. They
need at least to have some basic understanding of what leadership involves and of some of the dangers that beset it. Also if they are aware
that one day they may have to lead others, they are more likely to watch
other leaders and learn.

Among those who rule there is always a temptation either to dictatorship or paternalism, or both. Dictatorship is the refuge of the man
who is not sure of himself or of his authority. Unsure of his ability to
lead, he attempts to drive. He constantly asserts his authority and seeks
to enlarge it. He blusters because he cannot persuade. He holds a
tight rein because he cannot trust others. At the same time they learn
to mistrust him. He dare not allow dissent from his opinions for they
do not stand on their own merits but on his authority. The only way to
co-operate with him is to be completely submissive.

In paternalism the one in authority considers himself on a higher
level of knowledge, experience and judgment than the ones he com-
mands. He looks at them as his children and treats them in that way.
They are in no way his equals, so he does not feel it necessary to explain his decisions nor to justify his course of action. He expresses his
benevolence with little gifts or concessions of minor responsibility, such
as a parent might make to his child. He is persuaded that he always

acts for the best interests of those who are under him, even when they fail to appreciate it. If you try to co-operate with him you are soon made conscious that your efforts are like those of the small boy attempting to help his father carry a heavy suitcase. He may good-naturedly tolerate your efforts, but they are more of a drag than a help.

Perhaps paternalism is most commonly found in the missionary's relationship with the national Christians. Yet often it is also the attitude of the older missionaries toward the younger. They think it inconceivable that a young person without their years of experience should have anything to contribute to their understanding. In turn, the younger missionaries become convinced that the older ones have become fossilized, that they are afraid of new ideas and are a hindrance to the work. Of course neither one is true. Gray hairs do not necessarily indicate wisdom, and youthful notions are not always progressive. We need both to keep a proper balance. But we cannot have the advantages of both without able leaders who will avoid paternalism as well as dictatorship.

While we are discussing the relationship of older to younger missionaries we should also speak of another tendency. At times the older ones will "take advantage" of the younger. That is, they will assign to new missionaries the more tiresome and unpleasant tasks, on the ground that the new missionary should be doing some of the work and he is not yet fit for the more important jobs. To some degree this is not objectionable. But when the new missionary is required to do odd jobs instead of studying the language or otherwise preparing himself for his main ministry, or when he gets the impression that he is being turned into a personal "flunkey" of the senior missionary, it generates trouble. The fault may lie with either one. Younger missionaries are sometimes not willing to do their share of what needs to be done, or they feel that certain jobs are beneath them. On the other hand the older missionaries are prone to forget their own beginning days, and fail to realize that the younger ones can only grow as they are given real responsibilities.

We all need to realize that rulership is much more a responsibility than it is a privilege. The one who is in charge is responsible for getting the work done. More than that, he is also responsible for helping others to learn how to do the work in the most effective way and for guiding them in their efforts. He is as responsible for their failures as for their successes. This sense of responsibility is more wearing than the actual work. Not long ago a leading atomic scientist committed suicide. In his note of explanation he said, "I can't bear to go back to the lab. There are too many decisions to make, and I feel I'm not capable of making them. . . ."

Again in this matter of leading others the grace of humility is important. We need the lesson that Christ taught in Matthew 23:1-12: "One is your Master, even Christ, and all ye are brethren."

When you have charge of a station or a work, with others working under you, here are some suggestions that may prove helpful. First, it is always best to have a clear plan for the work. Then assign to the junior worker a suitable place in that plan. Never make him wait on your whim or convenience for the assignment of tasks. Be sure that he realizes that his part is meaningful and necessary. This may mean discussing the plan with him so that he can see how his work fits in. Give him real responsibility and let him know that you are trusting him to carry it out faithfully. And when you say that you are trusting him, do just that. Let him know that you may need to check up on his work once in awhile, but you certainly will not spy on him. Encourage him to talk with you about his work and take time to discuss its problems. Make sure he knows what is expected of him and don't hesitate to commend him for a job well done. Everyone likes to be appreciated, missionaries as well as others. And no one has ever yet demeaned himself by giving honest praise to another.

CHAPTER THIRTEEN

RELATION TO THE HOME CHURCH

A MISSIONARY has a twofold ministry: on the field and at home. On the field he is ministering directly to the people to whom he is sent. At home he ministers to the church that sent him through the devoted example he sets and the inspiration of the reports that he gives in one way or another. Sometimes the ministry to the home church may turn out to be as important as that on the field. That is why at times a mission may keep at home one of its best missionaries so as to represent the work among the churches.

It is strange that so often missionaries seem to be unaware of this double ministry. Many times the missionary will tell the home church that they are to labor together with him, that he could accomplish nothing without their help. Then when he gets to the field he fails to make their co-operation possible by keeping them informed. He acts as if he could do very well without anything but their financial support. He expects the church to minister to his material needs, and feels that it is a lack of vision and consecration on their part if the funds are insufficient. Yet his own responsibility to help give that vision and inspire that consecration never seems to enter his mind. The co-operation is all one-sided.

The missionary's ministry to the home church while he is on the field is through his example and the word that he sends home in letters, articles, pictures, etc. When he is on furlough, it is through a personal presentation of the same things, plus other things such as preaching, Bible teaching, counseling, etc., as he may have opportunity. Many a furloughed missionary has brought real refreshing to the home church, and incidentally has inspired increased confidence in his own work on the field.

MISSIONARY CORRESPONDENCE

1. *The problem.* In speaking about missionary correspondence, there is no need for us to give special attention to correspondence with your family and intimate friends. Neither do we need to say much about the necessary correspondence about business matters or mission reports. These are important, but they have little to do with the relationship of the missionary to his home church.

What we have in mind is your correspondence with churches and individuals at home who may have an interest in you or your work. It is the chief way you have of keeping in touch with those who are giving their support. In fact, apart from an occasional recording or radio message, it is almost the only way.

This is what makes it so important to keep up a *regular* correspondence. When you break contact for any considerable time, interest and support from the home church quite naturally decline. There are some loyal individuals who will still maintain their interest in spite of long neglect. And of course the church that has promised a certain sum each month will not immediately drop it. So you are not likely to be aware at once of the damage your negligence is causing. But the decline of interest is going on just the same, and it may seriously affect your support at just the wrong time.

Now here is the big problem. Just question any group of people and you are likely to find that three out of four are not very fond of writing letters. Some hardly ever write, except through necessity. Then remember that it is from such groups as these that our missionaries come. Missionaries are not normally any fonder of writing letters than anyone else. There are just two things that make them engage in it more than others. First there are the many new experiences that they want to share and doubtless a bit of lonesomeness for the folks at home. This is why many missionaries are better correspondents at the beginning of their service than they become later. Then there is the realization that for the sake of their ministry they must write. It is a part of the missionary's job.

Many a missionary finds letter writing a real chore. Like other unpleasant jobs, he avoids it as much as he can. In some cases he tries to justify himself like the old missionary to Japan who scathingly remarked, "I came out here to do missionary work, not to write letters." In other cases he simply promises himself that he will settle down to writing when he has his other work out of the way, or when he goes on vacation. But there is always something else to interfere. So he ends by writing only when his guilty feeling gets strong enough to oblige him to take the time for it.

It would probably be a great help if every missionary realized that letter writing is an integral part of his ministry. If he is an orderly person who likes to plan his work, that would mean setting aside a definite time for letter writing. If he is like many others who do not make clear-cut plans but do manage to keep their responsibilities pretty well in mind, he will still make a place for his letter writing with fair regularity. But if he is the sort of person who simply follows his own inclinations except when some duty becomes specially pressing, then even the realization that letter writing is part of his ministry will have little effect.

Because letter writing is a problem for many missionaries, and it can consume a great deal of time, there have been many attempts to simplify it. Often friends at home have volunteered to help the missionary as far as they could, especially in the matter of duplicating and mailing form letters. And missionaries themselves are always on the lookout for new techniques.

2. *Necessary personal letters.* Certain letters should always be personally written and with a minimum of delay. This is the case with gifts of money and other presents. Even when your reply is prompt, the time it took the gift to reach the field may be so great that the giver begins to wonder if it was lost. No matter how often they are told, people still fail to take into account the slowness of the mails. So a prompt reply is quite important, and a personal one. Never use a form letter to acknowledge such gifts. The donor may accept a form letter from the home office without complaint, but not from the missionary.

Perhaps we should put in this same category letters to your home church, when it helps support you on the field. Some churches have the helpful custom of duplicating such letters from their missionaries and distributing them to the whole membership. This benefits both the missionary and the church. But it should be a special letter to the church, not just a copy of the missionary's general circular letter.

Many personal letters to the missionary also call for a personal reply. Here the missionary has to use careful judgment. He knows that some letters don't call for any reply, and others do not demand a personal reply. But if he fails to send a personal reply to someone who is expecting one, he may easily lose a friend. Just a brief note may be all that is needed, but if those few words are personal they count for a great deal.

3. *Form letters.* We have already mentioned the circular or form letter, sometimes called a "prayer letter." It is the most prevalent kind of missionary letter in circulation today. In fact, if you mention "missionary letters" most people will think only of this kind. It is no longer open to question whether form letters should be used. They are being used and missionaries will continue to use them in spite of some of the complaints that have been made. Our only concern here is to show how they may be used more effectively.

a. *Why are they used?* The principal reason for the form letter is the large number of people with whom the missionary would like to keep in touch. Obviously there is a limit to the number of personal letters that any missionary can write. I am not sure that many missionaries have ever come very near that limit, yet the limit is still there. When a missionary has two or three hundred friends who would like to hear from him regularly, he is not likely to find time to write each one personally. And some missionaries have more than this on their mailing lists.

Another reason is what we might call the propaganda value of the form letter (using "propaganda" in its good sense). That is, the letter is sent to many who have not specifically requested it but who might be interested in what it contains. It goes to pastors and others in places of leadership, to missionary societies and prayer groups, to schools and a variety of individuals, usually missionary-minded Christians. Its publicity value is enough so that a number of missions take charge of sending out such letters for their missionaries. They will even run off extra copies to send to people who are not on the missionary's personal list but may be interested in the work.

Closely connected with these two reasons is the saving in time and money that the form letter represents. The saving in time is very real, and it is proportionately greater as the mailing list grows longer. The saving in money takes place only when the letters are sent third-class mail or when they are mailed in the homeland. Since such mailings are likely to reduce the effectiveness of the letter, the savings may be more apparent than real.

Some missionaries resort to the form letter when their personal correspondence gets so far behind that they see no other way of getting caught up. In a real emergency most people will understand and will not object. But don't repeat it! The form letter never really takes the place of a personal letter. If you send it to one who is entitled to hear from you personally, he will lay it to your lack of appreciation of him. Those who start out their form letters saying, "Please take this as a personal letter," are insulting the intelligence of their readers. They will accept an inferior substitute if they have to, but don't offend them by asking them to take it as the real thing.

b. *Basic principles.* There are five basic principles in sending out form letters that we neglect at our own peril. Thousands of dollars are wasted every month on ineffective form letters largely because they violate one or more of these principles.

(1) It is a letter. Don't confuse the form letter with a magazine article. It isn't. When your friend opens the envelope he expects a letter. Don't disappoint him. Your ideas for the article may be very clever and unique and still leave the reader "cold." A letter—even a form letter—has a character all its own. It differs as much from a magazine article as a conversation does from a sermon. A form letter should be a letter.

(2) It is a substitute. The form letter takes the place of the personal letter you would like to write if you had the time. It is a substitute for the personal letter. At first glance this seems obvious. But think through what it implies. No one ever offers for sale a substitute that bears no resemblance to the item requested. He always tries to offer something that is as near like it as possible. Why don't we do that with our missionary letters? There are at least seven things that mark a personal letter:

(a) Envelope personally addressed, either handwritten or typed.

(b) Sent sealed, by first-class mail.

(c) Posted from the field, or wherever the missionary may be at the time.

(d) Begun with a personal salutation.

(e) At least a portion that is purely personal included.

(f) Ends with a signature that is personally written.

(g) Letter either handwritten or typed by the missionary, or at his dictation.

If all of these features are present, you have a truly personal letter. Each one that is omitted decreases the personal nature of the letter. If none is present there is practically no personal element left. In fact, the only resemblance to a personal missive is that it goes addressed to an individual (which is also true of a magazine) and it originally came from an individual. It is surprising how many missionary letters fall into this last category of "completely impersonal." As substitutes for a personal letter they are failures.

(3) It must be read. It is not letters mailed but letters read that counts. Obviously the missionary who sends out 200 letters and gets 150 of them read is doing a better job than the one who pays postage on 500, of which only 100 are read. Yet few missionaries bother to find out whether their letters are read. They seem to take it for granted that they are. It would shock them to realize how many of their letters reach the wastebasket with scarcely more than a glance. But the shock would be worth while if it would get them to improve the quality of their letters. It is highly important to make sure that your letters reach their destination *and get read.* We will discuss this problem further as we go along.

(4) Its point of contact is personal. Even though the form letter is not a personal letter, people look to it for personal information about the sender. In fact, most of them are getting the letter because they are personally acquainted with him and have an interest in what he is doing. That personal point of contact is one thing that differentiates the letter from the magazine article. In the magazine article the person of the writer, if it stands out at all, is of secondary interest. In the letter it is primary. Even the events that the letter describes we expect to see in relation to the writer.

This personal interest is so great that we will often read a very poorly written letter from a friend just to get the personal information it contains. A person who did not know him so well would probably drop the same letter into the wastebasket. Yet in spite of the great value of this personal point of contact with the reader, many missionaries still omit any mention of personal affairs from their form letters. Probably they think the thing of greatest importance is the work and not their individual lives. In a sense this is true. But you are not going to get across the story of the work if you neglect the most important point of contact that you have with most of your readers. They are willing to see the work through you. You are the point of contact, the demonstration and the interpreter. You make the work live to them.

(5) It requires careful planning and preparation. There are missionaries who would never address a congregation of 200 or 300 people without very careful preparation, yet they will dash off a circular letter to the same number with scarcely a second look at what they have written. Actually it is much easier to do a good job when you have a living audience before you. You can see their reactions to what you say; you can sense any lack of interest; you can fit your manner of presentation to the people you see. But in writing a letter to go to so many people, you have to use your imagination to visualize them. What you can confidently say to one may needlessly offend another. But you won't know it right away. What you intended to say in a humorous way may not be understood that way, for the paper and ink do not convey the expression of your face nor the tone of your voice. Everything depends on those impersonal words and the impression they are likely to make on the one who reads them.

But at the same time that you are trying to imagine how several hundred people may react to what you are writing, you need to take care that your letter doesn't become so stiff and formal that no one will want to read it. It needs the warmth of human interest and the simple clarity of a personal conversation. Most people don't get these things in their form letters on the first draft. It takes careful composition, ruthless self-criticism, and a willingness to rewrite again and again until the product is satisfactory. Yet if the product is really good, no one will guess how many hours of toil went into it. This is true of most good writing.

c. *To whom should form letters go?* This is perhaps the easiest of our questions to answer. Form letters can very well go to all who express an interest in you or a desire to hear from you, and to whom you

do not need to send a personal letter. Even in this latter case you may
want to send your form letter besides the personal letter. Also, there is
nothing wrong in sending letters to people whom you may hope to
interest, even though they haven't actually expressed a desire to hear
from you.

d. *What is their purpose?* We need to remember that the mission
paper or magazine will convey a certain amount of information about
the work. However, it is largely impersonal, and in a large mission the
work of any individual is not likely to be mentioned very often. So the
missionary's form letter provides more detailed information for those
who are especially interested in him and in his part of the work. For his
home church and for others who want to pray for him it provides the
necessary information. Sometimes this purpose seems to be the principal one, so the letter is called a "prayer letter."

But missionaries often use the form letter also to maintain a somewhat personal touch with a large number of people. It is not only to
inform. It is also to keep up to some extent the bonds of fellowship. In
this it serves a purpose somewhat akin to that of the modern Christmas
card. It reminds our friends that we have not forgotten them, though
for a time we are removed from close contact.

And form letters are also used to stimulate, maintain and increase interest in the missionary and what he is doing. For the missionaries of
some of the faith missions this may be very important from a monetary
point of view. Their financial support comes from the gifts that are
sent specifically for them. So if they let the interest of their friends lag
through failure to correspond with them, their income is also likely to
decline. But many are not so concerned over their personal income as
they are over the spiritual support that is needed for the work. They are
deeply concerned for it themselves, and they want to share that concern
with others.

e. *What should go into such letters?* First of all they should contain personal information. We have already mentioned it as one of the
basic principles that the point of contact they make is personal. It is for
this personal information that most of your friends will look when they
first open the letter. It doesn't have to be tremendously important or
exciting. They are interested in knowing where you are, what you are
doing, and how you are getting along. It is not egotism to talk about

yourself and your family in such a letter, it is simply telling what people want to know. You are cheating your friends when you don't let them share with you in your joy over the birth of the new baby, or don't let them know of a serious illness that almost terminated your service, or don't let them pray with you when you have a crucial personal decision to make.

Of course you will include something about the work. But it should be information principally about the work as it relates to *you*. People are seldom interested in "the work" as an abstract thing. They are interested in the work of living people. They are specially interested in the work of people that they know. But in telling about your work, don't take it for granted that the people are already well informed about how it is carried on. A few may be; most of them won't be. Don't even take it for granted that they will remember what you wrote in a previous letter. That may be one that they didn't read, and very few will keep them to refer to. As far as possible, make each letter complete in itself. This means that you will not be able to tell a large number of events, but one story well told is worth more than a score that you can barely mention.

Besides these matters there may be others not related to you personally or to your work but that would be of interest or inspiration to those to whom you write. But don't take it for granted that what interests you will necessarily interest others. After you have been abroad for some time, you get a different perspective. This may make it difficult for you to put yourself in the place of the folk at home and write what will interest them. And if you say that your purpose is not to please the fancy of those who get your letters, let me remind you again that you may as well not write if you are not going to write letters that will be read. You can entice people to read your letters, but you can't oblige them, no matter how valuable the content is.

There are several things that should never be a part of the missionary circular letter. One is the sermonette that some feel duty bound to include. We used to receive letters from a missionary friend that we soon learned to start reading about halfway down the first page. He always sermonized at the beginning of his letters. We found that others of his close friends read his letters the same way we did, skipping the sermonette at the beginning. Actually the sermon is just as out of place in a letter as it would be in a private conversation.

Complaints also should have no place in the letter, whether complaints about the circumstances of your life, about your fellow missionaries, the people, the mission, or even complaints about the friends who don't write you. It might be different if such complaints accomplished anything constructive. But they don't. They only serve to put you in a bad light, as well as the persons about whom you complain. And if complaints about your nonwriting friends accomplish little, threats accomplish even less. I have known missionaries to write in their circular letters something like this: "We have written so many letters, and so few have taken the time to write to us. If we do not hear from you after you receive this letter, we shall have to drop your name from our mailing list."

Do you think that such a threat improved the situation? Not at all. The writers kept on writing, the nonwriters mostly kept silent and were dropped from the list, and the missionary lost even the one-sided contact that he had formerly had with them. Only a small fraction of those who receive, read and enjoy missionary form letters ever write a letter in response to them. Yet some of them give and pray regularly for the missionary.

Another of the things that we can do without in the missionary letter is what we might call "lists." This covers a variety of tiresome procedures. One is the prayer list. Now there is nothing in itself wrong with a prayer list. It can serve a very useful purpose. A number of your friends may appreciate your listing a number of definite items for prayer, though they probably represent a minority of your mailing list. The only objection is that such a list is not a letter and it shouldn't take the place of a letter. It can be inclosed with a letter, but it is not a substitute for it. Sometimes missionaries have arbitrarily tried to prepare a list of exactly 30 requests, one for each day of the month, and have used these lists for "prayer letters." The artificiality of such a plan is soon evident, and the number of requests calls for so much condensation that the people who get the list can't pray intelligently for half of the items.

Other "lists" include lengthy itineraries with no explanations, a calendar of events since you last wrote (maybe six months ago), also extremely condensed, and the like. Real travelogues are very interesting, but not the reading of timetables. And some letters are like last week's newspaper, neither recent enough nor ancient enough to be interesting. No one will want to know the details of your Christmas program next August. If you didn't write it soon after it happened, forget it.

Remember, too, that what you write in a form letter should always be in good taste. There may be a time when you will want to shock your friends out of a sense of complacency. But before you do it be sure that it needs to be done. Then be sure that you can do it skillfully, with a deft touch that will accomplish your purpose without offending. Otherwise the only effect will be that of disgust. There are sights and sounds and smells in some mission fields that will try the hardiest stomach. But is it necessary to write about them? In all probability your readers will simply be revolted, to no useful end, and they may even wonder why your mind dwells on such things.

f. *How should they be written?* If the form letter is a substitute for the personal letter, you want to make it appear as personal as possible. It is not easy to do this with several hundred people, some of whom are intimate friends while others are mere acquaintances. You will usually find, however, that very few will ever object that your letters are too familiar, even though they don't know you very well. The most common objection will be that your letters are too stiff and formal.

Of course the personal content helps to make a letter personal. Employ personal pronouns. Use "you" and "yours" wherever you can, and don't be afraid to bring in the "I," "me," and "mine." Try to bring your reader into the letter if you can. "Last year was a hard year," is very impersonal and leaves the reader out. "This has been a full year for all of us, hasn't it?" brings the reader into the picture and creates a more friendly, personal feeling.

Your letters should sound as natural as you can make them. You want your friends to be able to say, "Why, I can almost hear him say that!" That means cultivating a warm, conversational style. You have to cultivate it. It doesn't seem to come natural to most of us. Or perhaps I should say that our training in school has made us so conscious of what is "proper" in writing that we get stiff and unnatural whenever we pick up a pen or sit down to a typewriter. We have to work hard to get that stiffness out of our writing, to eliminate the vocabulary that we never use in ordinary conversation, and to sound as natural as when we talk.

And make your letters active. That doesn't mean that you have to sound as if you were always "on the go." Some of the most tiresome, monotonous letters come from missionaries whose work calls for a great deal of activity, while some of the most sprightly come from those who do a good part of their work sitting at a desk. The action should be in the letter itself. You can get some of this spirit of action into your letter by using active verbs wherever you can instead of the passive ones. But the matter goes deeper than mere form. When you look at things that have happened as if they were all completed in the past, your view is a passive one. If you describe them to others as if they were happening right now, you create more of a sense of action. The reader will feel that he is experiencing them right along with you. But don't let your action get bogged down with a lot of description or extraneous material. Stick to your one line of thought and make it move right along to the climax, if there is one.

Don't be afraid of a little emotion if it comes natural to you. Don't pretend an emotion you don't feel, but if you are sad or happy, apprehensive or joyfully expectant, let a little of it show in your letters—that is, if you would be likely to show it in a friendly conversation. This is another way of getting yourself into the letter, of making it personal. Most letters are too cut and dried.

Of course you are writing a letter, not a book, so your space is limited. A few exceptionally gifted writers can hold the readers' attention through four pages of material. But most of us are not that gifted. Two pages, not too crowded, is the most we should attempt. You ought to have many times as much to say as you can get in those two pages, but just store most of it away for future reference. Make the most of the space you have, but avoid giving your reader any sense of too heavy condensation. Don't try to crowd too much in. Take time to select your material carefully, treat it fairly, cut out irrelevant details and unnecessary words, and leave your reader with a sense of satisfaction instead of frustration.

g. *Special types of letters.* In writing their form letters, most missionaries like a little variety. They are sure that if they use the same type of letter every time the people at home will become bored. So from time to time they like to use some special type of letter that is different from what they have written before. This is not a bad idea, even though the need may not be as great as you think. That is, we prefer variety in our magazine articles, but when it comes to personal letters we don't usually think of them as belonging to one type or another, and we are too interested in the contents to worry about any monotony of style. But since missionaries will probably continue to think of their form letters as somewhat in the nature of a magazine article, we shall mention two or three types that are often used.

Perhaps the most common is the story type. That is, the major part of the letter is made up of one or more stories: stories of the work, story sketches of the people, stories of missionary experience, stories with or without a moral, stories that illustrate the thinking of the people, humorous stories, pathetic stories, stories from personal observation or experience as well as stories garnered from others. Everybody loves a good story. So there is a good reason why this type is popular.

But it may be true that some missionaries are too much on the lookout for good story material. Their anxiety to have a good story to tell may warp their sense of values in regard to the work. The thrilling, the spectacular, the exciting is likely to get more attention than the day by day "keeping everlastingly at it" that usually brings more substantial results. So be alert for useful stories, but don't let them swerve you from your main job, and don't yield to the temptation of coloring them up a bit, or using those that are of doubtful origin. And do learn how to tell a story. Some are not very good at telling stories orally. Or perhaps they just don't realize that there is an art to good story telling. But in writing everyone ought to be able to do an acceptable job. You have all the time you need to plan the story, to revise and correct it until it will be suitable for carrying just the impression that you want it to convey. Your stories will not be just for entertainment. They will produce impressions, paint pictures that you want your friends to feel and see.

Another type is simple description: description of a trip, a conference, a place, an event, a situation. We have called it "simple" description, but we don't mean that it is easy to do. The language should be simple, but the task of describing things in an interesting and forceful way is anything but simple. Too many people associate description with flowery language, the use of many adjectives, similes, metaphors and the like. Yet how many of these same people will have to admit that they seldom care to read such descriptive passages themselves.

I have just finished reading a missionary letter from Africa that is a model of descriptive prose. It is the description of a trip—in many ways not an unusual trip. Yet in simple language, interspersed with bits of conversation and glimpses of the writer's own reaction to what he saw and heard, it carries the reader along as if he were a part of a stirring adventure. You see the trip through his eyes. This is what description should be, not just an attempt to record the details of a picture, as a photograph would. Some photographs have so much detail that the main object gets lost in the picture. But good description should be more like a painting, where the artist omits some items, plays down others, and highlights the important part. He is successful when the viewer gets from his picture the same feeling that he got when he viewed the original scene.

Let me warn you that there are some descriptions that very few ever succeed in making interesting. Have you ever tried to describe a Bible conference? It is just as well if you haven't. Many missionaries have tried, and the account they give usually turns out to be a dull chronicling of the names of speakers and their subjects, statistics of attendance and decisions made, plus a liberal use of superlatives in a vain attempt to show the great spiritual impact the conference made.

Some of these conferences are indeed spiritual high points. But when you write that "the conference was simply marvelous," you really haven't said anything. Specifically what was "marvelous" about it? That adjective might cover anything from a reasonable successful program to a tremendous spiritual upheaval. Did it change your life? How? Can you tell what it was that changed your thinking in such a way that others will see something of its force? Were others affected? How do you know? All too often the result of a conference is an undefined feeling in the heart. It is real, but rather vague. As a result our attempts to describe it are vaguer yet. It may be the high point in your spiritual life, but it won't be a high point in your letters. You may do well to omit it.

There is a type of letter that we might call the "My Day" type. Most missionaries seem to try such a letter at least once in their career. Sometimes it is the result of inquiries from the home folks. They want to know what a missionary does, how he spends his day. We can under-stand their interest and would like to comply with their request. But it is not as easy as it sounds.

For one thing, it is hard to choose a "typical" day. Missionaries in some kinds of work have an established routine, but others don't. Like farmers, their work varies with the seasons, or it is subject to constant changes according to prevailing circumstances. No two days are alike.

Then, too, the missionary may be constantly busy, but he is afraid his description may sound as if his work is easier than it is. He wants to give his friends some idea of how busy a missionary can be. So he really doesn't take a typical day to describe, but one that is unusually full of activity. He may possibly succeed in impressing some of his friends, but that is all. His picture of missionary life is distorted.

Friends at home might be more understanding if they tried to write an account of their own daily activities. They might be surprised to see how insipid and unimportant some things look when they are written down. Of course they will object that a missionary's life must certainly be more interesting and varied than their own. And in some cases it is. But missionary life, like life in general, involves a great deal of patient plugging away at tiring jobs whose significance is not seen in a day or two. Teaching a group of ministerial students in Japan is not likely to differ much from a similar ministry in the United States. And the satis-factions and sense of accomplishment in the job do not come every day, as they might in an exploratory trip or in a series of evangelistic meet-ings. But the accomplishments are just as real, even though you wait months or years for them to become evident, and even though they don't fit very well into a "My Day" type of letter.

There are numerous other types of letters that may be tried on oc-casion. Sometimes a missionary will write a letter as from his baby son or daughter. If he can make it sound natural and not too artificial, most people will enjoy it. But it is not something that you will repeat often. Another missionary who travels a great deal may write his letters as a chronicle of the life of his car. This is more artificial and calls for more ability to keep it interesting. And others try other types that are even further from the ideal of the personal letter, such as the type that simu-lates a newspaper, etc. But if the same effort that is used in inventing unique types of presentation were spent in improving the presentation itself within the framework of a personal-type letter, more missionary letters would get read and accomplish their purpose.

h. *Form.* Even though you stick to the personal-type letter, there are a few things about form that ought to be said.

Make it look like a letter. Don't put on a heading, "April Prayer Letter" or "Circular Letter #27," and don't omit some sort of salutation.

Use generous margins and short paragraphs. Nothing discourages reading more than the sight of a solid page of crowded type.

Sketches, pictures, maps or diagrams sometimes add to the interest of a letter or make it clearer. Be careful, though, that they don't break up the written message in such a way that it is hard to read.

Some missionaries produce their letters on paper cut in unusual shapes or sizes or with unusual folds. These have a passing interest and can be attractive. However, they sometimes make it more difficult to read the message.

i. *How duplicate?* There are numerous forms of duplication in the United States, some of which call for expensive equipment but do a job that is hard to distinguish from personal writing. The fact that many companies will go to such an expense to personalize their circular letters should help the missionary to realize its importance. If the duplicating is to be done in the United States, it may be well to investigate some of these forms. On the field, however, there is usually not much choice.

The most common method of duplication is by mimeograph or some similar stencil duplicator. The major difficulty is that some do the work so poorly. The letters are too light or don't print entirely, or the page is crooked or the printing is poorly centered. Always clean your type before making a stencil. Be sure to use enough pressure on the "w" and "m" keys and not too much on the "o" and "e." Make sure that the ink gets equally to all parts of the stencil, even if it means thoroughly cleaning the drum and using a new cloth. And run off enough extra copies so you can throw away any that are imperfect. It is better to waste a few sheets of paper than spend postage on a poorly done letter and risk losing a friend.

Gelatine duplicators. There are several kinds of these, some of them using more than one color of ink. They are usually limited in the number of clear copies they can produce and many people don't care for the purple ink that is most commonly used. So comparatively few missionaries are using them for their form letters.

Printing (including multigraphing). This is the neatest form of duplicating and allows for an unlimited number of copies. However, if the type has to be set by hand it takes much longer than the typing of a stencil, and the printed letter always looks much more impersonal than other forms. Where the mission has its own printing plant, the missionaries sometimes find it economical to use it.

Every form of duplicating has its advantages and disadvantages. The important thing to remember is that no amount of attention to these externals will make up for a poorly written letter. It is the letter itself that is of prime importance.

j. *Addressing.* Obviously the closest thing to a personal letter is one with the envelope addressed in pen and ink or by typewriter. And it doesn't take nearly so long to address a couple of hundred envelopes as many seem to think. Letters from the field are almost always addressed this way. In the homeland, however, and sometimes at headquarters on the field, the addressograph can be used. Addressographing is always obvious and is a guarantee that the letter contains nothing personal. Even with an air mail stamp on the envelope, you know that if it were a personal letter it wouldn't have been addressographed. Addressographing is used exclusively for bulk mailings. The gummed label that is used for so many magazine mailings today is also used on some missionary letters. Though it is really not any more impersonal than the addressograph, it inevitably gives an appearance of cheapness that should be avoided.

As for the return address on the envelope, it doesn't seem to make much difference whether it is printed, stamped or written. Many purely personal letters are enclosed in envelopes with a printed return address. However, if the return address has a different name from that of the missionary who wrote the letter, look out. When a person receives an unsealed letter from a letter service, or from an individual whose name on the printed envelope is unfamiliar, he can easily conclude that it is just another piece of "throw-away" mail such as is cluttering our mail boxes these days. If he is busy he may never bother to open it. How could he tell it was from a missionary?

k. *Mailing.* The missionary who concludes that third-class mailing is more economical than first, because it costs less, needs to take a lesson from the business world. The out-of-pocket cost is indeed less, but the results from such a mailing are less yet. If you don't have time to read everything that is put in your mailbox, does the postage stamp have anything to do with the things you decide to open and read? Many tests have proved that it does. Other things being equal, foreign mailing is better than domestic, air mail is superior to surface mail, and first-class is far better than third. Printed permit mailings are at the bottom of the list. Though not everyone is a stamp collector, the unusual stamps, such as the commemoratives, seem to be more attractive to readers than the ordinary ones of the same denomination. One word of warning, though, lest you lay too much stress on this matter of mailing. It is highly questionable whether a first-class stamp adds much to a letter that is definitely third-class. There are commercial concerns that believe it is well worthwhile to send their form letters first class, and even airmail. But they make sure first that they have a letter that will live up to the extra postage they pay.

l. *How often?* Very few missionaries are able to get out a form letter to their whole constituency every month. Some do, but they are the exceptions. Neither do the people at home expect them that often. From a questionnaire sent out to a number of people who received letters from different missionaries, we found there seems to be remarkable agreement that a quarterly letter is best. That is, the period of maximum efficiency for the missionary form letter seems to be one every three months, *if it is regular.* This matter of regularity is even more important than the length of time. But when you go beyond three months, the interest drops off rapidly. A letter twice a year does very little to sustain interest, and an annual letter is scarcely more than a remembrance.

m. *Checking efficiency.* Do your letters get read? How can you tell? Is there any way of checking on their efficiency? This is the type of questions that very few missionaries ever seem to ask themselves. As we have already mentioned, they seem to take it for granted that since they sent the letters they are sure to be read. How utterly disillusioning it might be for some of them to learn the fate of their epistles.

It isn't easy to check on your letters, but it is important. There is no use wasting money on letters that don't accomplish your purpose. And if your letters need improvement, you ought to find out about it.

The difficulties you face in checking are similar to the ones a radio station faces. You have no paid subscription list, like a magazine, that will serve as an index. Many people will accept what you produce—may even enjoy it immensely—but will never let you know. You will have to guess at the reactions of the silent ones on the basis of what you are able to elicit from those who are more vocal.

Here are two or three tests. Do you ever get any replies to your form letters? Most people don't feel any obligation to answer a form letter, but a reply is a sure indication that it has been read. You will usually get at least a few replies if the letter is doing its job. Has anyone ever sent you a gift as a result of receiving your letter? You probably didn't ask for one, so it would have to be spontaneous. He might have been reminded to do it when your letter arrived, even without his reading the letter. But the chances are he read it. If he read it, then probably others did, too. Do you ever get any requests for your letters? That is, does someone who read a letter you sent to another friend ever ask to be put on your mailing list? Then you know that not only are some reading your letters but the letters are proving interesting to the readers. Do any of your friends in their personal letters comment on items contained in your form letters? Do they seem to show any acquaintance with them? If the answer to all of these questions is no, you can well question whether your letters are getting read.

Of course when you come home on furlough you can do a better job of checking through personal conversations. But remember that many people are too polite to tell you the whole truth.

Another way of checking is to put a request for a reply of some sort in your form letter. But even if your letter is getting well read, don't expect too many replies. Many people will intend to reply who never get around to doing it, even though they always read the letters.

n. *Keeping up the mailing list.* This is a matter that calls for continual alertness. With first-class mailings it is not too bad. The letters are either forwarded or returned to you when a person moves. Not so with third-class mailings. If they cannot be delivered to the first address on the envelope, they are dumped. Only if you are ready to pay a certain extra amount of return postage, and state so on the envelope, will they be returned to you. As a result, sometimes people are kept on the list for years after they have died or have moved elsewhere.

Check your list regularly for "dead wood." Don't be in too much of a hurry to drop them simply because they haven't written in a long time or otherwise expressed their interest. But if you have good reason for doubting whether they are still interested, don't hesitate to cut them off. Some do not wish to offend you by asking that their names be dropped. Some missionaries try to revise their mailing list by enclosing with their letter a return post card that is to be filled out and sent in. Even so, some people forget to mail the card, and others think it was meant for somebody else; you already know that *they* are interested.

If your letters are being sent out from an address in the homeland, your problem is increased. A few people will write to that home address, but most of them will write to you on the field. Then you have to make sure that you relay the information to the one who gets out your letter, making allowance for all the delays and misunderstandings that may arise.

o. *Combined circular and personal letter.* This letter belongs in a class by itself. It has been proved by experience to be very useful, but most missionaries seem to feel it involves more time than they are willing to spend.

The idea is simply this. Suppose you wanted to write to every one of your friends personally. The great bulk of your letter would be largely the same in every case. You would probably tell the same experiences, and very much in the same way. Why not mimeograph this part of the letter to avoid repeating it over and over? Make it a little over a page in length, omitting the salutation and conclusion.

Then, carefully adjusting the margin on your typewriter to fit the mimeographed material, dub in a personal salutation and add to the end any special personal remarks you want to include. It may be a line or two, or it may be two or three paragraphs. Then close with your complimentary conclusion and a personal signature. Such a letter will have practically all of the distinguishing marks of a personal letter and will almost always be accepted as one. Yet by mimeographing the bulk of it you have saved a great deal of the time and effort involved in the purely personal letter. It has most of the advantages both of the circular and of the personal letter.

Of course it is not necessary to add a personal paragraph in every case. But even though most of them don't contain that personal addition, they do have the personal salutation and the personal conclusion, and this makes them much more personal than the usual circular letter. The receiver knows that the writer was thinking of him personally, that he is not just an anonymous member of that vague company of "Dear Friends" to whom the form letter is addressed.

One plan is to save up the personal letters the missionary receives that don't require a prompt reply, and answer them all with this quarterly letter. In this way the missionary may even save time over sending the usual circular letter *plus* the necessary personal ones.

Of course some missionaries do jot a personal note on the side or back of their current circular letter and let it do duty for a personal reply. As a personal note it is acceptable, but there is no surer way to get the reader completely to disregard what is in the circular. The advantage of the combination letter is that the personal items are in the body of the letter, so that the whole thing usually gets read.

4. *Recordings.* The letter is not the only way by which today's missionary may keep in touch with his sending church. There are several recording devices, especially the tape recorder, that he is finding increasingly useful. Of course it demands that the missionary have a workable recorder with him on the field, and also that the church have a means of playing the recording at home. But both these things are becoming common. Today the missionary can render a periodic report in which the tone of his voice may be as expressive as the words he uses. He may still feel quite stilted before the microphone, but in most cases his language is freer than it would be if he had to put it all down in writing.

Recordings, of course, are generally used where groups are involved: churches, missionary societies, Sunday School classes, etc. They are much less useful for individual communication. Also, they do require preparation. Nothing is more boring than for a whole congregation to sit quietly listening to an imperfect transcription of the missionary's voice as he talks on and on with no particular plan to his talk. A recording should be made as carefully, perhaps more carefully, than a sermon to the congregation. More carefully, we say, because you don't have the advantage of your visible presence to put it across.

5. *Photographs.* Practically every missionary takes pictures, whether for his own use or to help in presenting his work to the supporting

churches. He may use some of his pictures in his letters. Occasionally one or another gets into the mission publication. He sends some to friends and relatives. But most of them are kept until he comes home on furlough. He then is likely to use them in his meetings in the churches to illustrate some of his work on the field.

Every missionary takes pictures, but they don't all take good pictures. Modern equipment makes good pictures more possible than ever before, but you need more than good equipment. Some missionaries are actually overequipped. That is, they have expensive cameras that they don't know how to operate, light meters that they have difficulty in reading, filters and extra lenses that someone insisted would be useful but whose purposes they don't quite comprehend. Some of them never take a picture except in good sunlight, with the sun directly behind them, and at distances of fifteen feet or better. A fixed-focus box camera would probably serve their purposes about as well as the most expensive camera, and with less worry. The expensive cameras are for those who want to try for the more difficult shots or want to work at the finer details of the photographic art.

a. *What pictures should be taken?* Remember that we are talking not about pictures for your personal remembrance but those that you can use in your relation with the church at home.

Obviously you will want pictures of the work you are doing. If your work is varied this will give you a wide scope. But not all types of work are easy to represent pictorially. Always take more pictures than you expect to use, so you can cull out the inferior ones. One picture is seldom enough to represent adequately any type of work. If you can get a series of pictures that will tell the story, so much the better. Of course you have to know what story you want to tell first. Then use your imagination to figure out how to picture it best.

Pictures of the people will certainly be helpful. But here the missionary makes one of his most common mistakes. He takes them almost always in groups, lining them up and posing them in a stiff and unnatural way. Such pictures are seldom interesting to those who don't know the people. Unfortunately, the missionary sometimes tries to make up for this by telling the story of each one in the line, and he only succeeds in adding to the boredom.

Groups are not necessarily bad, especially if you can picture them in some normal activity. But take also some individual pictures, including closeups that will show the features. Take them engaged in their usual activities so that they will be truly representative. Too many look for the strange and unusual, when what we want is that which will show the ordinary and the usual.

In some places you will have difficulty in getting people to let you take their pictures. They don't understand your purpose, or they are superstitiously afraid of the "shadow-catcher." Never take a picture to hold the people up to ridicule, and try not to give them the idea that you think they are objects of curiosity. Many of them will understand if you explain that your friends are interested in seeing how they live, since it is different from our ways. They, too, are interested in the way other people live.

The question of taking pictures of religious rites is a delicate one. In some public ceremonies in the open air there may be no objection at all. In other cases the mere attempt to take a picture may stir up violence. Even among Christians there is often objection to taking pictures of a solemn service of worship. Take care not to offend, for picture taking has only a secondary place in your work. Don't jeopardize your main purpose just for the sake of a picture.

Scenery. The church at home is interested in knowing what the country looks like as well as the people. So it is perfectly all right to take pictures of the scenery. But remember that things may not look the same in a small picture as they appeared to you in real life. It takes experience and imagination to figure out ahead of time what your finished product will look like. Perhaps the biggest mistake is to try to get too much into the picture, or to take pictures at too great a distance with nothing in the foreground to give depth.

b. *Planning the picture.* Many amateur photographers belong to the "see and shoot" school. They shoot whatever takes their fancy at the moment, without worrying about lighting, background, composition, etc. Ordinarily their pictures show this lack of planning. And when another gets more interesting pictures, they are likely to lay it to his better equipment, or at most to his possession of some elusive knack that they have not inherited. Actually it is more often the result of careful painstaking study and experimentation. Many commercial photographs that look so easy and natural are the result of countless hours of work, plus long experience, and a number of shots that fizzled or didn't suit the exacting artist.

Most good pictures are planned, even though they appear quite natural. This is not to discount the occasional "lucky" shot that a photographer may get on the spur of the moment. These so-called "lucky" shots usually come to those who have had long experience in the work, and they are not the usual thing. There are times when you have to take what you can get without any opportunity to plan. But planning gives a better picture.

The logical thing is to decide what story you want your picture to tell and then figure out how best to get it. It doesn't always work out in practice, though. Sometimes you see a scene that suggests to you the possibility of a story. The story comes after the picture. In either case the picture is not just a picture. It is related to a story, a story that you think is worth telling.

Generally speaking, unposed pictures may seem to be the most interesting. But good ones are sometimes hard to get. You have to take them with whatever background or lighting is present at the time. And if the subject knows you are taking his picture, he may insist on posing regardless. If the subject is in motion, you have to anticipate what his position will be when you snap the shutter. And he may not move in the direction you want. Or someone else may step in between. But the unposed picture does have the advantage of great naturalness.

On the other hand, posed pictures are easier to get, and with care they can be made to appear quite natural. There is certainly nothing wrong in a posed picture, if the story it tells is true. In a posed picture you have control of the lighting, the background and the composition. And you can repeat the shot as often as you need to in order to get what you want. Of course your major problem is to make it appear natural, with none of the stiffness or artificiality that we usually associate with posing.

If you are taking a picture of scenery, buildings or other inanimate objects, you will do well to include a person, or at least an animal, so as to give the picture life.

If you want your picture to tell a story it ought to suggest action, either physical or mental, if it doesn't actually portray it.

To show the size of any object, include a person or some other object of known size for purposes of comparison.

Shadows are as important as light in a picture. Pay attention to them and try to visualize how they will appear in the finished picture.

Watch out for the background. It can spoil an otherwise good picture by detracting from the main subject.

Don't try to get too much into your picture. It is sometimes said that the best picture is one from which nothing can be removed.

Don't feel that you have to take all of your pictures from waist level or any other level. Experiment with other positions for different effects.

Our general tendency is to stand too far off from the main object and diminish its importance in the picture. Try standing closer so that it dominates the picture.

These are just a few suggestions that we hope will be of help to missionaries. For the actual mechanics of picture taking there are any number of good guides that can be purchased. There are also books on pictorial composition for the one who is willing to take the time to study it carefully. Actually I suppose the average missionary's greatest lack is an ability to see a picture in his mind's eye before he tries to take it with a camera. It is a matter of vision and imagination, plus enough interest to keep on studying and trying. Some missionaries have done some excellent work in what for them is just a sideline.

c. *Moving pictures.* The judgment of experience has not favored the taking of moving pictures by the average missionary. It is not only that he lacks training and experience to do a good job. The problem arises in the nature of the motion picture itself: by its very nature the motion picture must have sequence. It must tell a connected story from beginning to end. It doesn't have to be the sequence in which the pictures were taken, but the pictures do have to be related to one another in some way. This takes comprehensive planning, rather than the accumulation of isolated shots over a period of several years.

Besides, the taking of such pictures is expensive. It would be a great deal less if 8 mm. pictures were suitable. But for public showing you need 16 mm. film, which means a more expensive camera and an expenditure of roughly four times as much for film. Not many individual missionaries can afford to do much along this line. More commonly the mission undertakes the production of motion pictures, though it may call for the co-operation of capable missionaries if it cannot afford to hire professionals.

CHAPTER FOURTEEN

RELATION TO THE NATIONALS

TERMS USED

A STUDENT FROM AFRICA came to my office one day and very politely requested, "Can't you get the people to stop calling us 'natives'?" I knew what he meant. I knew something of the resentments that have grown up among other peoples because of their treatment by Europeans and Americans. And those resentments have sometimes found a focus in that term "native." All too often the one who talks of the "natives" does so with an air of condescension. They are an inferior group, a group to be looked down on, sometimes even a despised group.

Of course there was little enough that I could do. One man could scarcely change a custom that has grown up through years of usage. Missionary leaders have been trying to do away with this term for years. But they have not been entirely successful. People still say "natives" and probably will continue to do so. The term "nationals" has a strange sound to them and often requires an explanation. All this I explained to my African friend, assuring him of my own sympathy with his viewpoint. We do need to make a change, but a change not so much of words as of attitudes.

The word "native" has in itself no sense of depreciation. It refers simply to one who was born in the place. We are natives of the country where we were born. A plant is native to the place where it originated. And we continue to use the word "native" in this very acceptable sense. But it is also true that in our dealings with people not of our own group the word has taken on some additional connotations. Even in American society, the sophisticated city dweller is likely to speak with

162

disdain of "the natives" in the country place where he spends his summer vacation. And many of our American tourists are notoriously disrespectful toward the people whose lands they visit, lumping them all together as "the natives" without regard to nationality or civilized status. The usual implication is that they are inferior.

Unfortunately we don't have another general term that can fully take the place of "native." "National" has been used for a number of years and in some cases is very suitable. The evil connotations of "native" haven't yet been attached to it. But "nationals" would hardly be accurate in speaking of the native peoples of Angola, who are governed by the nation of Portugal. How then would you differentiate between the Portuguese settlers and the Africans?

However, we are on perfectly safe ground when we use national, racial or tribal adjectives for the people. The indigenous inhabitants of Japan certainly prefer to be called Japanese. The people of Chile take pride in being Chileans. And in Africa south of the equator the term "African" is not objectionable, though it is often wise to be a little more specific and speak of the Kikuyu, the Akamba, etc.

ATTITUDES

As we have said before, the fundamental problem is attitudes rather than words. But words are the expression of attitudes. So be careful with the words you use. But at the same time give much more attention to your attitudes. Some people seem to know how to use all the right words, but they never gain the confidence of the people. Others make embarrassing slips now and then, but the people good-humoredly overlook them, for they say, "His heart is right." Most people are rather quick to sense whether a person likes them or not. They can be deceived, but usually not for long.

Two missionaries were visiting a town in Venezuela together. A young mother entered the house where they were staying, carrying her baby girl, a child born out of wedlock. Both missionaries spoke to the mother, and the second one also played a little with the baby.

When the mother had gone on, the first missionary remarked to his companion, "I just can't 'make over' these children of sin." The other simply replied, "Well, she's a cute little thing; and after all, it isn't her fault."

That night, after the evening service, the second missionary overheard the mother talking to her baby outside the house, as mothers will. "Mr. E. doesn't like you," she was saying, "but Mr. C. does!" The first missionary had not said a word to the mother about it, but she had accurately sensed his attitude.

Sometimes missionaries, when they first reach the field, are overly sensitive about doing things just right. They are constantly afraid of doing some little thing that might offend the people. Of course it is far better to be this way than to be overly careless. We do want to avoid all offense if possible. But to relieve a little bit of the worry and tension, let me say that a manifestly friendly attitude will do far more than a punctilious observance of all the rules. People are usually ready to overlook minor errors on the part of persons who like them.

What we are talking about is not that "put on" air of friendliness to everybody. Rather we mean sincere and evident respect for the other person as an individual, and a willingness to get to know him so as to be friends, if we can find a common basis for friendship. You can't like people until you have seen them and met them; but you can come to them with a willingness to like them. You can let them know that you want to be a friend, and if it doesn't work out it won't be through lack of willingness.

It seems as if this should be easy for a missionary. After all, he is going abroad because he wants to do good to others. But such a presumption is poorly founded. There are many missionaries who find it difficult to learn to like the people. There are some like the one who is said to have written home, "This would be a wonderful place, if there weren't so many natives around." There are missionaries who can put on a good front of being friendly to the people, but secretly they despise them and they avoid being with them any more than is necessary.

How can this be? It is not hard to understand. In the first place, some of these people are not very likeable—no more so than are some Americans. And you don't like a person simply by determining that you are going to like him. Especially when he has habits that constantly grate on your sensibilities. Then, after all, he is different from you. It will take time for you to get used to his ways of thinking and acting. And if you think that adjustment is too much of an effort, you never will really get to feeling at home with him. Besides, his language is so different, and at the beginning maybe even his appearance is frightening to you. How much we fear the strange and the unusual! And then there are many who go out "to do good" in the same way that some people dispense charity. Out of their abundance they are condescending to make a contribution to those who are less fortunate. They are willing to give, to give generously and even sacrificially, of what they possess. But they do not give themselves. And "the gift without the giver is bare."

How little people seem to realize some of these things! How little they appreciate the importance of self-respect to an individual, and not only self-respect but a measure of esteem from others! How often they offend, even in their most unselfish acts! "How can a person accept our gifts and still resent us?" they say. "Why aren't they more grateful?" And all the time, if they only stopped to think, they know that they would do the same thing if they were in the others' place.

We all resent being made to feel inferior. We resent having to accept another's gifts solely because of his pity for our condition. It wouldn't hurt so much if he helped us simply as a friend, saying, "Maybe some day I'll need your help." We know that day may never come, but we realize that he wanted to help us as a friend, taking no glory for what he did, expecting no recompense, not even a "thank you."

We are not saying that the missionary is going to admire all that he sees in the people. Far from it. He is realistic enough to know that some are scoundrels. So was he, or so would he have been, if Christ had not got hold of him. That is the secret of the whole thing. By nature he is no better than these others to whom he goes, though he may have been born in more fortunate circumstances. But in Jesus Christ he has found One who could revolutionize his life, transform it, ennoble it. He has a new life in Christ, but it isn't like a treasure that he can dole out to others less fortunate. He has no way of giving it to them. All he can do is introduce them to the One who saved him. He is confident that Christ can do the same thing for them. He really wants them to know his Saviour, for he knows what it would mean to them. But if they finally do accept the Saviour, they owe the missionary nothing. Rather, in giving them the gospel he was only paying his own debt, a debt that was laid on him when he received the new life. He is not trying to win adherents for his church. He is trying to get people to reach out for themselves and take hold of Christ—or rather let Christ take hold of them—so that they can enter into real life.

So the attitude of the missionary should not be that of one who goes to others to get anything, whether followers, or merit, or rewards, or praise, or appreciation. It should be that of one who gives, who gives because he must give, who learned to give from the One who "so loved the world that he gave his only begotten Son."

We cannot take it for granted that the people will understand this benevolent purpose, no matter how sincere we are in it. They have been deceived before, and they will look for the catch in our offer. The world cannot understand anyone who gives without a reasonably sure chance of reaping a profit. Even the so-called "spiritually minded" Orientals are constantly seeking for gain, though it may not be the sort that is calculated in dollars and cents. It is still true that "the natural man receiveth not the things of the Spirit of God; for they are foolishness unto him." But whether the people understand it or not, it is the only attitude that can make our relations with them what they should be.

Our relation with the people is of utmost importance in the work we are called to do. They are quite naturally suspicious of an outsider, not to say a foreigner. They will not be ready to trust any offer he makes them, to believe any message he gives them, to give allegiance to any Saviour he recommends to them, unless they first have confidence in *him.* All of his work revolves around this matter of confidence. Once it is lost, once the people become antagonistic to him, no matter how true his message may be, his work is done.

It is for this reason that the missionary needs to take special care in his early days, so that the first impressions are good. First impressions are often lasting impressions. Of course a poor first impression can be changed. But it is much harder to change it than it is to make sure of a good impression to begin with. A good rule is to be quick to hear and slow to speak, quick to see and slow to act. Be more ready to learn than to teach, more ready to hear another's viewpoint than to expound your own. Then when the time comes to speak your own piece, they will be more ready to listen, for you will speak with a background of understanding.

"FACE"

One of the serious mistakes that Americans make in their relations with Orientals is overdirectness. We sometimes pride ourselves on "calling a spade a spade." We believe in being frank to the point of bluntness. We believe that "saving face" is a form of hypocrisy.

There may be something to say for this view in the field of ethics. Perhaps it would be better all around if people spoke out frankly, if they weren't so concerned about "face." Undoubtedly it would make our relationships with one another much less complicated. They might sometimes be less friendly. But at least we would know just where we stood.

However, what we might prefer in theory may be very unwise in practice. We are called on to deal with the people as they are, not as we think they ought to be. They are deeply concerned about "face." It is ingrained in them from their earliest years. To make them "lose face" is the most serious offense possible. As they see it, it is not an excess of truth that inspires such an action, it is an excess of animosity. If you want to keep a man's friendship you always try to "save his face." It is only your enemies that you try to make "lose face," and then only under great provocation.

So resist that impulse to "bawl out" your servant, or that clerk in the store. If you must correct him, do it privately, so that he will not lose face before others. Better still, take a positive approach and suggest to him a "better" way. He will understand and will also appreciate your consideration. Moreover you can build up a reservoir of good will toward yourself if you will show appreciation for things that are done well. The warm breath of praise opens many a heart's door that is tightly closed against the blasts of criticism.

BASIC STUDIES: PSYCHOLOGY AND ANTHROPOLOGY

Good human relations are always based on understanding. They call for understanding on both sides. Suspicion and doubt and fear and distrust have to be reduced or eliminated. Each one has to know what he can count on the other to do. You don't have to believe alike. But you do have to respect one another and know what you can expect from each other.

This means, then, that the missionary in particular needs to know the people among whom he works. He needs to know them as human beings, and he needs to know them as members of the cultural group to which they belong. It is one of the fundamental laws of teaching that the teacher must know his pupils just as much as the subject matter he is to teach. In a sense the missionary is a teacher. And he must certainly know the ones he is to teach. Jesus Christ Himself, the greatest of missionaries, "knew what was in man."

The missionary needs to know psychology. That is, he has to know how people think and act, and why. He needs to know what motivates them, what inhibits their actions. He needs to know how sin has warped their thinking, how error gets control of their wills. These and many other things he needs to know about man in general. Taking a course in psychology in school will not give him an adequate knowledge of man. While such study is good as far as it goes, often the student fails to relate knowledge gained to actual experience. And many of the keenest students of human nature have never had the advantage of such a college course. In fact, interesting and informative as some of the college textbooks are, we still feel that the Bible itself is superior as a source book for the study of human nature.

In psychology we study the inner experiences of man *as man*. The study of his life as a member of a cultural group we usually call anthropology. In some things all men are alike, both physically and spiritually. There are, for example, a few differences in the appearance and physical structure of the different races of mankind. But when a doctor is called to remove from a man his infected appendix, he doesn't have to know his race in order to know where to cut. The similarities in anatomy are far greater than the dissimilarities. On the other hand, there is a multitude of things in which men differ from people to people, and even man to man. Anthropology is interested in those traits that are common to one group of people, and in the comparisons between the various groups. So a missionary needs to know something about what we call cultural anthropology. At the very least he needs to gain an understanding of the particular group with which he is working.

It is this lack of understanding that has often blocked the attempt of missionaries to make much of an impression on the peoples to whom they have gone. To use a modern term, there has been no communication. The missionary has thought he was teaching one thing; the people have understood something else. The missionary has expected the people to react in a certain way; their actual reactions were quite the opposite. Sometimes he has succeeded in getting them to conform to all the externals of the faith, but inwardly they seem to have changed scarcely at all.

What is the purpose of the missionary's study of anthropology? Let us put it simply. It is *to enter into such a sympathetic understanding of the people that he will be able to show them what Christ can mean to them in the circumstances in which they live.*

The missionary's motivation is not just curiosity, you see. He is not interested merely in knowing strange and unusual customs. There is a definite purpose and a spiritual one. The missionary is persuaded that Christ can meet the needs of all men everywhere. But the circumstances are different from place to place. Sin is the fundamental problem, but it shows itself in a bewildering variety of ways. So the new life that comes through Christ is likely to show itself in different ways among different peoples. We are not called on to show people what Christ can mean to them if they happen to be Americans living in an American society. They are not Americans and most of them will never see America. Their type of life is different, their temptations and problems in many ways are different. "If I accept Christ, what will it mean in my life?" asks the tribal chief in the Amazon jungle, the witch doctor in Africa, the moneylender in India, the student in Japan, the soldier in Formosa. They want definite help, as did the people who came to John the Baptist in Luke 3 saying, "What shall we do?" And the missionary is only prepared to help them if he knows the circumstances of their lives.

How do we get this knowledge, this understanding? There is no substitute for direct contact with the people. We need to be with them not only at church or in school or on the road, but in their homes. We need to gain their confidence, so they will reveal to us their problems, their anxieties, their joys and hopes and ambitions. That may mean long continued contact, for people do not open up their hearts to new acquaintances. It means patiently building up a friendship on the basis of mutual respect and confidence.

How can a missionary expect to carry out his ministry if he never sees the people in their homes? How can he help them meet their problems if he never sees them in the circumstances where those problems arise? At the very best he can never completely understand them, for that would mean his becoming one of them. But the more he can share with them in their daily life, the closer he will come to that ideal.

Of course it is possible to live with people for a time and still not be aware of the reasons why they act as they do. The good missionary will usually be observant. Even more, he may show a positive curiosity. It was stated some years ago that cultural anthropology was "almost a missionary science because of the contributions of missionaries to the study of other peoples." The missionaries observed, they asked questions, and they recorded their observations for the information of others.

Sometimes they made mistakes, for they weren't all accurate observers. Sometimes the people deliberately misled them for one reason or another. And sometimes they just failed to understand the information they received or the significance of the things they witnessed. Just to avoid some of the most common pitfalls that may trap the unwary observer, let us put down seven rules for accurate observation.

1. *Listen more than you talk.* Remember that you are trying to learn, not to instruct.

2. *Learn to ask questions without appearing too inquisitive.* If people think you are too inquisitive, they will do one of two things. Either they will give you no answer or they will give you the wrong answer. Quite often it is the latter.

3. *Don't read your own ideas into your observations, and don't ask questions to prove your point.* You are after facts, not confirmation of your own preconceived opinions.

4. *Record your observations at the time instead of depending on your memory.* It is remarkable how things that are quite vivid to us right now become blurred with the passing of a few days.

5. *Don't exclude any fact because it doesn't seem to fit the general pattern.* Maybe your idea of the pattern is all wrong. Facts are facts, whether we understand how they fit or not.

6. *Patiently check every observation for possible errors.* We can't emphasize this too much. Even eye witnesses can be mistaken.

7. *Don't set down as general principles what may be exceptional cases.* An American stole a visitor's wallet. Are all Americans thieves? Don't call a thing "typical" unless it characterizes most of the people.

In saying there is no substitute for personal contact with the people, we didn't mean to imply that there is no value in a formal study of anthropology in the classroom. On the contrary it has at least two real values. First, it gives an understanding of the basic principles needed to understand any people. Then, it teaches what others have already found out and verified about a wide variety of peoples. For the prospective missionary, then, two courses are specially useful. One is a general course in cultural anthropology. The other, if he knows the field to which he is going, is a course in the ethnology of the particular people he wishes to reach. If the second is not available, there would still be value in a study of a related people, always understanding that even two closely related peoples may have wide differences in their culture.

So far we have spoken about culture but we have not defined it. Some say that culture is man's reaction to his environment. Others say that it is man's learned conduct as opposed to that which is instinctive or innate. And there are numerous other definitions more technical and less simple. This much is sure, man's culture is the most variable thing about him.

The following dozen items are some of the subjects commonly treated in a study of the culture of a people:

1. *Customs associated with birth.*
2. *Language.*
3. *Initiation into the tribe.*
4. *Means of subsistence, occupations, etc.*
5. *Housing.*
6. *Education, arts and crafts.*
7. *Marriage customs.*
8. *Family relations.*
9. *Community relations.*
10. *Relation to other groups.*
11. *Practices associated with disease, death and burial.*
12. *Religion and magic.*

There are a number of problems in the study of anthropology from a missionary point of view. We might say to begin with that some anthropologists, though their science is one of the newest, are firm believers in the *status quo.* That is, they seem to take the attitude that what is, is right. They are sure that every element in a culture serves a useful purpose and therefore we should not try to change it. On the other hand, some missionaries take the opposite attitude. To them, everything in a heathen culture that is not found in our culture is wrong. We must bring these other people around to our way of thinking and acting. It is a part of our missionary job. Of course neither of these views is correct. It is hard to say which is the more damaging to sound missionary endeavor.

Note first that a culture is usually a well-integrated pattern of beliefs and practices. Each one is tied in with the others in such a way that you cannot make any major change in the culture without affecting the whole pattern.

However, we also need to note that no culture is perfectly stable. All are changing in one way or another. Some are more fluid, while others are extremely conservative and resistant to change. But all are subject to change. And some of the changes are quite sudden and violent, apart from any Christian missionary work. Note the changes taking place in China today.

We should acknowledge that most elements in a culture do serve a useful purpose, or at least one that the people think is useful. Perhaps we should qualify this and say rather that their original intention was to serve a useful purpose. With the passing of years and the coming in of other changes, some have outlived their usefulness. Others have been perverted and have been made to serve selfish ends.

Religion, of course, is a part of the culture of a people. Not only is it a part, but it affects many other parts. You cannot change a man's religious beliefs and leave the rest of his culture as it was before. A change of religion inevitably means a change in other phases of a man's life.

But not all elements in a culture are affected by religion to a noticeable degree. A change of religion, for example, does not necessarily involve a change of occupation. It may have no effect on the traditional methods of earning a living.

The missionary is a missionary of the Christian faith, not of western culture. We have often heard this in recent years, yet the practice of some missionaries shows they have not comprehended it. At least they seem to have found it difficult to determine just how much of what they were preaching was an essential part of the faith, and how much came from their cultural background with little or no support in the Biblical revelation.

The problem of the missionary is to replace a heathen faith with the Christian faith, and then to guide those who accept the gospel in applying it to those parts of their culture that are inconsistent with Christianity. To do this he has to know what is really anti-Christian in a culture and so must be changed, and what may be considered neutral and so may be left alone or perhaps adapted to Christian purposes.

It is not always necessary to do away even with practices that have anti-Christian associations. Sometimes it is possible to substitute for them some similar practices that have a distinctly Christian content. It is to the missionary's advantage when he can do this. However, the attempt is not without danger. By this means sometimes pagan practices have found their way into the church of Christ.

It is neither necessary for the missionary to alter his gospel to suit heathen tastes, as some would have him do, nor to destroy completely the heathen culture, as other uncompromising enthusiasts seem to want. In some societies extensive changes have to be made, because so much of life is controlled by non-Christian religious ideals. Sometimes these changes are little short of revolutionary. Hence the missionary is accused of "destroying native culture." But there is nothing else he can do and remain true to his faith. In other societies, however, the necessary changes are much fewer. It is much the same as with individuals. The new birth that is made possible through Christ means a basic change in the person. But that change is not so apparent, not to say spectacular, in the youth who has led a respectable life, as it is in the confirmed "down-and-outer."

The missionary needs to realize that the changes made are the fruit of a new faith, not the source of it. The changes themselves are of little value, and may even be harmful, if they do not proceed from a changed heart. This has always been a problem in missionary work, and always will be. There are many who adopt "the forms of godliness but deny the power thereof." To some people Christianity is only a newer and more powerful form of magic. If you speak the right words and go through the right actions—that is, if you follow the formula—you will get the supernatural results. How difficult it seems for us all to realize that it is the heart that counts! To use Christ's own terminology, it is the spirit that gives life, not the flesh.

Relation to Law and Authority

There was a time, when colonial rule was much more widespread than it is today, when the missionary's relation to law and authority had only an indirect bearing on his relation to the people of the land. But the situation has been changing. Increasingly the missionary is having to deal with self-governing states. So his relation to law and authority does not involve other countries but is only a part of his relation to the people of the land.

The principle is the same, whether under native rule or rule by a colonial power: "Obey them that have the rule over you"; "Render unto Caesar the things that are Caesar's." There is only one ground for disobedience: when obedience would mean violating the higher law of God. There will still be many questions difficult to decide. But above all things the missionary needs to avoid giving the impression that he considers himself above the law, whether as an American or as a missionary. Sometimes in making his decision he forgets that there are others who are following not only his teaching but his example. He needs to guard against creating disrespect for the law among his followers. When we go to any country outside our own we must realize that we are not lords of the land, but guests. The guest does have certain rights, but it is not one of those rights to do as he pleases without regard to established rule and authority.

We have said that the missionary does have certain rights under the law. He is not wrong when he sees fit to claim those rights, just as Paul claimed the rights of Roman citizenship on more than one occasion. However, he should not do it in a contentious spirit and should set a good example to the national believers. Beware of claiming any special rights that may have been granted to foreigners under duress. Such a practice may build up a backlog of bitterness that later on will vent itself against the missionary's work when the rights are withdrawn. We have seen this in the Orient where for years westerners insisted on rights of extraterritoriality, exemption from local jurisdiction. Even more, it is questionable whether a missionary should ever take advantage of his privileged position to intercede on behalf of the national Christians.

His intercession may indeed succeed for the moment, but it will earn also a measure of resentment. In addition, the Christians then become inseparably linked in the thinking of the people with the foreign power the missionary represents. In a sense they become denationalized without actually choosing to do so. Even though it is permissible, it is not always wise to claim your rights under the law. Sometimes you can accomplish a great deal more by suffering wrongfully, though of course it is hard to see at the time. Before acting, always weigh the possible results of your action.

Treat officials with the courtesy and respect that their office calls for. However, look out for any appearance of political favoritism. The missionary who allows himself to become involved in local politics is sowing the seeds of trouble. Though his friends may be in power at the moment, when they are turned out the missionary may be turned out with them.

Custom often calls for a visit to the local authority when you first reach a place, and also at the time of departure. Don't neglect these courtesy calls, even though you may not care for them. You have a witness to bear to the officials as well as to others. Maintain as friendly relations with them as the circumstances will allow, without becoming too closely identified with the party in power. Even when they do not accept your message they may accept your friendship, and this will be an important help in the work.

The American missionary is both a missionary and an American. He cannot avoid this dual relationship, nor is he free from the responsibilities that pertain to his American citizenship. For example, he is expected to register his presence in the country at the nearest American consulate and to keep his papers in order. He is responsible to report any marriage, birth or death in his family within a reasonable period of time. His sons are subject to registration for the draft. He is subject both to the local laws that govern all residents in the country, and to international treaties that govern that country's relations with the United States and its citizens. If his rights as an American are infringed, he may appeal to the American diplomatic official to intervene in the case. He should be careful, however, to make such appeals only in exceptional cases. They identify the missionary more closely with American interests than with the Christian missionary cause.

Property rights are a most frequent source of trouble. That is why many missions require that all real property be held in the name of the mission itself, and not in the names of individuals. In some cases the missionary has to agree that if he buys any such property with his own funds, or uses his own money to improve the property, the property and all improvements automatically come into the possession of the mission. Then in the case any litigation arises, the mission will handle the matter and not the individual missionary. This avoids a great deal of difficulty. In some cases, in order to have legal standing the mission must be officially recognized or even incorporated within the country where it is working. Even where incorporation is not actually required it may be advantageous.

BUSINESS RELATIONSHIPS

1. *Honesty.* We take it for granted that the missionary will be strictly honest in all his business dealings. Of course this doesn't mean that he can't be a good bargainer. There is no particular merit in letting oneself be imposed on. There are many places where haggling over the price of an item is expected. In fact, bargaining is a part of the game, and the seller who gets his first price may be really disappointed. "Let the buyer beware" is the rule in all too many places, so you may need to be constantly alert to avoid being cheated. But avoid any accusation of cheating if you possibly can. The Orient is not the only place where you have to be concerned about "saving face." If you ever do have to make any open accusation of wrongdoing, be sure that you have the clearest of proofs. It is better to suffer yourself to be defrauded than appear in the light of a false accuser.

2. *Loans.* In the matter of loans to the people, remember that Polonius' advice to Laertes is still good: "Neither a borrower nor a lender be; for a loan oft loseth both itself and friend, and borrowing dulls the edge of husbandry." You can easily turn a friend into an enemy by lending him money that he eventually is unable to return. Sometimes it is better to offer a small gift in place of a larger loan. The loan might turn into a gift anyway. It is a handicap under which all American missionaries suffer, that everyone thinks they are rich. So we shall constantly have to expect requests for money in one way or another. Sometimes missionaries are able to insist that all requests for financial as-

sistance be handled by the deacons of the church. The missionary then makes his contributions to the "deacons' fund," along with those of the national Christians. There is less likelihood that the deacons will be imposed on than the missionary. They are usually better acquainted with their own people and their needs.

3. *Workmen and servants.* Christian organizations in the homeland have an unenviable reputation for paying substandard wages. This does not particularly commend the gospel that we preach. However, the reason usually given is the lack of sufficient funds to do better. On the mission field, on the other hand, the missionary often has an income far in excess of that of the nationals. It is probably small according to American standards, but in the eyes of the people it removes any sound objection he might have to the paying of standard wages to his employees. The only acceptable policy is to pay at least what the local wage scale is for similar work. In places where wages are excessively low he ought to do more.

In various countries where the missionaries are serving today, governments have been passing laws for the protection of the workers. Undoubtedly in some cases they have gone beyond what is reasonable, and sometimes it works a hardship on Christian organizations. Yet it is strangely disturbing to listen to missionaries who have long been used to cheap labor as they complain about even the modest increases that are sometimes demanded. We would expect the missionary to be in the forefront of those who are trying to help the national improve his standard of living.

Then, too, there is the matter of such benefits as days off, suitable working conditions, hours of labor, etc. Is it right to expect a house servant to be on the job seven days a week, with no time off for her own purposes? Is it a sufficient excuse to claim that others do the same thing? We are dealing here with a field where there is often much friction. All unknowingly the missionary may make demands that the nationals feel are unreasonable. On the other hand the missionary is irritated with what he considers to be the incurable laziness of the national and his irresponsibility. There needs to be some sort of an understanding. The missionary in particular needs to take care that he doesn't harm his work by appearing to exploit the people.

In most places where the missionary hires workmen, he may properly require them to attend a daily devotional service, even if they are not Christians. That is, he may require them to attend so long as he does not require them to take an active part in the service. However, he should never use employment as a lever to force conversion. Not only should he avoid any open attempts of the sort, but he should avoid giving the impression that conversion is the sure way to employment or to preferment. Christ Himself had little confidence in those who followed Him for the loaves and fishes, and they were the ones who soon turned against Him.

The question of having nationals, and especially servants, eat at the same table as the missionaries is not easy to solve. Much depends on the local situation. There are places where no one considers it in good taste and where even the servants themselves much prefer to eat apart. This is particularly true where their tastes are very different from those of the missionary. But they will naturally resent being made to feel like menials. Really it isn't so much a matter of eating at the same table as it is of the over-all attitude and actions of the missionary. True democracy goes deeper than the question of where one may properly sit and eat. It involves mutual respect that will show itself in a hundred different ways. And if that respect is lacking, the formalities will be meaningless. Having the right spirit, the missionary can always work out the details of his own situation in a satisfactory way.

ADOPTIONS

There are numerous situations in which a missionary feels moved to adopt a native child. Very commonly it is a missionary couple who have no child of their own but long for one. In their own country they would probably adopt a child; but when they are in missionary service it is often difficult to get the necessary permission. Usually the child they are considering is an orphan, or a castaway or unwanted child. Sometimes it is a parent who asks the missionary to take the child, and he finds it hard to refuse. This is especailly true where there are no orphanages. The thought in mind usually is that the child will get proper care and training if the missionary has him. Then one day he may develop into a Christian worker among his own people. It seems like an effective way to get national workers.

No matter how reasonable it all seems, some missions from long experience have adopted a rule against any formal adoptions. Some of the reasons why they oppose the practice are these:

1. When a missionary adopts a child, he removes him from his own environment and rears him as an American. You would hardly expect anything else. Yet this puts him in an ambiguous position. He doesn't usually gain full acceptance as an American among Americans, yet his own people no longer feel that he is one of them. In a sense he has become denationalized, and the possibilities of his becoming a leader among his own people are comparatively small.

2. In the earliest years, and while the family is on the field, some problems are hardly noticeable. But when the youth comes to a marriageable age, he faces a dilemma. To marry an American, if it is possible, presents all the problems of a mixed marriage with the possible social ostracism that it involves. To marry one of his own people may be almost as bad. He has become accustomed to an American standard of living and may have been educated far beyond the level of his own people, especially of the women, so the marriage would be unequal.

3. On furlough, or in cases where the foster parents may have to leave the field, there is a serious problem of adjustment in American society. Children of different races may be objects of interest in a missionary meeting, but in the local school and playground, and in other social affairs, their presence is often resented. Then the children suffer. Whether we approve of it or not, racial discrimination is a reality in American society.

LOVE AFFAIRS

Love affairs between missionaries and nationals, even of the most diverse races and cultures, are not unusual. The causes are not hard to find. (1) The missionary goes to the field at the normal age for marriage, or slightly beyond; (2) he is already predisposed to a love of the people by the very nature of his ministry, even though it is a love of a somewhat different kind; (3) and after he has been on the field awhile, the differences of race and culture tend to fade and he thinks only of individuals; (4) besides, there is a special attraction when both are interested in Christian service; (5) and finally, away from eligible young people of his own nationality, and oppressed by loneliness, he does things that under more normal circumstances he would not consider.

These affairs are of serious concern to the mission, though the young people usually think only of themselves. In the event they get married, the mission has to face the question of their official status. Shall the national be received into the missionary body, regardless of suitability, qualifications, or the opinions of the others? When an American couple applies, both have to be accepted by the Board. Shall one continue to be a missionary while the other is not? Officially that might be possible, but in actual experience it is unworkable. It is not as if missionary work were just a secular job that one could engage in entirely apart from the other. The work involves them both, and the two are really one.

Then there is the matter of the mission's relations with the people. They probably do not expect the missionaries to intermarry with them. But if a love affair does start and then is broken off, it may cause a strong reaction. Don't the missionaries think that they are good enough for them? And homeland relations are involved, too, since the mission is held responsible if it allows the affair to go on. Some missions have tried to avoid some of these problems by a set policy: any one desiring to marry a national must withdraw from the mission. But even that rule has not always succeeded in discouraging such marriages, and it has been considerably less than successful in obviating all the difficulties.

These mixed marriages have sometimes succeeded, though usually they don't. There are always problems of adjustment to one another in marriage. And these normal problems are multiplied when racial and cultural differences are added.

The ones who are usually lost sight of, and yet are most deeply concerned, are the children who come of such a marriage. It is the common lot of half-castes that they are neither accepted by the father's group nor by the mother's. They grow up in either society with the bitter feeling of not belonging. And their problem is accentuated when they reach a marriageable age. Whom can they marry?

Missionaries also need to take warning that they are not immune to temptations on the mission field. Sometimes love affairs have ended in something less honorable than marriage. A freedom of courtship that may not seem dangerous in our American society may open the door to immorality elsewhere. It has happened all too often. If we know this we can be forearmed.

CHAPTER FIFTEEN

RELATION TO THE NATIONAL CHURCH

IN ANOTHER PLACE we shall talk about the indigenous church, what it is, what it involves, and some means of accomplishing it. Here we are going to presume that such a church already exists, or at least that it is on the road to becoming indigenous. Very few people will dispute today the idea that the aim of missionary work should encompass the establishment of churches that are self-propagating, self supporting and self-governing.

"Fraternal Workers"

The question discussed in this chapter has to do with the relation of the *missionary* to the national church. Here we meet a new type of worker called a "fraternal worker." He is not a missionary in the usual sense, though in other ways he is. He is sent out by his church or denomination, but he is sent at the request of the church in the field. When he reaches his field of labor, he will serve under the direction of the church rather than the mission. In some cases the mission as such has been dissolved. It no longer carries on any work of its own.

The ideal that has stimulated this development is excellent. It is not only the recognition that a strong church exists in many fields. It is also the recognition that that church is a responsible body of believers, capable of directing the work in its own field on a par with the older churches, yet still needing some help from them. In other words, the mission church has come of age.

Where such an arrangement exists, the problem of the missionary's relation to the church is greatly simplified. He is not a representative of the mission. He belongs to no organization on the field that might in any way compete with the church for his loyalty. He is a worker loaned to the church to serve at its pleasure and under its direction. His own church will supply his salary and perhaps many other expenses, but the authority over him on the field is the national church. The church stands supreme and alone, with no competition from the mission, though it is still partly dependent on the mission for funds and personnel.

In many ways this is good. The fraternal worker finds it necessary to come to understand the people perhaps better than did some of the older missionaries. He cannot impose upon them his ideas, unless they see that they have merit. Unless he is making a useful contribution to the work, the church may request his withdrawal. Often he can give much more attention to his special ministry instead of being tied up with details of administration. Even more important, he stands before the people as their invited guest and helper, instead of an aggressive foreigner who has thrust himself upon them.

As we have said, this arrangement greatly simplifies the relationship of the missionary to the church. Previously such relationships could become very complicated. Anyone who has ever sat in a meeting where mission and church tried to come to an understanding on their respective spheres of responsibility knows something of those complications. What is the mission's job, once the church is a going concern? Should the missionaries have any voice in the church councils? Should the church not have a representative on the governing council of the mission? Who should decide on the opening of new works? What can the church do about a missionary who is objectionable? Does not the comparative wealth of the mission put it in a place where it can dictate to the church?

But though this new arrangement seems theoretically so ideal, and though it almost does away with the former friction between mission and church, there are objectors who believe that it has some fundamental weaknesses, and others who feel that in some cases the action was premature. What are some of the objections? Let us put them in the form of questions. First, is the national church really mature enough for such a responsibility? It is not a question simply of handling its own affairs. It is a matter of carrying forward a work that is admittedly too great for its own resources. In doing this it must make the best use of considerable well-trained personnel from the outside. And will it necessarily be more judicious in its handling of the foreigners than were the missionaries in their direction of the nationals? It is also called on to administer large sums of money from abroad, perhaps far greater than its own total offerings for the work. Is it prepared to handle those funds wisely, and in such a way that the church abroad will be willing to continue sending? Or is its autonomy more apparent than real, when it must continue to depend so largely on support from abroad? "The one that pays the piper calls the tune."

Second, will the church press forward the work, or will it consume all its energies in administering what is already begun? As we have said, the present work is far beyond the capacities of the church to maintain alone. Hence the continuing need for personnel and funds from abroad. Is the church able to provide all the leadership needed for the direction of the present work, plus that which will be needed to press forward into new areas? Is this not expecting too much from a church that was reportedly suffering from a shortage of leadership even before? Is there any magic in full autonomy that will automatically produce leaders?

Third, does not the plan completely disregard the operation of the Holy Spirit? It sets up a single proper channel for all activities. Everything must be channeled through the national church organization. The organization must decide when it is time to begin a new evangelistic effort, where it is to be and who will carry it on. It will decide what new movements from abroad will be allowed to enter its area. The church abroad will frown on attempts by any of its members to enter the area except by invitation of the national church organization.

It is all very logical, but does it not presume that the Holy Spirit will always work through official channels? And does not history teach us otherwise? And even though the church succeeds in keeping full control of the activities of its own group, what about other groups that may feel led to enter the area? In many areas today the most vigorous, rapidly advancing groups are not the closely organized "old-line" denominations. They are the more loosely organized groups where allowance is still made for the possibility of individual guidance by the Spirit. They frequently go off into excesses, but they are *alive and growing*. These groups will not refrain from pressing into an area where they believe there is a need, simply because an autonomous church already exists there. That church may not represent more than one-tenth of one per cent of the population.

But unquestionably the "fraternal worker" represents a significant move toward a great ideal: not simply the ideal of an indigenous church, but the ideal of a world-wide Church where each member stands ready to assist the others according to his ability, and to receive from the others inspiration and help according to his own need. There are no longer "sending" and "receiving" churches, for the stream is beginning to flow in both directions. And workers from one foreign field are being sent by their own church to assist in another. Even the distinction of "older" and "younger" churches is being dropped in an attempt to emphasize the equality of all within the Church universal.

PRACTICAL COUNSEL FOR MISSIONARIES

But in most missions we still face the problem of the relationship of the missionary to the church and of the mission to the church. In some cases that relationship may be spelled out by mission policy or by agreement between the mission and the church. In others, especially in independent missions and in pioneer areas, much depends on the judgment of the individual missionary. Let us give here a few words of counsel to the individual missionary.

1. *The missionary is not a local pastor.* This does not mean that he will never have to serve as a pastor. At the beginning, of course, he is the only one who can shepherd the believers. So he will have to accept it as a part of his missionary responsibility. But the very nature of his calling is much broader. The pastor is concerned about shepherding one flock; the missionary is concerned about multiplying the number of the flocks, each one ultimately to be under its own trained pastor. The pastor's work continues indefinitely; the missionary's work, if it is successful, has an end. Unless the missionary can see clearly this broader scope of his ministry, he is likely to tie himself down to a single congregation and thus limit his usefulness as a missionary. He may make a very good pastor, but he was called to be a missionary.

2. *The missionary is both an evangelist and a teacher.* We are not talking about his specialized activities. We are referring to his essential

character. He is an evangelist in the sense that his constant aim is to
see others come into the light of the gospel of Christ. If this is not
his desire he is no missionary, regardless of his appointment and his
activities. But he is a teacher in the sense that he aims also to prepare
others to do the work that he has begun. He may be a teacher of
evangelists, a teacher of teachers, a teacher of medical workers, a teacher
of any one of the ministries that he may carry out on the field. We
often say that a missionary's chief job is to work himself out of a job.
But he can only do this as he teaches others and sets them the proper
example. So, fundamentally, the missionary should be concerned both
with evangelism and teaching.

3. *The missionary is the contact man between the church and the
mission.* The church and the mission should be separate entities from
the very beginning, for each has its own distinctive work to do. But
during the time that the missionary also serves as pastor of the church,
the mission predominates. It is always a temptation to the missionary
to prolong that period more than is necessary. Still, even after the
church has its own national pastor and church organization, it will for
a long time have need of some services from the mission. It will not at
the very beginning, for example, be able to take over the training of its
own leadership. Neither will it be able to provide its own literature.
And in a variety of other ways it will need help. The missionary is the
link through which that help is made available.

It is just here that we run into difficulties. The job calls for a great
deal of tact and discernment. Yet not all missionaries are so gifted. As
the church grows toward maturity, it will resent any attempt at dictation. But at the same time it is likely to expect more in the way of material help than it ought to have. The missionary has to try to understand the church's point of view and show himself as sympathetic as
possible. And he must also try to get the church to understand the
mission's situation. It is a task that calls for broad understanding and
exceptional patience.

4. *The missionary can be very helpful as an adviser to the church.*
That is, he can if he has earned their confidence. The simple fact that
he is a missionary does not make him acceptable as an adviser. It is
strange how some fail to see this. He has to demonstrate his ability.
He has to show that there is a likelihood that he will be able to help.

He has to win their respect for his good judgment. And most of all he has to know how to counsel without dictating. This means that he has to know how to respect their judgment even when he does not agree with it. The best counsellors are often the most unobtrusive. They depend on the force of their reasons rather than on the authority of their position.

5. *The missionary should be an inspiration to the church.* This is a challenge to the best that is in us. We may not understand how we could inspire anyone. But if our going forth into missionary service was an inspiration to the church at home, cannot that same spirit of dedication inspire the church on the field? Have we to any degree lost that spirit of devotion and self-sacrifice? If so, let us seek to renew it. For that is just what the national church needs. It is not our sermons alone that inspire. It is the example of our lives, especially the spirit that appears to motivate us and the dedication that we exhibit. An Indian leader, while contending that "the evangelization of India is not to be conceived any more as the responsibility of foreign missionary societies," goes on to add, "The Indian Church is not spiritually ready to discharge its evangelistic responsibility." So he says that one of the greatest services a foreign missionary can render to the church "is to help in the coming of a revival in the Indian Church, help the Indian Church to become fit and ready to receive a great outpouring of the Holy Spirit."[1]

6. *At the church's request, he should be ready to serve in any way that is consistent with his calling.* Many a missionary is serving either permanently or temporarily with the national church and even at times under its direction. It is not necessary for the mission as such to cease operations in order to co-operate in this way. However, the missionary should be careful not to accept even a minor job that can be performed by a national. Sometimes nationals are glad to have the missionary take over a routine job like that of caring for the funds, because of his efficiency and proved honesty. (And if anything goes wrong it is easy to blame the missionary.) Yet usually there is no good reason why the people themselves should not bear that responsibility. Let them do it.

7. *A final word.* The missionary should count himself a part of the church and show it by his conduct. By this we don't mean that the missionary has to surrender his membership in a church in his homeland.

[1]Rajaiah D. Paul, "Missionary Activity in Present-Day India," in *Revolution in Missions*, Blaise Levai, ed.

If a dual membership is not permitted it may come to that, but we are not concerned here about the formalities of church membership. Whether ex officio or in some other way, the missionary should be identified with the church and recognize its authority. He should not count himself outside the church and above it. There should not be one code of conduct for the nationals in the church and another for the missionary. If he is in the fellowship of the church he should also be subject to its discipline. It is useless to talk about the missionary's identifying himself with the people in other ways, while he disregards this most important of all identifications. Did not Christ Himself give us such an example of complete identification (Phil. 2)?

CHAPTER SIXTEEN

OTHER RELATIONSHIPS

O F THE OTHER RELATIONSHIPS that concern a missionary in his life and ministry, we are going to single out only two for special consideration: the relation to other foreign residents, and the relation to missionaries of other societies.

RELATION TO OTHER FOREIGN RESIDENTS

Most large cities throughout the world today have their foreign colonies. Many of the smaller places also have a few foreign residents. What should be the relation of the missionary to these people? Should he pass them by? Often they have no Christian ministry. Are they no part of his concern?

Some of the foreign colonies are large enough and interested enough to form their own churches and secure full-time pastors. The major problem is with the smaller groups. Some of them may be touched by the ministry of the national church, but that is exceptional. More often if the missionary does not reach them they are not reached. Many of them are in as desperate need of spiritual help as the people among whom they live. Here is a challenge to the missionary's real concern for souls. He must not overlook those from his own country who need his ministry. Some missionaries have done excellent work of this sort.

But there is also another problem. It is not the problem of neglect but of excessive attention. It is dangerous for us to show a preference for the company of those of our own nation. It is an attitude that is very likely to alienate us from the very people who are our primary concern. This is especially so when those with whom we associate are not known for the Christian character of their living. Does an unbelieving American count for more in our eyes than a believing national? The people watch us to see. They do not expect us to shun our fellow countrymen, but they are very quick to note any preference we may show for their society.

RELATION TO MISSIONARIES OF OTHER SOCIETIES

Whether we like it or not, mission societies have multiplied rapidly in recent years. Those who once had the field entirely to themselves have witnessed the coming of others, some to help and others to compete. No longer can they count on being the sole representatives of Christianity. They must take into consideration these others and their work, whether for good or ill. They will necessarily have some relationship with them, or at least have to assume some attitude toward them. Of course this is far from a new problem in missions, but it is becoming increasingly important as the number of missions grows.

Perhaps we should divide the missions into three groups: those whose position is so radically different from ours that any co-operation is practically out of the question, such as the Roman Catholics and certain heretical sects; then those whose differences are such that we would find it hard to work together in the gospel, yet we would not openly oppose them; and finally those who differ from us only in some of the lesser matters. We can hardly make these divisions any more precise, for there are some groups that are much more tolerant than others.

1. *Relation to those whose work we oppose.* Perhaps the most common attitude toward this group is that of avoiding contact with them as much as possible. There is very little common ground, so there is not much basis for fellowship. Co-operation is out of the question, for the aims of one are opposed to the other. You cannot entirely ignore them, for their work touches yours, but you do not seek any contact with them.

But while we say that this is the most common attitude, we are not sure it is the best. Even for purposes of opposing their work, might it not be better sometimes to come into direct contact with them so as to understand their position? Do it tactfully and courteously, of course. A Christian is a gentleman at all times. But you can converse with them without in any way compromising your own position. Of course if you are inclined to "lose your head" in such a discussion, then avoid it, for it can do no good.

It is not only for understanding your opponent's position, however, that we suggest a direct approach at times. Rather, we should always consider the possibility that those who are in error may be reclaimed from that error. We are trying to win the heathen to a faith in Christ; should we not also try to win those who are just as lost, even though they bear the name of Christian? Admittedly it is more difficult to win a missionary of such a group than a simple follower. Yet does that free us from making the attempt? Sometimes the attempt has succeeded.

At all events, as we said, the missionary should comport himself as a Christian. The Protestant missionary who, in a rainstorm, refused to pick up a Catholic priest in his automobile, did his cause far more harm than good. He was demonstrating bigotry rather than fidelity. It is true that often the missionaries themselves are the objects of bigoted persecution. Yet Christ Himself said, "Do good to them that hate you," and Paul makes it even more specific when he says, "If thine enemy hunger, feed him; if he thirst, give him to drink." This is the Christian way.

2. *Relation to others who differ from us.* Here we run into questions that are far from easy to answer. They involve the whole issue of tolerance, co-operation, fellowship, and even the relative importance of various doctrinal and practical matters. The individual missionary's attitudes are often based on his own particular religious background and training. Some missionaries have scarcely known any Christian fellowship outside of their own denomination. Christianity and their denomination seem to them practically synonymous terms. Others who are personally just as deeply committed to Christ come from churches where there is a great deal of latitude in doctrine, have been trained in interdenominational schools, and have friends in a variety of different churches. These different backgrounds of course affect their attitudes on the mission field.

At a student missionary conference several years ago, a young woman asked why it was that her denomination was so unco-operative with others. The answer was simply this: "When you are sure that you are absolutely right in every detail, then every one who differs from you must be wrong. And if you believe that his errors are important, how can you co-operate with him in spreading error?" There are two basic assumptions here, you see. One is that you have a perfect comprehension of the whole truth and could not possibly be mistaken in any detail. The other is that "truth is truth" and no error can possibly be unimportant. When you make these assumptions, you must of necessity stand alone.

We shall always have people of this sort on the mission field. Missionary work calls for real dedication, for single-mindedness. Rajaiah Paul, an Indian Christian leader from whom we have quoted before, has written, "Whatever may be his other qualifications, a missionary must be someone who is utterly convinced of the truth and the universal validity of the Christian message. A half-hearted Christian . . . cannot be missionary in any real sense." So we need not concern ourselves overmuch with those who are too "broad-minded." Not many of them enter the missionary ranks. But we shall always be confronted with the problem of those who go beyond the assurance of "the truth of the Christian message" to an assurance that that message is precisely what they understand it to be and nothing else.

But most missionaries are not quite so close-minded. In fact it can probably be said that missionaries as a whole are more tolerant, more ready to co-operate than the groups they represent at home. On one occasion, several years ago, a certain group of missionaries received orders to cease co-operation with another group with whom they had worked together for some years. The only reason they received was, "We [at home] do not co-operate with those people."

So for most missionaries the following suggestions should be of some help in their relationship with those of different societies.

a. *First get acquainted with them.* This in itself will avoid many a misunderstanding or wrong judgment. How readily we criticize people we have never met! How often we judge them on the basis of unverified rumors! How quick we are to believe unfavorable reports about those who are different from us! Get acquainted with them. Then if you find reason to oppose them you can do it on a sound basis, not on mere hearsay.

b. *If on acquaintance you find in them a kindred spirit, enjoy their fellowship.* It will do you both good. You will probably also find it helpful to discuss some of the problems you have in common. Not long ago a Southern Baptist missionary in Nigeria wrote of his fellowship with an Anglican missionary. He said that on certain matters of doctrine they were far from agreement, but he found the Anglican "a real missionary." He couldn't help admiring him for the work he was doing with only a fraction of the material help that the American enjoyed. Such personal friendships are not uncommon on the mission field. They are good for the work of the Lord.

c. *Wherever possible, co-operate.* This individual co-operation between those who respect one another's ministry is the strongest basis for co-operation on a larger scale. Notice that we do not say that it is always possible, even among those who enjoy a certain amount of personal friendship. But where it is possible, and in the measure that it is possible, it will not only strengthen the ties of friendship but it will do good to the work. It may be simply that you invite the other to preach for you on occasion. Or it may be that you both work together on the production of a piece of literature that you both need. But the example that you set of Christian unity will not be lost on the people.

We need to mention, however, that there are times when even such personal co-operation is precluded by mission policy. In such a case, even though the policy may not seem to you to be wise, the only thing to do is conform. There may be a good reason for the policy. At any rate you should not break the unity in your own mission to secure a small measure of co-operation with those outside. Such failure to co-operate need not mean any lessening of the personal friendship.

d. *If it is not possible to co-operate, avoid stirring up unnecessary antagonisms.* Sometimes the other will not be so considerate. He may deliberately spread harmful tales about you and your work. He may seek to win away your converts or prejudice your standing with the government. He may try to stir up differences between you and your supporters at home. All of these things have been done. Yet you are not permitted to retaliate in kind. It might be possible to bring even stronger accusations against him and his work. But in such an exchange neither side would win. The major sufferer would be the work of the Lord, the new believers who would be caused to stumble by this strife between those who profess to be missionaries of Christ. It is not easy to have your good evil spoken of. And there are times when you must answer your accusers. But do avoid the sort of controversy that will only deepen the rift between you. There are those who appear to delight in strife, but "the servant of the Lord must not strive."

e. *Above all, watch out for jealousy.* It may lead you to belittle and harm the work of the other, but it is at the same time digging the grave of your own. Jealousy is only the other side of the coin of selfishness. We are jealous of the successes of others because we want them for ourselves. We resent the progress they make if we are not able to duplicate it. We are afraid that the attention they receive will detract from our own glory.

Look at the work of the other soberly and honestly. It will have its flaws. Every work does. But look at its over-all results. Is it accomplishing a praiseworthy purpose? Is it bringing honor to the Lord? Are the people whom it reaches becoming worthy servants of the Lord? Would you be ready honestly to praise it yourself, if you did not belong in another camp?

Then do so. Rejoice in what it is accomplishing. There is no surer cure for the disease of jealousy. And then get to your own work and see about improving it. You don't build up your own by pulling down that of the other. Get busy. And if he is using some effective methods, don't be too proud to adopt them or to adapt them to your own purposes. None of us is really original. We are all using things we learned from others. Jealousy is the lazy man's way out. The industrious man will be spurred to greater efforts by the successes of others.

PART FOUR

The Missionary's Work

CHAPTER SEVENTEEN

MANY PATHS—ONE GOAL

WHAT IS YOUR WORK going to be as a missionary? What jobs will you have to do? To answer such a question is almost impossible. Missionaries do too many different things. And they work in too many different fields. But we can safely say that you will probably do some things that you hadn't counted on. Without much question you will face some jobs for which you haven't had any special preparation.

There are really not many occupations that are completely foreign to missionary work. Just mention any job that a Christian can properly undertake. Then look in the records. You will probably find somewhere a missionary who has done that job. He may be engaged in it right now.

For example, missionaries often have been explorers. David Livingstone was only one of the many. They have tried to avoid getting entangled in political affairs. Yet in primitive areas like the Pacific islands they couldn't avoid it. Kings and chieftains asked them to be their advisors. Sometimes, like Christian Friedrich Schwartz in India, they were asked to carry out delicate diplomatic missions when no one else could be trusted. It was a missionary, Guido Verbeck, who helped to write the constitution of modern Japan.

From William Carey and Robert Morrison to the present day, missionaries have served in large numbers as linguists, grammarians and translators. Until fairly recent years cultural anthropology could almost be called a missionary science. Not only missionary schools but a number of great universities owe their origin to missionary initiative. Healing, from the roadside dispensary to the city hospital, has played an important part in missionary work. It was missionaries who called attention to the woeful plight of the lepers and who still carry much of the burden of their care.

Missionaries have taught arts and crafts to Africans. They have taught agriculture to Indians. They have engaged in famine relief in China. They have helped with refugee problems such as came with the partition of India. Often they have had to become architects and builders. The jinriksha is a missionary invention. Road building by missionaries is not uncommon. Missionaries have operated boats of various kinds. Some of them are piloting airplanes. They pioneered radio broadcasting in at least one country and are using it widely in 'others.

It is true that you will not find all of these activities in any one field. No one missionary engages in them all. But the work of a single mission station is usually many-sided. In fact, this diversification presents the missionary with a serious problem. He can easily dissipate his energies in a variety of very useful activities. Then after awhile he wakes up to find that he has lost his way toward his main objective. He is busy—constantly busy—but the things that he does don't seem to contribute much to his purpose in being there. And when he realizes this it creates in him a sense of frustration. What is the good of all this ceaseless activity?

Inevitably the sincere missionary will come to the time when he asks himself, "Why am I here? What did I come out here to do? Am I moving toward a goal? Or am I just drifting in spite of all my busyness?" And if he can't find a satisfactory answer to these questions he is likely to give up, defeated.

No work is going to succeed that does not have a goal. This much is obvious. You are not a missionary just for the sake of being a missionary. You expect to accomplish something. But what is it? Some missionaries, and even some missions, are very "fuzzy" in their thinking about their goals. They are not sure just what their objectives are. They have never taken the trouble to define them. Or they may claim to be pursuing one goal while they readily allow themselves to be turned aside into a number of other paths. At any rate they do not set before themselves a fixed objective and then make all their efforts contribute to that one end. They are not "single-minded."

This single-mindedness is very important in missionary work. It is possible to follow many different paths to reach your goal, but the goal must be a single one. Only so can you make progress. Knowing what you want to accomplish, you can choose the best ways to do it. And if one way is blocked, you can choose another that will reach the same end. Your varied ministries are only means to an end. No matter how good they may be in themselves, if they don't help you to reach your goal they can be a serious hindrance to your purpose. This has actually happened in places where education, for example, has become an end in itself. Some mission schools are missionary only in the sense that a mission society is responsible for them and mission funds support them. They have long since ceased to serve any valid missionary purpose, but they continue to drain off valuable missionary manpower and resources. They have lost sight of their goal.

And just what is this single goal? To use the words of Christ Himself, it is that men "may know thee the only true God, and Jesus Christ, whom thou hast sent." This involves knowing Him, not in the sense of being acquainted with His name or His deeds, but knowing Him through personal acquaintance and fellowship. It is to get men to know Him, to put their trust in Him, to let their lives be dominated by Him.

This is not so shallow an aim as simply "preaching the gospel." Preaching the gospel can become purely mechanical. It can be divorced from any deep concern for the people. It can lead to a false sense of accomplishment, when the Word is preached where it should be, but without any assurance that it is understood or that it has reached the hearts of men. In fact, the preaching of the gospel is not an end in itself. It is simply one of the chief means for reaching the real goal. The real goal is the regeneration of men.

This goal is also more comprehensive than "to establish the church." We should not despise the church. It is a part of God's order. We need it for Christian fellowship and mutual inspiration. We need it for the witness it can give to Christ before the world. Yet when we make the church itself the final goal we open the door to lifeless formalism. Association with the church takes the place of the life-giving association with Christ. We become more concerned with details of organization than with vitality of faith. And because our particular church is only one of many, we are likely to labor more for the building up of our own group than for the increase of the Body of Christ.

Or should I say that we are likely to confuse membership in our society with membership in that mystical Body?

But at the same time this goal is more restricted than that of "building a new world." The regeneration of society is certainly to be desired. But abstract, impersonal "society" has no existence apart from the individuals who compose it. Society may be something more than simply a composite of the individuals who compose it, but it is still true that the attitudes of those individuals determine just what it is going to be. The successful politician doesn't depend on swaying "the public." He gets out and shakes hands and kisses babies, and he has his precinct workers contacting individuals. So in mission work any regeneration of society will have to come through the individual regeneration of those who compose it. And it will inevitably come in the measure in which the individuals are truly regenerated. To labor for a regenerate society composed of unregenerate individuals, or to hope that through the regeneration of society its members will be changed, is vainly to beat the air.

To some this may sound like excessive individualism. They are persuaded that the kingdom of Christ will never come if we depend on the one by one method. It is too slow, too selective. We must in this modern day use a mass approach to get large-scale results.

To this we answer that we are simply following the Master Himself. He not only called individuals; He seriously distrusted the crowds who professed to be on His side. In John 6 He not only ran away from such a crowd, He later deliberately made it difficult for them to follow Him by giving His message on the bread of life. After that most of them left Him.

Our goal is the regeneration of men and women. This will involve preaching as a method. It will involve the church as a body of those who have been regenerated. It may even result in extensive changes in society, when large numbers of people, or people in influential positions are changed. But it is their regeneration, their salvation, that is our one great goal.

This does not mean that the missionary himself will do all the work. He may be the first, but he should not long be the only evangelist. He is not a lone taper from whom all the others will have to light their lamps. He should rather aim to be like the match that starts a conflagration. His goal should be to kindle others in such a way that they in turn will ignite still others. His ultimate aim should go far beyond his personal ministry, and even that of his society or church. It should be nothing less than the spiritual regeneration through Christ of "all who will," by every possible means.

As you go out to the mission field, you need to have your goal well in mind. It will determine your strategy and your tactics. But don't make the mistake of thinking that such a goal is easy to reach. You will only be disappointed and become discouraged. The enemy is very powerful. There are numerous battles and thousands of skirmishes in this warfare. There are retreats as well as advances. Sometimes there are long and wearisome campaigns with little visible result. And when you win a battle or capture a strong point, always remind yourself of your ultimate goal. Don't let the enemy lead you into an ambush or trick you into resting on your laurels. He doesn't have to defeat you in open battle. If he can turn you aside or cause you to take your ease, he will do just as well. From time to time you will do well to take a new view of your objective. Then see what you are actually doing in the light of that goal. It will help to keep you on track and will give a deeper meaning to some of the routine duties you must perform. The effective missionary will always take time to take aim.

CHAPTER EIGHTEEN

EVANGELISM

WE BEGIN OUR STUDY of missionary work with evangelism. Evangelism is the very heart of that work. All other missionary activities should in some measure contribute to it. From it these other works all derive their significance.

DEFINITION AND PURPOSE

Evangelism in its broadest sense includes all attempts to make known the Christian message, the gospel, and to persuade men to accept it. In this sense all missionary work is evangelism. But we often use the word in a more restricted sense: referring to a direct and open proclaiming of the gospel, accompanied by an appeal for men to accept it. It is in this sense that we use it here.

The purpose of evangelism is very simple. It is to bring men into the vital relationship of personal faith in our Lord and Saviour Jesus Christ. But this is not a purpose that can be achieved easily. Success in evangelism will require presenting the message in a variety of ways in order to make it clear to the people with whom we deal. It is not enough to convince them that the Christian faith is a good thing. We must persuade them that it meets an urgent need and that it is highly desirable. But even that persuasion will fall short if it doesn't result in a definite acceptance of the life that Christ offers the one who believes.

It is just here that the missionary feels his own insufficiency. He learns that he must depend on the operation of the Spirit of God. Often he is able to persuade men of the truth of his message. Sometimes he is even able to get them to join a Christian church. But he knows they haven't entered into a vital experience of personal faith in Christ. Yet this is his real purpose.

TYPES OF EVANGELISM

In general, evangelism may be classified according to three types: personal evangelism, public meetings with an appeal for a personal decision, and group or "mass" evangelism.

1. *Personal evangelism.* The work of evangelism is never complete until the individual makes a personal commitment to Christ. And the most widespread and effective means of getting that commitment is through individuals dealing with individuals. Sometimes the personal approach is made first, though the final decision comes in a public meeting. At other times the order is reversed. But often the whole matter is handled man to man. In any event the personal element, sooner or later, plays an important part.

Every missionary should be first of all a personal evangelist. In some fields you won't be able to carry on any other kind of evangelism. But even where you have more freedom you will find it basic to the building of the church. There is no use thinking about reaching the crowds if you are not interested in the individuals who make up the crowds. Neither can you get the nationals much interested in personal evangelism if you don't engage in it yourself. The day will come when they will be doing the bulk of such work, for every Christian should be a witness to others. But the missionary is never relieved of the obligation to do what he can. And you will usually have opportunities, no matter what your special ministry. It is true, however, that some do have more opportunities than others.

Personal work in other lands does not differ greatly from that at home. The major differences are as follows. Your approach will have to fit the customs of the land. You will have to face some arguments that are different, since the religious background of the people is different. And you are going to face a stronger prejudice, since you are a foreigner. But you need the same spirit of concern for others and the same tact in dealing with them. You must have the same clear understanding of the faith and ability to present it to others. You need the same dependence on the Spirit of God. And in many cases you will find a surprising similarity of spiritual problems and ways of thinking about them.

2. *Public meetings with a personal appeal.* What we call "evange-

listic services" in the homeland are also held in many mission fields. But we shouldn't suppose that they are the only kind of public meetings held. There are many times when our stylized service of songs, prayers, Scripture reading and sermon would be quite out of place. The message is primary; the other items may be so strange that they would detract from it.

There are times when a whole village may be brought together to hear what the stranger has to say. There are other times when the meeting must be like our street meetings, with all the distractions and competition. There are times when a missionary can join a group and unobtrusively turn the discussion into the channel of the gospel. There are other times when large campaigns can be planned to meet in tents, theaters, stadiums or other such gathering places.

What we need to remember is that *our accustomed order of service was not ordained of God. Our message is.* Our whole purpose is to find the most effective ways of presenting that message.

The value of the public meeting is that it enables you to reach a whole group of people at the same time. It also may allow you to give a more complete and orderly exposition of your message than would a private conversation. But it calls for a definite "follow-up." A single public message is far from enough. Even a series of messages is not enough. There must be both diligent sowing and patient watering. Through lack of watering the sowing can easily be lost. That is one of the grave dangers of mass movements. There are not enough skilled workers to care wisely and patiently for the tender shoots.

The appeal for a decision is something on which veteran missionaries disagree. They do not question the need for it. They only dispute the time and manner of calling for it. It is possible to be premature in asking for a decision. You must lay a basis for a decision first, so it will appear reasonable. But it is also possible to be too hesitant about making an appeal, when the people are ripe for it. We have somewhat the same situation in the homeland, with one exception. In non-Christian lands people seem to be less hesitant about making an open and vocal profession of faith, once they have made the decision. Therefore, many missionaries object to the common American practice of asking for a show of hands to indicate acceptance of the message. "Among our people," they say, "everyone would raise his hand, and it wouldn't mean a thing!"

3. *Group evangelism, or mass movements.* When we talk here about group evangelism, we are not thinking of what some people call "mass evangelism." That is, we are not thinking of large union evangelistic campaigns such as those carried on by Billy Graham. These are included in the previous class. What we are thinking of is the attempt to win a whole community as a unit.

Such an approach would not work in a society like that of the United States. We are too individualistic. But there are other societies where religion is considered a community affair. A man in such a society doesn't change his faith on his own initiative. He wouldn't dare. It is a matter to be decided by the group as a whole. We know that in our historical background there were times when the king determined the faith of his people. So it shouldn't surprise us that such a philosophy still holds in many parts of the world.

The basic idea of group evangelism is to get the group as such officially to adopt the Christian faith. Admittedly there will be many who are unregenerate. But they are now formally within the Christian fold. The way is open to perfect their understanding of Christian truth, to make effective in their lives the faith that they profess with their lips. The major opposition has been removed. The tremendous weight of community opinion is now on the side of Christianity.

This group approach is seldom deliberately used today. It was much more common in the Middle Ages. It was also used by Spanish and Portuguese missionaries in their great period of colonial expansion. But more recent mass movements have usually come without deliberate attempt. In India a large proportion of the Christians came into the church through mass movements. Yet the missionaries themselves did not plan the movements.

There are some who believe that we should make greater use of group evangelism today. They contend that it is the most effective strategy. If ever the world is to be won for Christ, they say, it can never be by calling the believers out one by one. It must be by large-scale movements. In line with this, some of them faced the open door in Japan at the close of the war with extreme optimism. Here was a people disillusioned with its former gods. The nation was ripe for conversion.

If only the emperor himself could be converted, Japan might become a Christian country.

It was not an impossible idea. Perhaps its greatest weakness was that it left out of account the work of the Spirit of God. It is not our persuasiveness but His power that changes men, even emperors. And He exercises that power "as He will," not as our ambitions dictate. But the method has worked before. Chiefs and leaders have been converted and their people have followed them. In many cases today, people will tell the missionary who brings them the gospel: "We would like to believe, but we can't do it alone. If you will only get our leaders to believe, then all of us will believe."

Whether or not we think that the group approach in evangelism should be emphasized, we do need to realize that there are certain dangers inherent in all mass movements. It may seem an advantage that the whole community as a unit becomes Christian with very little disruption. But what about the leadership? The former political leaders may not be fit spiritual leaders. And the former religious leaders may offer little in the way of Christian leadership. Natural talent is not a sufficient substitute for the gifts and calling of the Spirit. And the danger is even greater that the conversion may be very superficial. It is a tremendous task to try to raise a nominally converted community to a full understanding of Christianity and a real personal commitment to Christ. It is all the more difficult because they already think of themselves as Christians.

Yet mass movements do take place. Perhaps in tightly knit communities we ought to expect them. At any rate the dangers they present should not lead us to disregard or discourage them. We need to be alive to the challenge and the opportunity that they present. Dr. Clough, of the American Baptist Mission in India, was excessively cautious when the great mass movement began in his territory. He was afraid that many might be seeking to get into the church for unworthy motives. So he withheld baptism. If the urging of others had not finally prevailed, that excess of caution could easily have lost to his mission the greatest opportunity it ever had. Again the important thing is to discern in such a movement the work of the Spirit of God.

MEANS USED IN EVANGELISM

1. *The Christian life.* The strongest basis for evangelism is the example of a Christian life. It is true that Christian living alone will not bring conversions unless there is an explanation of the source of that life. But as a demonstration of the truth of the Christian message such a life has no equal in effectiveness. We need to remember that most people are not interested in abstract theology. They want to see its outworking.

The life of the missionary himself is always under observation. It surprises him at times to learn how much the people seem to know of what goes on in the supposed privacy of his own home. Grouchiness, laziness, self-indulgence, etc., cannot be hid. He is constantly under inspection. His only safeguard is the utmost sincerity in living the kind of life he preaches.

But even when he lives on a high spiritual plane, the people are likely to discount his example. The reason is very simple. He is a foreigner. He is not like them. He lives the way he does because that is his nature. It is easy to think this way when the missionary is the only foreigner they have known. So his example is not so effective as it would be if he were a national.

This is what makes the Christian living of the early converts so very important. These are people like themselves, people they have known before. Their lives will speak powerfully, either for or against the gospel. So give careful attention to these early believers in any place. Don't be too hasty in taking them in if there is any question about their sincerity. Labor with them with more patience and devotion than over any sermon. They will be living sermons. Paul speaks of some of his converts as "My little children, of whom I travail in birth again until Christ be formed in you." This intense concern should be ours, and with the same objective.

2. *The spoken word and its limitations.* The spoken word is the chief means used in evangelism. This has always been so, since Bible times. It will probably continue to be so. This is one of the main reasons why a missionary needs to know how to use words. It is also the reason why he needs to learn well the language of the people. In presenting his message he must be able to talk to them clearly and convincingly.

There are of course various ways of using the spoken word. A private conversation is not a sermon. There are some preachers that are poor conversationalists. On the other hand there are some people who are very effective in personal work but poor in the pulpit. We can use words in a coolly logical way to convince, or we can use them in a passionate way to stir the emotions. Often the differences are not so much in the words themselves as in the force that the personality of the speaker gives them. Sometimes we need to see the speaker to get the full force of what he is saying.

But the spoken word does have limitations. One is the number of people that you can reach with it. In direct personal evangelism you can only reach a limited number of people during a full lifetime. By public meetings you can increase that number greatly. But even so the number is limited. Unless you have mechanical help the strength of your voice will only be enough to reach a few hundreds in any one meeting.

Another limitation is the transitoriness of the spoken word. No matter how earnest and able the speaker is, the audience seldom gets more than a fraction of what he says. He hopes that it gets the important points. And of what it does get, it retains an even smaller fraction in the active memory. What are you able to tell of the sermon that you heard last Sunday? This is why teachers soon learn to repeat important statements more than once. Even so they know that some will still hear wrong. If listeners have nothing to depend on but the spoken word, only rote memorization or constant repetition will keep them from error.

We can overcome some of these limitations in part by our modern inventions. The public address system is a great boon. With it the speaker with an average voice can address several thousand people instead of a handful. They may not get the finer shades of his voice, and those who are farther away will not be able to see his facial expressions. Still, these losses are comparatively minor. The public address systems are also not limited to fixed locations. Some are made to be mounted on automobiles or trucks. They can either have their own source of power or depend on the car battery. Some are portable enough to take to places where trucks cannot go. Often they can be used to draw a crowd. One missionary in Africa wanted to reach some pygmies but had trouble locating them. Finally he put his speaker up in a tree, tuned it to top volume, and broadcast an invitation for the pygmies to come to that place. In about an hour they came in. They had heard the "big voice from the sky."

Radio broadcasting also helps to overcome the limitations of the human voice. Radio carries the voice much farther than any public address system and potentially to many more people. The size of the audience is limited only by the number of people within range who have access to radio receivers and want to listen. They usually listen individually or in small groups, and there is no precise way of knowing how many they are. Of course the speaker and the audience are not visible to each other. This, however, is a handicap mostly to the speaker, who misses seeing the reaction of the listeners to what he is saying.

Another aid, which you can use alone or over the radio, is recordings on discs or tape. Like radio, recordings do tend to be impersonal. But they also enjoy a unique advantage. You can use them over and over, and they always say the same thing in the same way. A Lisu tribesman remarked about a gospel recording, "It must be true; it always says the same thing!" Besides, the recordings only require the presence of the speaker once: at the time when the original recording is made. After that you can make an unlimited number of copies.

Disc recordings are especially useful. They can be used wherever there is a record player of any sort. They do wear out, but they can be reproduced in any quantity from the master record. Christian nationals who are not themselves preachers can use them effectively in evangelism. And the records can continue their ministry even after the missionary or national worker is gone.[1]

3. *The written word.* Evangelism by the written word has both advantages and disadvantages. It lacks the presence of the speaker and the emphases and shades of meaning that his voice can portray. Everything depends on those little black marks on white paper and the way the reader interprets them. The meaning he gets isn't always the one the writer intended. This is where the skill of the writer shows up. While we can tell how many copies of a message we print and distribute, there is no way on earth of telling how many read it. In some places we know that very few people read at all. But here the few

[1]Gospel Recordings, Inc., of Los Angeles, Calif., has shown to missions around the world how useful this aid to their work can be.

who can read will read aloud to a group of others. And often where writing is scarce the written word is the more highly valued.

Writing has a number of advantages. The potential audience for a single message is almost limitless. Mr. Moody's messages on *The Way of Life* are still moving hearts in many countries more than half a century after his death. Even today letters come addressed to him as if he were still alive. The written word, too, can penetrate where the living messenger would not be allowed. It needs no passport, and if men try to block it they find that it is one of the easiest things to smuggle. Its message can be read time and again. And the cost per person reached is probably less than by any other means.

There are three major problems in developing a literature program. The first is the writing of suitable works. Not many are talented along this line. Writing is not the same as speaking. Good speakers often turn out to be poor writers. And some of their best sermons are very ineffective in print—they are too wordy and repetitious and lack the personality of the speaker. The second problem is financing, since literature for evangelistic purposes can hardly be expected to pay for itself. Yet people at home have less interest in providing for a multitude of written messages than for a single living messenger. The third problem is distribution—getting the message into the hands of those who will read it.

The distribution of tracts is the most common way of using the written word. The principles of doing it are largely the same as in the homeland, with one exception. In many fields the tracts are more gladly received. In some places missionaries even dare to toss tracts from a moving car, knowing that people will pick them up and read them. However, it is always much more effective to distribute them personally to those who have been interested in some other way. Remember that an attractive, well-printed tract is always more effective than a dozen cheap, shoddy ones. People get their ideas of Christianity from the appearance of the tract as well as from what it says. It is well to note, too, that tract distribution is something that nationals can do even more effectively than missionaries.

Colportage, the selling of books from door to door, is another effective way of spreading the gospel. The one who has paid for a book, even if only a small price, is more likely to keep it and read it than the one who got it free. Such a work almost always needs to be subsidized. It cannot be expected fully to pay for itself. But because it does bring some financial returns it costs less than free distribution and gives better results. In some fields, notably Latin America, the Bible colporteur has often been the pioneer, the one who opened the way for settled missionary work. Sometimes the reading of a Bible sold by a colporteur has resulted in the establishment of a church apart from any other missionary endeavor. Colporteurs need not be preachers, but they do need to know the books they are selling and have a clear understanding of their faith, since they will often be engaged in discussion.

Newspaper evangelism has proved useful in some places. It calls for a fair rate of literacy among the people and a good circulation of newspapers. The method is to secure space in the newspaper, usually by paying advertising rates, and put in a Christian message for the readers. Always include an address to which people can write for further information. And it is a good idea to offer a larger work on the same subject to those who will write in. A major problem is that many writers don't know how to prepare this kind of article. They fail to attract and hold the readers' interest and get him to act. Unless they can do this the money is wasted.

Periodicals of an evangelistic sort are also very useful. Many a mission publishes its own. In some cases several missions in the same field will co-operate in a single publication so as to get better quality. Only a few such papers get a wide circulation outside of their own area. Many combine evangelism and Bible teaching, so they can be used with Christians or non-Christians. The better ones are able to maintain a subscription price that covers a large part of the costs. Others are distributed free. The problem of editorship, either missionary or national, is a large one as is the problem of getting a steady flow of material of a usable sort. Many papers depend a great deal on translations from the English or on reprints from other papers. If a subscription price is charged it calls for more office help to keep the records and care for mailings to individual subscribers.

Mail service is often a great help. In some countries all papers published within the country may pass through the mails without charge. In other countries they are given a special reduced rate. This makes it possible at small expense to use the mails to distribute papers to any whose names you get. John Ritchie used this plan with real effect in opening new areas in Peru.[2]

4. *Visual aids.* Evangelism is often more effective when you use one of the many types of visual aids in supporting and illustrating your message. Object lessons are appreciated by adults as well as by children. Flannelgraph lessons are perhaps more useful with children, but not necessarily so. Remember in both cases though that the lessons we use with American children or adults may not fit in with another language or culture. Some of the items we use in object lessons are meaningless elsewhere. The same thing applies to slides or filmstrips. You need to choose or prepare them with care.

Motion pictures can be used where you have electricity. However, there are very few to be had in languages other than English, except some of the Moody films. The cost of some of these visual aids is enough so that they need to be used rather widely to give good returns on the investment. You can sometimes rent films from a depository or agent, as in India.

GROUPS THAT CALL FOR SPECIALIZED EFFORTS

Not all groups, even in the same country, can be reached in the same way. Sex, age, race, occupation and other factors may make it advisable to plan specialized efforts to reach some of these groups. The number, size and importance of the groups differs from field to field. The following are some that are common.

1. *Women.* In some places it is possible to present the message to men and women in mixed groups. In others, however, the women must be reached separately. There is even such a thing as a separate women's language which it is improper to use with men. In India and some Moslem countries the seclusion of women makes a separate women's work necessary, and it must be done entirely by women. Even in lands where a separate work is not essential, separate meetings for women have a real value.

2. *Children.* Child evangelism has assumed a new importance in recent years. A variety of special methods for dealing with children has been developed and special organizations have been formed. Some of them have extended their work to the mission fields. This new interest

[2]John Ritchie, *Indigenous Church Principles in Theory and Practice* (Westwood, New Jersey, Revell & Co., 1946).

comes partly because we realize that the final success of our work depends on the second and third generations. It is also partly because children are usually responsive and we want to reach them before they become indifferent and hardened by sin. Often, too, we can reach adults through the children.

3. *Youth.* We have found in this country that youth has its own problems that we cannot meet by the usual adult approach. The same is true in other lands. However, in some places there is no distinct period that can be labeled youth. The reason is that the period of childhood is hardly over before the young person is expected to take on the responsibilities of an adult, including the establishing of a family. In such a place a special youth work is all but impossible. Elsewhere it can and should receive attention.

4. *Students.* In some countries the students in the colleges and universities are a smaller group than here at home. But they are a group from whom the leaders of the country are likely to come. They are more politically aware than a similar group at home. Yet they face problems similar to those of college students anywhere. They are learning to question even those things that have been hallowed by long tradition. But along with their skepticism they often have a high idealism. Whether they are good students or not, they pride themselves on their intellectual abilities, so the approach that would work with a poor illiterate would never win their respect. In some places a mission has set aside one of its best missionaries for full-time work with such students.

5. *Persons of mixed blood.* In our missionary thinking we seldom give much attention to those of mixed parentage, such as the Eurafricans, Anglo-Indians, etc. Their lot is often hard. They are seldom acceptable among the people of either parent. They incline to follow the customs of the one they think superior, but they may be socially ostracized by that group. There are larger numbers of these people than we think, and there is often need of special efforts to reach them.

6. *Immigrant groups.* Though we are conscious of our own immigration problems, we seldom realize that other countries have similar problems, and sometimes in more acute form. Just as the Hawaiians have become a minority in their own islands through immigration, so the Chinese are coming to outnumber the Malayans in Malaya, and the

Indians are outnumbering the Fijians in Fiji. In other lands, while the threat is not so great, there are very large immigrant colonies, such as the Indians in East and South Africa and the Slavs in Brazil. The work that is planned to meet the needs of the native population will not often meet the needs of these immigrants from other lands and cultures. Occasionally special missions are sent to them from abroad. More often, if anything is to be done it must be done as a special project by the mission already in the field.

7. *Jails, hospitals and other public institutions.* Evangelism in these institutions is very similar to that carried on in similar places in the United States. The conditions differ and liberties may be much more restricted, but in general the same principles apply.

8. *Military forces.* Many military commanders recognize the importance of moral instruction for their men. In a few cases they are free to permit direct religious instruction by the missionary. In many others a tactful missionary may get an opportunity to give instruction in morals and so open the way for personal inquiries about the Christian faith. An outstanding example of this is the work of William Strong of the Soldiers and Gospel Mission in Chile. In lands where there is compulsory military service, this presents an unusual opportunity to reach a large part of the male population. The one who engages in it, though, must combine great discretion with a real evangelistic zeal.

DIRECTED EVANGELISM

In logical order, the first evangelistic efforts are made by the missionary, and the ultimate objective is evangelism by the people themselves. However, there is always a period of transition. The very first converts will do personal evangelism on their own, and they may even engage in other types. And there will probably also be a time during which the nationals will carry on some evangelism under the oversight of the missionary. The abrupt transition from "all missionary" to "all national" is not good. There needs to be a time of preparation and guidance. By directed evangelism we mean evangelism carried out by nationals either under the direction of the missionary or with his active counsel.

Every missionary has the chance of taking part in this directed evangelism, if he has so much as one national to work with him. When he is dealing with a non-Christian he can encourage the national to lead the way. He will find it hard to keep quiet when he thinks he can do a better job. But keep quiet he must, unless there is an unmistakable need for his help. Afterward, if necessary, he can tell the national how to do better.

Where the missionary is guiding or counseling a church, he has even greater opportunities. He can encourage the church to set up a definite evangelistic program as a part of its ministry. He can guide them in their planning for it and instruct them in some of the tested methods.

Where he is in charge of a Bible institute or seminary, such work is a part of his responsibility. It is not enough to train people in an understanding of the words of Scripture. They also need training in the practical expression of Christian truths. Often they carry on practical Christian work at the same time as their studies. Sometimes the studies are interrupted for a short period of field work. At other times the vacation periods are used for such things as evangelistic campaigns, house-to-house visitation, etc. This experience doesn't reach its full effectiveness unless the missionary or teacher is along to guide and counsel or correct.

At times the missionary can help a whole district to set up an evangelistic program. The missionary himself should not take on any more of the detailed work than he has to, but he should not stand aloof, as if advice were the only thing he could give. The inspiration of his example is important. But if he can encourage the churches to set up their own evangelistic program, so much the better.

CHAPTER NINETEEN

ITINERATION

Its Place in Missionary Service

ITINERATION is not actually a separate phase of missionary work. Rather, it is involved in several phases of the work and concerns the ministry of a variety of missionaries. Some types of missionary work are confined to a single locality, such as school teaching. However, where the missionary is responsible for a district, whether as a general missionary, an educational supervisor or a doctor, he faces the problems of itineration. He cannot stay at home and handle the work as it should be done.

Not many find itineration easy. It involves more than mere absence from home and "living out of a suitcase." It is a strain constantly to be meeting new people, new problems, new situations. The missionary's visit to a community may be the only one they will have for a year, so they stay with him until late at night and appear again early in the morning. He has little rest and less time to be alone for meditation and prayer. In many places, too, travel conditions are very trying.

But wide itineration is the basis for successful work. In the beginning it is the way to set the gospel fires burning over the widest area. And after churches are formed it is the way to nourish their growth and direct and encourage their activities. Even a verbal report given at headquarters by the leaders of the church is no substitute for a personal visit by the missionary.

Planning an Itinerary

It is very important to have a comprehensive plan for your itinerary. Include in it not only the places you are going to visit and the time to be spent in each, but as far as possible the things you want to accomplish in each place and for the whole trip. You will almost never carry out the full plan, since unexpected situations always arise, but you accomplish much more with a clear plan than without it.

In some places you will need to plan your travel with careful regard to the season and the time of month. Rainy season traveling may be out of the question or subject to serious hazards. You may not have to regard the phases of the moon when you travel only in the daytime. But if you are thinking of meetings in country districts, you won't get a good congregation at night in the dark of the moon. There are places, too, where the population is sparse at certain times of the year. For example, there are fishing villages in Alaska that are almost depopulated of men when the fishing season is on.

The time you stay in any place depends on conditions. The people often want the missionary to stay longer than he can. On the other hand, the missionary sometimes makes his visit too short to accomplish much. Other people are not as restlessly active as Americans. Even where there is a church established, they often will not let the missionary know all about their problems as soon as he arrives. It takes time to get them to open up their hearts. It may take an even longer time for the missionary to see the situation in its proper perspective.

Seasoned explorers sometimes say that thrilling adventures are a sign of poor planning. It is certain that many a missionary boasts of narrow escapes that were really the outcome of his own lack of reasonable care. In going into unfamiliar territory get all the information you can ahead of time. Even in highly civilized countries you can get into some awkward situations by not making inquiries about routes, schedules, facilities, costs, etc. And do pay attention to the warnings you get from those who have had experience. Occasionally they may be mistaken, but more than one missionary has lost his life by disregarding such warnings.

What you take along in the way of equipment and supplies depends on your means of travel and the purpose of the trip. Travel on horseback may limit you to what you can carry in a pair of saddlebags, unless you take along a packhorse. But a car or truck provides room for a much larger amount of baggage. In some places extended tours mean the taking of enough equipment to both house and feed the missionary party. It is much better when the missionaries can secure adequate local accommodations.

Consider your need for a musical instrument. Many missionaries like the accordion because it can be taken where pianos and organs are not available, and with less difficulty than a folding organ. Take enough literature, even if it means leaving behind some article that would cater to your comfort. In some areas a few tablets for purifying water are a wise precaution. Such things as a first-aid kit, a needle and thread, and a few simple remedies take little space and help a lot.

MEANS OF TRAVEL

It might seem unnecessary to deal with means of travel here. After all, the missionary uses what means are available. But the matter isn't as simple as that. There are often several means available and the missionary must choose. And sometimes he is tempted to ask for additional equipment to facilitate his travel without checking to see if such a plan is really wise.

There are two things to consider besides the means available. One is economy in money, time, and health. The other is the accomplishment of your purpose. The matter of economy is very complex. Considering money alone, there are times when airplane travel may be cheaper than travel by land. The airplane sometimes covers in an hour a distance that would take a week by land. So though the cost is high per hour it may be low for the trip. The matter of time is even more deceptive. It is not merely a question of how many hours can be saved. It is also a question of how valuable those hours are. What will you do with the hours saved? And for reasons of health, the trip to the field by ship may be preferable to that by air, but on the field a trip along jungle rivers by canoe is certainly harder on the health than a trip by air. Between some types of transportation, though, there is little to choose. It is up to the missionary to estimate the cost and the advantages.

The accomplishment of your purpose involves other questions. The one who is eager only to get from one place to another will probably choose the most rapid and comfortable means of transportation if he can afford it. This is true of those who are planning to reach only the major centers. But the missionary who is really trying to cover his district finds that this is not satisfactory. The airplane skips all intermediate points. The automobile reaches only those that are along the roads. And their very speed communicates itself to the spirit of the missionary, who becomes too impatient to pause for a leisurely chat along the way, chats that often produce spiritual results. It is not without reason that other people accuse the Americans of always being in a hurry, but often for no particular purpose.

Travel by plane, car, boat, etc., raises the question whether it is wiser to rent such vehicles, pay passage in them, or to own them. Also, if they are owned, should each missionary have his own, or should they be the property of the mission? Some seem to think that every missionary should have his car, jeep, station wagon, truck or something of the sort if he can raise the money to buy it. This is far from true. No one will ever admit that he is extravagant, but these things are sometimes extravagances.

Here are some things to keep in mind when considering the purchase of vehicles for transportation.

1. *Are there commercial lines available to meet most of your needs?* (This has ruled out missionary aviation in some fields.)

2. *What is the actual over-all value to the work of such a vehicle?* That is, how much is it needed and how often? An occasional trip does not justify a capital expenditure of several thousand dollars or more in goods that deteriorate rapidly whether used or not.

3. *What are the costs per mile of operation?* Gas and oil are only a part of the costs. There are taxes and license fees and insurance. There are repairs and replacements to be made. There is housing to be provided. All of this in addition to the original cost and import duties. In the case of airplanes there are landing fields to be built and maintained. In the case of boats there are dockage facilities to arrange for.

Several years ago Missionary Aviation Fellowship made a careful estimate of the cost of operating a lightweight plane in Latin America. They said in their report, "Fly the plane 75 hours a year (that's a lot for *individual* use—it represents nine thousand miles) and the *total* hourly cost is actually *triple* the running expense." It only costs two-thirds as much *per mile* to operate a plane for 100 hours as it does for 50. And you can cut even this amount in half if you operate it for 300 hours or more in the year. In other words, individual operation is very expensive.

4. *What are the costs in missionary manpower?* That is, how much missionary time must be used in operating and maintaining these vehicles? Is there any other trained personnel that you can use? It is poor accounting not to include the value of the missionary's time in your calculations.

5. *There are two special considerations we ought to mention.* Often the possession of a vehicle opens the door to impositions by the nationals. They don't see why you shouldn't accommodate them by taking them where they want to go—without charge, of course. And then there is one other intangible that we must count in. Perhaps the possession of a car is slightly expensive for the amount of work you can do with it. But it enables the family to get away occasionally for some needed relaxation that they might not otherwise get. Or else it assures the missionary that he can make his trips at times when commercial passage is not available. We cannot always evaluate such things in terms of dollars and cents. They do need to be considered. But it is poor stewardship not to pay attention to the dollars and cents.

ASSURING THE RESULTS OF AN ITINERARY

An itinerary is not a chapter in the work that closes when you reach home again. In many things it is only a beginning or a step along the way. A leader was chosen in a certain place. You would be foolish to forget about him and his problems as soon as you leave. Or the beginning of a solution to the problem in a certain school was found while you were there. It will work if the plan is carried through. It is still your concern after you are far away, or should be.

Few of us are gifted with such exceptional memories that we can recall all the events of an extended itinerary after it has ended. This means that some sort of record must be kept along the way. In some missions this is one reason why each missionary is required to keep a diary. It is useful both as a record of what was done and a reminder of things that need further attention and prayer.

A single trip has very limited results unless it is followed up. The missionary may not be able to make another visit to the same places as soon as he would like, but his return should not be left to chance or to the inspiration of the moment. It should be definitely planned. In the meantime he is wise if he arranges to receive more or less regular reports about the progress of the work. A careful steward keeps well informed.

Of course follow-up work is not entirely dependent on the return visit of the missionary. Sometimes it is possible to follow up an evangelistic campaign with a more extended ministry of teaching by another group. Sometimes the people are started on correspondence courses that will help them go on. The important thing is that the seed planted should be watered and cultivated.

CHAPTER TWENTY

CHURCH ORGANIZATION

THE ONE GREAT AIM of missions is evangelism. But from the results of evangelism comes the church. So church organization is one of the most important activities of the missionary.

BASIC PRINCIPLES

We can avoid a great deal of confusion in our thinking about church organization if we make one basic distinction to begin with—a distinction between the "visible" and the "invisible" Church. Or perhaps we could call it the distinction between the Church and the churches. It is the distinction between the Church as the Body of Christ and the churches as organizations of those who profess to be followers of Christ. This distinction we commonly find in Protestant theology but we seem to forget it in common practice.

Membership in the Church of Christ is by birth, not election. It is by the operation of the Holy Spirit in the human heart, bringing about man's regeneration, or the "new birth." It is an entirely miraculous work brought about by God Himself. Man's part is in the presentation of the message, the gospel, in the demonstration of its power in his own life, in the earnest pleading for its acceptance. But he can go no further. It is the Holy Spirit who must incline the heart of man to accept the message. It is the Holy Spirit who must accomplish his rebirth. It is Christ to whom he is joined in this act.

The one who has believed the message of the gospel, who has put his trust in Christ and through faith has been united to him in the new birth, is by that fact a member of the Church of Christ. He needs no acknowledgment on the part of men. He does not go through a probationary period, a catechumenate. He does not have to wait for the ap-

222

proval of a church group. He may be lacking in knowledge, in an understanding of what this new life involves, of what God expects from him. His outer man is very much the same. It is the inner man that has been changed. That inner man begins at once to change the believer's conduct. He does not change it all at once. The new man is still in the body. And that body through long practice has been habituated to another type of life. But he may still speak of himself as "a new man in Christ Jesus." He is a member of Christ's Body, the Church.

But membership in the Church of Christ means also membership with others who are in that Body. We are not just an aggregation of believers individually joined to Christ by the new birth but independent of each other. We are members of Christ *and of each other.* We have no choice in the matter. We cannot select those with whom we should like to be united in this Body. We have no power to admit one nor to reject another. It is only by God's grace that we ourselves become members. We must recognize that same grace and loving wisdom in the calling of others who shall form a part of the Church. We may not understand His choice. But it is our understanding that is at fault, not His wisdom. We may feel that some are not worthy to be a part of His Church. But we have forgotten our own unworthiness, that no one is worthy and perhaps we least of all. Regardless of our differences, regardless of the fact that all of us retain habits that are displeasing to others, God has seen fit to join us to Christ by faith, and to make us by that act also members of one another.

We recognize this in theory. We know that it is the teaching of the New Testament. But living in accordance with this truth is another thing. It is not merely a matter of forgetting denominational differences, important as that may be. Neither is it simply a matter of overlooking racial and national backgrounds. Positively, it is the recognition of real faith, the recognition of the life of Christ in another, regardless of any circumstance. Like me, he may not have come to the measure of the fullness of the stature of Christ. But that is not the question. While he may be farther away from the ideal than I, what does it matter? The principal thing is, "Does the Spirit of Christ dwell in him? Can I," to quote the words of another missionary, " 'recognize real faith even when it is accompanied by an almost untutored conscience?' "

Such an attitude is not ecumenicism. It is not indifferentism. It is not the world church. Primarily it has nothing to do with any organizational activities. It is not opposed to them; it simply is not concerned with them. It is concerned only with recognizing those who have received the same gift of life, who enjoy the same spiritual parentage as we. If we recognize the existence of spiritual life in others, then we must acknowledge that we are both members of the same Body, the same Church of Christ; and regardless of our differences we have a family relationship to one another.

And what does that relationship mean? To some extent we have it explained by Paul in I Corinthians 12 and Ephesians 4. He admits that some members are "more feeble" than others. But he contends that these feeble ones also "are necessary." Every part of the body is needed for the functioning of the body as a whole. "The body is not one member, but many," yet "there should be no schism in the body." Each member has its place and its ministry. And with the help that each one supplies, the body itself grows.

The churches are a different matter. Some have gone so far as to question whether they are really necessary. But they have been with us since the days of the Apostles, and most Christians would not question that they perform a useful function.

Ideally the churches should be only the visible organization and functioning of the Church of Christ in this world. But that ideal has never been attained. From the very beginning there have been some who have entered the churches without the experience of regeneration. Perhaps Simon Magus would be an example. On the other hand the churches have often been hesitant about receiving those who were already members of the Body of Christ. It took Barnabas' intercession to get the Jerusalem church to receive Paul. And the acceptance of Gentile believers without the performance of Jewish rites was for a long time a bone of contention in the churches, even after the Jerusalem Council.

We need to face the churches as they are, not as they should be. They are groupings of individuals who profess a common faith in the Lord Jesus Christ. In most cases today their association is voluntary. They will admit others to their group either through action of the group itself or through its representatives. They determine their own standards for acceptance, though most of them will contend that those standards are taken from the Bible. They usually have the initiatory rite of baptism, though its practice differs from group to group, and some dispense with it altogether. Many of them are committed to a definite creed or confession which they believe represents Christian teaching. Others allow a wide latitude of belief within certain broad limits. Some are strongly organized with a definite hierarchy. At the other extreme are those who lay claim to no organization, though they do have an organization of an informal sort. Some are very vigorous in promoting the interests of their group. Others are more static. Some are limited to certain racial or national groups. Some occur chiefly among people on a certain economic or intellectual level. Others are much more inclusive.

The differences between the churches are myriad, though some are more basic than others. Yet every one that claims to be a Christian church claims in some sense to represent the invisible Church of Christ. It is not our purpose to examine those claims. We want only to see how their claims affect their conduct.

There are very few who try to identify themselves completely as the Church of Christ. That is, there are very few who would say that only in their church may one find those who have been truly born again. Where that is the case, it explains why they cannot possibly compromise in any way, why they cannot enter into such a thing as a comity arrangement, why they must insist on full conformity to the pattern that they have established, even in the newest congregation that is formed.

But most Protestant churches will admit that others outside their group may be sincerely Christian and truly born again of the Spirit. They believe that their doctrines and practices are closer to the truth than others. They would prefer to see others acknowledge this and join with them. But they do not deny the real faith that others seem to have in spite of their errors. In some cases they would not even claim that the others are in error, but only that their own procedure is preferable. In other words, most Protestant churches acknowledge the difference that there is between the Church of Christ and the churches.

If we look at missions and its problems in the light of this fact we notice some amazing things. In the first place, whether or not our small church is represented there, the church of Christ is to be found in almost every nation under Heaven. Oh, it is a small and weak church in some places, so far as numbers and influence are concerned! But the church is there! And that means that Christ is there in the church. What happens to our idea of "closed doors," then? It means that very few of them are closed in the absolute sense. There are very few doors behind which Christ is not to be found. The closing is only against the free flow of help between members of the same body; or perhaps we ought rather to say it is against the entrance of foreign members of the Church of Christ. Ostensibly it is an action against foreigners rather than against Christians.

And because the church is there, we see that any other members of the Church of Christ who enter must take account of those who are already present. This does not necessarily mean co-operation. But neither should it mean conflict, if that can be avoided. If we recognize them as true members of the Church of Christ, in spite of the errors into which we may think they have fallen, then we must respect them for the sake of the One who dwells within their hearts and ours. We must seek to avoid offense and the rousing of any harmful competition. Our aim should be the increase of the Church of Christ, not of our own particular church.

On the other hand, this does not mean that those who are already there have a monopoly on the work of evangelization. There are no monopolies in this field. The insistence of some of the leaders of the Indian Church that to it, and to it alone belongs the task of evangelizing India is ill-advised. That it has the primary responsibility and the major opportunity is unquestionable. That the evangelizing efforts of others should not be used to cause schism in the Body of Christ nor to hinder its growth, we also do not deny. But the evangelizing of all men everywhere and at all times is the privilege and responsibility of everyone who is himself a member of the Church of Christ. You see, we are speaking here of evangelism in itself, the winning of men to Jesus Christ, not to some particular church.

But some cannot see that there is any difference between winning men to Christ and winning them to our church. Do they not need the fellowship that the church provides? Do they not need its instruction so that they may not fall into error? Do they not need its help in a variety of different ways?

It is here that confusion in our thinking is revealed. The answer to these questions is both yes and no. The new member of the Church of Christ does need fellowship with other members. He should expect it as one who now belongs to the same Body. But he does not need a restricted fellowship that limits him only to those other members with whom the evangelist happens to be in heartiest accord. He does not need a circumscribed fellowship whose limits were determined by the arguments of men who lived in another day and in a different country and may have little to do with him. He needs fellowship with Christ and with all who are in Christ.

He does need instruction, too. He needs to know the Word of God. He needs to know how to let it speak to his heart and advise him in his daily conduct. He needs to know something of its glorious, unsearchable depths. He needs to learn to look to the Spirit, the author, so that He may illumine his understanding to know what he needs to know. But he does not need instruction that will confine him to a certain "system" of Biblical interpretation based on the logic of men and reduced to terms that will allow their minds to comprehend it. He does not need instruction that will reduce his sense of adoring wonder in the presence of the God whom he worships, and make him wonder instead at the learning of the men who are his instructors. He does not have to have the errors of other groups all spelled out for him, with the precise arguments to be used in combating them. He needs to learn to sit at the feet of the Holy Spirit of God, the One whom Christ promised to be his teacher, and let Him teach.

We are all too distrustful of the Holy Spirit. We say it is His work when a soul is born again; but we act as if it were ours. We try to win men to the Lord Jesus Christ by our own efforts instead of asking Him to use us to do it, or perhaps even to do it without us. And when men are won, when they are born again into the family of God, we act as if we ourselves were responsible to see that they are kept secure, that they do not stumble along the way. Yes, the Holy Spirit can teach them—but first we must make sure that they are well grounded in the faith (our faith). Otherwise He might allow them to be deceived, to be misled.

All of this sounds quite visionary, quite unrealistic. Yet we cannot get away from the fact that it is scriptural. And we are impressed with the way Paul put it into practice. It is not Paul's methods that we need to imitate today; it is Paul's spirit that we need to have. Read the first three chapters of I Corinthians in connection with what we have just said. Note also the example of his ministry from the day that Barnabas and he first set out together. We would call him unrealistic and visionary to a high degree. He seemed to think that there was some great, inherent power in the gospel he proclaimed that would do wonders of itself. He seemed to believe that the Holy Spirit was a reality, a Person who took an active part in the affairs of man, and especially in the affairs of the Church of Christ. He was opposed by his own people, the Jews, was laughed at by the Greeks, and was jailed as a disturber of the peace by the Romans. He sometimes got great crowds to listen to him speak, but the number of those in any one place who turned to Christ by faith does not appear to have been large. Yet before he went to Rome he could write of "having no more place in these parts." He had no organization on which to lean. The little groups of believers, mostly people from the lower classes, many of them unstable, were scarcely the sort of movement that would make the great Roman empire take notice. But to Paul the Church of Christ was a living reality whose power was not the power of men but of God.

THE INDIGENOUS CHURCH

We cannot approach this matter of church organization without at once facing the question of "the indigenous church." In recent years the term has taken on the nature of a shibboleth. It appears with monotonous frequency in every missionary discussion. It is solemnly mouthed by young students who presume that it is the very essence of missionary wisdom. Every self-respecting mission claims that its objective is "to establish indigenous churches." And many Bible schools go so far as to list the subject as a separate item in the curriculum.

This in itself would not be bad if those who used the term understood what it means, or if they all used it in the same sense. But they don't. To some the term "indigenous" means little more than "self-supporting" in a financial sense. Others are aware of the three "selfs": self-propagating, self-governing and self-supporting. But they consider the church indigenous if it has a national pastor, no matter how much under the thumb of the missionary he may be. One mission writes of the indigenous churches it is founding at the same time that it is pouring huge sums of foreign money into the operating of these churches. Obviously the term means different things to different people.

What is our ultimate objective in the church? Unquestionably it is *a vital, flourishing church, grounded in Jesus Christ and carrying on a full, active ministry, in fellowship with other churches but not dependent on them.*

This differs in important ways from the usual definition of an indigenous church. That definition in its classical expression is summed up in the three selfs that we mentioned above. They do indeed make a church indigenous, if by indigenous we mean something that carries on a self-contained existence without reliance on outside help. But that is still far from our ideal. There are churches that are completely indigenous, yet spiritually dead. There are some that are indigenous but so completely self-centered that they have no effective witness. There are churches that are indigenous but have departed from a strictly Christian foundation. And there are many churches that are sincerely Christian and indigenous but are scarcely able to keep up a poor, struggling existence where they are.

The church on the mission field is like the son in a family. In infancy he has everything done for him. In childhood he begins to learn responsibility by being given certain jobs to do. In adolescence he needs guidance and help, but he resents dictation or being made to feel dependent. In maturity, if he has been guided successfully through the first three stages, he has full responsibility for his own life and that of the children he may beget. But he is still in the fellowship of the family. At times he will seek counsel of his parents, or in emergencies even material help if they can give it. But he is not fully mature until he, too, helps others. We are speaking, of course, of the normal son with wise parents.

Following out this simile we come to a number of conclusions. If the infant is brought to birth but is then abandoned, it may die unless others take it in. How many churches have succumbed because their life had scarcely begun before they were abandoned to their own resources! And if too early the son is made to fend for himself, he may develop a strong spirit of independence, but he loses out on his education and faces life with inadequate preparation. We are confronted with many of these adolescent churches today. They have been cast adrift or have revolted against parental authority with the thought that independence would solve all their problems. It hasn't, and rightly or wrongly they have been inclined to blame their parents for their lack of sufficient preparation for independent living. And then there is the adult who has broken fellowship with his family. He is indeed a lonesome man. And so is the church that willfully alienates itself from others in order to be indigenous. On the other hand we must remember that an overly protective parent not only weakens the character of his son; he also fails to prepare him for a useful life in the world. It takes carefully balanced judgment to be a good parent. It takes the same to be a good missionary.

Now let us come back to our objectives for the church. We want a church that is a mature church, able not only to support itself and direct its own affairs but also to beget children and care for them properly. We want it to be a healthy, strong church, well nourished in the Word of God and fervent in spirit. We want to see it not only in fellowship with other churches but contributing its part to meet the world's need for the gospel of Christ. Of course it will support itself and govern itself, but it ought also to see to the training of its own children, to the preparation of its own ministers. It may be a small minority in its own land and concern itself little about political affairs, but its stand on spiritual and moral issues should reveal the insight and judgment that comes to those who have sat at the feet of the Saviour and have long walked with Him (Acts 4:13).

Our ideal, then, is not the indigenous church, self-contained and independent. It is rather the ideal of the Body of Christ as Paul presents it in I Corinthians 12 and Ephesians 4: each part completely subject to the Head, reliably performing its own tasks, but working in harmony with the other parts of the Body. The great word to describe adequately the indigenous principle is not selfish independence but humble interdependence.

PUTTING THE IDEAL INTO PRACTICE

It is far easier to state an ideal than it is to show how we can realize it. In fact, we may seriously question whether any church has ever attained the ideal we have expressed. But this does not argue that the ideal is wrong or that we should not keep it before us. When the Lord said, "Be ye holy, for I am holy," He apparently set before us an unattainable ideal. Yet He did not retract it. It is still His command.

In recent months several missionaries have inquired about books on the indigenous church. They have complained: "All that I have read have dealt with indigenous church principles, but they don't tell just how to put those principles into practice. Isn't there a book that tells us how to do it?"

Really what those missionaries have wanted was specific instruction in what to do in their particular situation. This they will never find. Situations vary too much. Missions and missionaries vary too much. What one missionary may be able to do effectively another may be incapable of doing. What one would like to do, his mission may not be in favor of doing. And then, of course, any mission's procedure will be influenced by the actions of others in its neighborhood.

Also, the missionary faces several limitations in what he can do. One is his denominational affiliation. This may determine for him the type of church organization that he can use. Another is the mission society rules. The Korean mission of the Presbyterian Church, for example, early established some rules for missionaries in relation to the churches. They forbade, among other things, the giving of financial aid in the construction of church buildings.

Then there is the missionary's own lack of authority to experiment or make changes. A younger missionary working under the supervision of an older missionary may sometimes secure permission to experiment. But if the older missionary is unsympathetic there is little that he can do.

And then there are the actions and attitudes of other missionaries. When they are of his own mission he may try to persuade them to cooperate with his plan. Or he may be able to try it out on a limited scale and demonstrate that it works. But if he tries to act independently he is headed for trouble.

When the problem involves another mission it is even harder to solve. Suppose you determine to follow the indigenous principle of expecting the national churches to pay the salaries of their own pastors. But a neighboring mission continues to pay its pastors with funds from abroad. If the salaries are the same, you may have only a slight rumble of discontent from the churches that have to pay. But often the ones paid with foreign funds get a much more generous salary. Then you face the possibility that your pastors may be enticed to leave for the better salaries elsewhere. It has happened more than once. And don't lay the blame on the pastors. How many pastors in our own country "feel called" to another pastorate that offers a higher salary?

Now we do not say that all of these things are bad in themselves. For the missionary his denomination's view of the church is probably right, his mission's rules are wise and necessary, and he should not have authority to make changes indiscriminately. All we are trying to show is that these things do place a limit on the freedom of the missionary to devise his own plans for church organization on the field.

Yet it is possible to be a little more precise in our statement of principles than we have been. There are some specific suggestions that we can make. They may not be valid everywhere. In fact, some missionary leaders may question a few of them. But in general we believe that they have proved helpful.

1. *New work.* The missionary who goes into a completely new area is to be envied. He can start at the bottom without having to adjust his program to what others have done or are doing. But there are not many in this position. Neither is there any assurance that the present-day missionary, with all that he might learn from the experience of others, will do any better than those of the past century. Methods, after all, are always subordinate to the spirit. A zealous missionary, motivated by the love of Christ and anxious to be led by His Spirit, may accomplish much in spite of poor methods; while the one who knows all the methods but is lacking in that motivation and that guidance will accomplish little that is worth while. We must put first the Spirit of God. Without Him we can do nothing.

Obviously the first work in a new area is to sow the seed. Evangelism is basic. It may be through preaching, through medical work, or in limitless other ways. But the immediate objective is to win individuals or groups to the Lord Jesus Christ. We can do nothing about a church until there is a body of believers to form the church. Naturally this work of evangelism will be carried out first by the missionary. It is no place for the missionary who shrinks from direct evangelism.

However, it is never too early to begin preparations for the church. We know, for example, that we cannot build a strong church on a foundation of illiteracy and ignorance of the Word of God. The church will need hymns, too, and other literature. So we do well to start at once on these things. Fortunately they are not only essential for the church that is to be, but they are valuable instruments in the primary work of evangelism. Evangelism and Bible translation go hand in hand, with one supporting the other.

In some fields there are converts within a short time; in others it may be several years before the first believer rejoices the heart of the missionary. There are places in some difficult Moslem fields where years of witnessing have produced too few believers to organize a church. Some of the individual Christians are mature believers who should be associated with the missionary in the work, but the church as an organization is still future. Until a church can be formed the missionary will need to continue as an evangelist and a pastor.

But there are two things that can and should be expected from every believer from the beginning. They are witnessing and giving. Everyone who has become a follower of Christ should also recognize his obligation to witness for Christ. No one should receive pay for such witness. Every Christian should want to do it. Also the new believer should be taught to give of his substance to the Lord. We missionaries have often failed in this. The people are so poor that we have taught them to receive but not to give. Then later we have complained that the church does not take seriously its financial obligations. Let the people from the beginning learn the blessedness of sacrificial giving.

How large should a group of believers be before you organize it as a church? Opinions differ. How much of an organization do you need or want? We Americans tend to overorganize. We try to get a fixed form of organization too soon. We overlook the fact that the earliest believers are not necessarily the best leaders. Organization should be designed to meet needs, as in the selection of the first deacons in Jerusalem. And the needs are not always the same in every place. Organize when there seems to be a real need for it.

One of the things that complicates the picture is that the missionary often sets up his permanent residence in the place where he has his first group of believers. So long as he is there, they are not likely to feel the need of organization very soon. The missionary can handle what needs to be done.

In places where the missionary resides only temporarily, the example of Paul might be appropriate. The trouble is that we don't know enough about his procedure. He seems to have stayed long enough in each place to gather a small group of believers, but we don't know how large. The only organization he used at the beginning was the appointment of elders. They were usually appointed some time after his first evangelistic trip. Later on we find mention of deacons, but with no explanation of how they were chosen. All that we really know is that after a group of believers was gathered, some of their number were appointed as lay leaders of the group, after the fashion of the Jewish synagogue. Yet the missionary continued to feel a responsibility toward the infant church, visited it as he was able, and sent it words of counsel and instruction.

Paul's experience as a very successful missionary can give us some very useful principles for today. We see that it is not necessary for a missionary to stay constantly with a church until it is mature. If he can stay with it until it is well established, as Paul did at Ephesus, it is a good idea. But it is not necessary to stay until it has complete church organization of our American type, including a paid ministry. Some provision for the continuance of the work is needed even where the missionary can stay only briefly. But the plan should be simple, like the appointment of the elders, and if possible familiar. Also, though the missionary should plan to keep in touch with the new congregation, he should not keep the strings in his own hands. This may seem risky to some, but if the foundations are well laid it is the best long-range policy.

A church cannot be completely indigenous from the beginning. It needs too much in the way of instruction and guidance from those who are older in the faith. But men like James Fraser in southwest China have shown that it can do more than many missionaries believe. It takes only a few months for an infant to insist on holding his nursing bottle. His first attempts at feeding himself with a spoon are pretty sloppy, but it is the way he learns. And infant churches, too, can make rapid progress.

There is no reason why, when the group gets too large to meet in a home, it cannot provide its own meeting place. There were no church buildings in New Testament days, but they don't seem to have been handicapped by it. The meeting place does not need to be elaborate, but there is no particular merit in making it ugly and barren of all adornment. Neither does it have to "look like a church," according to our ideas. It can well conform to the local style of architecture. The people who gather there should have the comfortable feeling that it is their place of worship, not that they are guests in the foreigner's domain.

And there is no good reason why the church should not be able to run its own affairs, after a short period of tutelage. Some may think that tutelage refers to drill in parliamentary procedure, details of church management and the like. But it doesn't. It refers to instruction in the basic principles of Christian living as we find them in the Scriptures. Details of procedure should evolve from those principles, not the other way around. "Seek ye first the kingdom of God and his righteousness" was not spoken in this connection, but it is still applicable. And if we fear that the church will go off on a tangent, we show either our lack of confidence in the Holy Spirit or our doubt that the church is His creation.

There will be problems, of course. There will be mistakes made, some of them serious. But no one has yet proved that the church's mistakes are more common or serious than those made by the misison or the missionary. The missionary who arrogates to himself the privilege of making all the mistakes is cheating the church out of a most valuable learning experience. We never choose to make mistakes, but when they come they teach us valuable lessons.

We have already said that from the day of his conversion every Christian should be expected to witness. This witness should be voluntary and unpaid. It is the spontaneous product of the new life within us. Self-propagation is the most basic of the three selfs. It is the first one to put into practice before even a church is formed.

Some would say, then, that if the church does these things it is fully indigenous from the start. It already has the three selfs. But if that is your understanding of the term it is still far from our ideal. It is like calling a little boy a man. He has the potentialities of manhood. He has some of the characteristics of a man. He is on the way to becoming a man. But he is still a boy, with a boy's need for help, guidance, instruction, normal growth, and maturation.

The new church has the three selfs, but in a limited degree. It is self-propagating as far as spontaneous personal witness is concerned. But it is not yet ready to send forth and support its own missionaries, to stimulate the formation of other churches and guide them in their development. It is self-governing in its own intimate affairs. But it has not yet been tested on the larger fields of life—its relation to other churches and to the world outside. It is self-supporting to the extent of keeping up its own place of worship and a few other immediate expenses. But when it finds it wise to secure the services of a full-time pastor it is pressed to the utmost to provide his meager salary. It can hardly think of doing anything more. And what of the need for further instruction? Who will teach its Bible teachers? Who will train its pastors? Who will supply its Bibles, write its literature, compose its hymns? Until the church itself is ready to do these things it is not completely indigenous.

What we missionaries need to realize is that some of our work in a new area will be quickly taken over by the church. Some will be taken over only gradually. But our aim should be that ultimately all of it will be in the hands of the church. The only exception will be the voluntary services that any servant of Christ will perform wherever he may be. There need never be any end to the works of love that a Christian may perform wherever he sees a need, even if he is a foreigner.

Our role as missionaries, then, must be something like that of parents. "He must increase, but I must decrease." We must try to recognize the changes as they come and adapt ourselves to them. We are going to have to make concessions, one by one. If we make them wisely at the right time we shall keep the confidence of the church. In fact it will seek our counsel, knowing that we respect its right to decide. And when it comes to full maturity we shall be in closest fellowship.

2. *Work already established.* Though we have spoken extensively about the ideals for *new* work, we realize that most missionaries today face an entirely different situation. They go to fields where the church is already established. They may establish new congregations within their area, but the pattern of the church is already set. It may have been designed on sound principles. It may not. It may simply have developed through a combination of circumstances. But at any rate it is there. And it has to be faced.

This is where the missionary will have to begin, with the church as it is. He can't start all over again. He has no authority to change the basic pattern of organization. He can seek to persuade the church to change certain procedures or to adopt more worthy goals. But the major changes he can make on his own initiative have to do with his own attitudes and his personal actions. These are in themselves important. In fact, though we have spoken of the missionary's limitations, we ought to say that there is a great deal that he can do within those limitations. It depends on his abilities as a leader.

The first thing to do is to have your objectives clearly in mind. Know what the ideal is. Keep it before you. What kind of a church do you want eventually to see? What kind is it now? What is your relationship to it? Is there anything you can do to help it toward that goal of a mature church? It may not be much, but do it. Your own attitude will help others. And review your objectives regularly to see what progress has been made.

Right orientation is the important thing. Besides your final objective you need to have certain principles as landmarks to guide you.

a. *Look for the Spirit's guidance.* We would not make so many mistakes if we put aside our own notions and took time to let Him show us how to glorify the Saviour (John 16:14).

b. *Don't do anything you can get a national to do.* Perhaps you can do it better. But how will he learn if you don't let him do it? This is not laziness but good teaching.

c. *Continue your sincere concern.* Turning over responsibility doesn't mean forgetting the matter. Find out how well it is done. Rejoice with the national in his successes. Pray with him in his problems. Hold yourself ready to counsel and guide. But don't force your ideas on him. Here is where you can show real leadership.

d. *Remember that a strong church must be a church instructed in the Word.* Push the study of the Scriptures for all of the people, not just for a few. "Mind not high things, but condescend to men of low estate." Be ready with patience to instruct the dull as well as the brilliant. The church must be able to feed on the Word. So as a corollary the church must be literate. Help it to attain that status.

e. *A living church is a witnessing church.* It should be active in propagating the faith. It should be missionary. Are you? Can you inspire it by your example along this line?

f. *A healthy church is a clean church.* This calls for church discipline. But it should be self-disciplined. Even if you as the missionary should be allowed to administer discipline, don't! Discipline should arise from the offended sense of righteousness of the church. The one who is disciplined is likely to feel resentment. If he is disciplined by the missionary it is because he is a foreigner. His own people will feel sorry for him. If he is disciplined by his own people it is because they are Christians. He will feel the stigma of condemnation by those of his own kind. It is much more likely to lead to repentance, which is the objective of discipline.

g. *A strong church is a giving church.* No matter how rich or how poor, people need to be taught to give. It is never too early to begin. But let them see the results of their giving as well as the need for it. Never relieve them of a burden that they can carry, simply because you have more money than they. But remember that there are limits to what they can do. Outside help is often needed for the extra load, for emergencies. But it should be neither offered nor expected for the regular expenses. And let the people handle their own funds.

h. *Finally, the church does not live to itself.* It is only a part of the Body of Christ. It needs fellowship with other parts, especially those in its own neighborhood. No one is in a better position to promote this fellowship than the missionary. He is likely to be in touch with more churches than anyone else and can view them in perspective. If conferences and conventions are not already being held, he is the one in the best position to take the initiative to get them started and to lay the groundwork. But he should remember that his own work is very temporary. The gathering should be for the churches, not the missionaries. And he should never attempt to control the churches through the conference.

How can you bring a church to a sound indigenous basis that was not started that way? This is the problem in many fields. It is a problem beset with pitfalls on every side. No one has the perfect answer. In fact, it is really not a problem that the individual missionary should try to solve by himself. It usually concerns the whole mission and should be worked out in consultation. We can only give a few words of general counsel.

Don't attempt to solve the problem by unilateral action. That is, if you believe you ought to make a radical change in your policies, don't do it except by agreement with the church. If you have taught the church to depend on you for certain funds and services, you are morally obligated to consult with them before cutting them off.

During the Great Depression a certain mission found its funds for the support of national workers reduced almost to nothing. It called a conference of the workers and announced that the mission would have to cut off most of their support. If they wanted to serve without pay or get the churches to support them, that was their right. The workers withdrew and held a session of their own. Then they returned to the mission with their decision. They rebuked the mission for not letting them know what the situation was until such drastic action was needed. Some of them would continue and trust that the Lord would provide somehow. Others would have to resign, but didn't know where they could secure employment in such times. The church was not ready to take on such a responsibility yet. Why hadn't the mission let them know before?

In this case the suddenness of the action was one of the greatest causes of hardship. Such changes should not be made suddenly. The people need time to prepare themselves for the new situation. They need to be taught stewardship. They need to find out what their own capacities are. Sometimes a mission has spread the process over a period of five or more years, withdrawing twenty per cent of foreign support each successive year until the whole burden is on the national church.

But before you are in a good position to do anything at all about making a change, there is a job of salesmanship that must be done. Does the church see that a change is needed? Do the missionaries themselves understand why it is needed? In a day when nearly every missionary conference re-echoes with the words "indigenous church," we have been astounded at the number of young missionaries on the field who seem to know nothing at all about the matter. And there are others who misunderstand the principles, or for one reason or another oppose them. There is a need that the missionaries themselves come to an agreement on what they want to accomplish. And there is also a need that the church see that the change will be for its own benefit as for the Church of Christ. This is no small task.

When both the missionaries and the church see the need for a change, when both are willing to work patiently together for the unselfish good of Christ's Church, a workable plan will result. It may not be perfect. It will doubtless have a few flaws. Some corrections may need to be made. But given the will to make it work, it will work.

CHAPTER TWENTY-ONE

TEACHING

IMPORTANCE

TEACHING IS WITHOUT DOUBT the broadest field of missionary work. Nearly every missionary is involved in it in one way or another. And it touches practically every other phase of missionary activity. So we are not going to limit our discussion here to the formally organized schools. The subject is too big for that. It is too basic.

1. *Understanding.* Even the evangelist needs to be a teacher. What good does it do to move men to accept Christianity if they don't understand what Christianity is? He may insist that he told them all about it. But did they understand? It is not truth presented but truth understood and appropriated that counts. Teaching means causing them to understand.

2. *Establishment.* A believer's firmness in the faith depends on truth viewed and confirmed from various points. A single stay will not keep a mast from toppling if it gets wind from an unexpected quarter. So a strong church is a well-taught church. Paul knew this when he said to the Ephesian elders, "I have not shunned to declare unto you all the counsel of God" (Acts 20:27).

3. *Development.* Conversion is only the beginning of the Christian life. You can't achieve fullness of Christian comprehension and maturity of Christian living in a single day. Teaching provides the means for Christians to develop.

OBJECTIVES

There are some who look at education as an end in itself. People, especially backward people, need to be educated. If we give them education we are performing a useful service, regardless of the uses to which that education is put. However, the true missionary of Christ has no such blind faith in the efficacy of education. He knows that it is only a means to an end. Some of the greatest enemies of Christianity are exceedingly well educated. But they use that education for purposes quite foreign to those that we have learned from Christ. So we need to define the objectives that we have as missionaries in our educational work.

1. *We are primarily interested in the spiritual instruction of the church.* This is basic. It involves not only the leaders but all those who have put their faith in Christ. Paul speaks of this ministry when he says, "I kept back nothing that was profitable unto you, but have showed you, and have taught you publicly, and from house to house" (Acts 20:20).

2. *But we are also interested in the training of Christian leaders.* A mission leader with more than half a century of experience in the field has remarked, "The highest work of the missionary is to train such men, send them out, stand by them, help them solve their problems, and keep in closest touch with them." In his instructions to the young missionary Timothy, Paul wrote, "The things that thou hast heard of me among many witnesses, the same commit thou to faithful men, who shall be able to teach others also" (II Tim. 2:2).

3. *And there is also a need to train the people in the fellowship and ministry of the church.* The individual not only has a relationship and responsibility to God, he also has similar obligations toward other men. The church is the divinely ordained means of fellowship among Christians and of ministry to the unconverted.

4. *Finally, in order to attain these first three objectives, we find it necessary to teach some other subjects.* But we should always keep them subordinate to our main objectives.

DIRECT INDOCTRINATION

1. *General.*

a. *Expository preaching.* All preaching is to some extent teaching, though in some the teaching element is small. Expository preaching attempts to teach the Word of God to the people and on that basis appeal for decisions. In good hands it is very effective and builds a strong church. But it demands ability, time and effort on the part of the preacher. Otherwise it can become very monotonous, as the preacher tries to explain self-evident or well-known truths, or when he presents random thoughts as he reads verse by verse.

Given equal ability and a willingness to work, the missionary will find expository preaching the most valuable sort in his ministry to Christian believers. One thing should be remembered, that to present the truth in the clearest and simplest terms is very important. Often the people understand much less than we think they do because we take too much for granted. Also in good teaching there must be repetition. Only a few will get a statement the first time it is made. But remember that there is one sort of repetition that dulls the hearing and another sort that has a cumulative effect.

b. *Sunday Schools.* It is inconceivable to some that at the beginning of the past century many Americans thought the Sunday School was an invention of the devil. Today it is the one means of religious instruction that multitudes have ever had. And it is now common in all countries where Christianity of a Protestant sort is found. It may be called the right arm of the church. It has even been imitated by some non-Christian religions.

There are some differences between Sunday School work at home and on the field. In most fields there is an acute shortage of printed materials. In some, the pupils don't yet know how to read. So, much more has to depend on purely oral instruction.

In addition, the shortage of teachers is much more serious than at home. New converts from heathenism, with no background of Christian civilization and no acquaintance with Sunday Schools, cannot be expected to become teachers overnight. This means that a program of teacher training must begin as soon as possible if there is to be a Sunday School. Finally, it is not always possible to use the standardized lessons, so the missionary may have to plan his own.

c. *General conferences or conventions.* These gatherings of Christians have numerous values, one being systematic Bible instruction. In some places, notably Korea, large gatherings for Bible study have played an important part in the life of the church. They are planned for some central location at a time of the year when most people may be able to attend. Each one is expected to provide for his own keep.

Ordinary occupations are laid aside and attention is concentrated on the study of the Word.

d. *Correspondence courses.* More than ever before, correspondence courses are coming into use today. This is because of the great increase in literacy and the extension of postal services at reasonable cost. The major problem in these courses is the correction and examination service. If this responsibility is added to the work of the already over-burdened missionary, it is not likely to be cared for properly. It calls for the services of those who will give it first place in their attention. The work can be simplified in the preparation of the lessons. Questions of an objective sort can be graded by the use of a key sheet and do not call for the employment of highly trained graders.

e. *Radio Bible classes.* Radio Bible classes are valuable not only for evangelism but also for the instruction of Christians. As a part of the teaching process and a check on its effectiveness, students should write in for the lesson outlines and should take a final examination which is graded at the radio station. A small fee may be charged for enrollment and a certificate issued for successful completion of a course.

2. *Teaching of special groups.* As we have already said, there is some instruction that is intended for the church membership in general. But there is also a need for special instruction that is aimed at particular groups within the church. We are going to mention four such groups that call for special attention.

a. *Children.* First of all there are the children. The kind of instruction that would be very effective with adults often fails to reach the child's heart and mind. We need to use a special approach, a different set of methods, to reach the children. We have already mentioned child evangelism. The instruction of the children must continue along the same lines.

Of course there is some instruction in child evangelism. It usually includes quite a bit of Bible memorization together with some explanations. The Sunday School, too, although it commonly includes all the age groups, often has its principal ministry among the children. They are usually taught separate from the adults.

But there are some means of instruction that are just for the children. One is the Vacation Bible School. This has become a common feature of our church life in the homeland. To some it may come as a surprise to learn that it has also been adapted to use in the mission fields. In a sense it is largely a product of our American culture with its three-month vacation from school for the children. But the special methods that have been used in connection with it have proved effective in their own right. They do not depend on the formal vacation for their usefulness. Vacation Bible School teaching is being used even among children who have no school from which to take a vacation.

Something of the same sort occurs in connection with "Bible camps." In evangelical circles at home these camps, when properly conducted, have proved one of the most effective means of instruction as well as of evangelism among the children. Many a missionary can point back to a Bible camp where he first made his decision to prepare to be Christ's messenger to other lands. We sometimes think that the major attraction of these camps is to get out into the open, away from the cities and what we think of as "civilized" life. In some cases this may be true. Yet the camps attract a multitude of children from the rural areas as well. And somehow on the mission field, even where this attraction is nonexistent, the missionaries who have tried the camps have been delighted with the results. They have turned out to be quite popular. Of course if they live up to their name they give a good amount of Bible teaching as well as good fellowship and recreation.

b. *Young people.* For years the young people were a neglected group in the church. They were no longer children, nor did they appreciate being treated like children. Yet the older members of the church were not ready to give them an adult part in the church's organization and work. Then came the young people's society of Christian Endeavor, followed by a number of other youth organizations. They grew rapidly because they met a real need. There is a similar need in many of our mission fields. Alert missionaries have realized this need and have pushed the training of Christian young people through young people's societies.

We talk a great deal today of "learning by doing." It is a sound educational principle. It was also a central idea in the beginning of Christian Endeavor. Dr. Francis E. Clark, founder, proposed that the young people in the church should have a meeting of their own, where they could learn to express themselves and carry on worship without the embarrassment of the presence and participation of their elders. They would plan their own services, learn to develop Christian and Biblical topics, and win other young people. Yet they were not to be independent of the church. They were simply to carry on a specialized ministry within the church. It was to be a sort of training school to prepare young people to be more effective members of their church.

The same need may not be so obvious with the first generation of believers on the mission field. But the real success of any mission work will be seen in the second and other succeeding generations of Christians. And it is just here that the youth work demonstrates its value. What good does it do to reach the children if we cannot keep them through the adolescent period? And a church that depends for its existence on a constant stream of adult converts is one day likely to find the stream dry up. What is the mainstay of our older and stronger churches? Isn't it usually the children and grandchildren of Christians? We must find ways not only of keeping them but of instructing them for their future responsibilities. Young people's work is not an adjunct to our regular church work; it is a vital part of it. This is as much true in foreign missions as it is in the home field.

c. *Women.* In almost every field special organizations for women are found in the churches. In general they follow the pattern established for such organizations in the United States. In some countries, however, they have a more important place, since women may not be permitted to take part in a meeting of men or may not profit from it because of their inferior education.

d. *Men.* The need for a special men's organization is not so often felt as it is for the women. The men usually run the church. At times, however, a special group like the Fishermen's Club may catch on and have a useful ministry in promoting personal evangelism.

3. *Leadership training.* There is no more important ministry than that of training nationals to take over the work that the missionary has begun. The permanence and ultimate success of the work on the field depends on the national ministry. Many recognize this in theory but do not find the means effectively to put it into practice.

When the work can be carried on by a volunteer who can at the same time support himself at his trade, the matter is comparatively simple. But as the churches grow there comes a time when workers are needed who will give their whole time to the ministry. It is sometimes possible to employ one of these volunteer workers full time by providing the necessary funds to release him from the need of following his trade. But more often this does not work out. The reasons are various. The man who does well in a part-time ministry may already have reached his peak of usefulness. To employ him full time adds very little to his ministry. It may even leave him discontented, for he misses the change of occupation his trade afforded him. Then, too, the volunteer worker may have reached an age when he is not likely to improve much with further study. His success in a limited field does not indicate how well he will do in a greatly enlarged field with new problems and challenges.

So there is a need for the training of younger men whom the Lord may call, men who may be expected to qualify for a full-time spiritual ministry. In this our problems are multiplied. First is the problem of bringing the young people to such a measure of dedication that they will hear the Lord's call to such a ministry. This is not easy when governments and commercial enterprises offer an able young man so many more material inducements to enter their service, and he can still be a Christian and render voluntary part-time service. It means real sacrifice, and it is made doubly difficult when he fails to see in the missionary any example of a similar sacrifice.

A missionary in Africa wrote about how few of the graduates from the mission school were considering going into Christian service:

> Too well these young men know the pittance received by the so-called outschool "teacher" in lieu of salary. They are Christian boys. They know the need for men to carry the gospel to those still sitting in darkness, and they want some volunteer to go. But, after all, a bush evangelist has no prestige, no recognition, no honor—and adolescent Africa craves all these.

Then of those who do offer, there is the problem of deciding which ones should be accepted for training. Leaving out of account those who may be looking for an easy way of making a living, there are still many who do not realize the demands of the ministry and would never make effective workers. The missionary's judgment in this matter is seldom the best. The one who appeals to him may not be the one who will be acceptable to the people. And he may not know the young man as well as his compatriots do. The solution? Look for some evidence of the

Lord's calling. Is he already active in such Christian work as he can do? Has he shown the initiative a leader must have? Do his own people respect him? Sometimes this last can be answered by their willingness to help support him in his training. Even so there will always be some mistakes made.

Finally there are the practical problems of the kind of training that should be provided, financing, supervision, etc. We shall consider some of these in discussing the types of training schools.

How do you train leaders? There are three different ways: through instruction, through example, and through giving them actual experience in leading. Every good training program will give them all three of these elements. But even so there can be a variety of plans for carrying out the task.

a. *Individual fellowship.* The training of the Twelve by Jesus was an example of this sort of training. They lived with Him, listened to Him, watched Him and worked under His personal direction. It was an effective means of training, and in the hands of a good teacher it still is. Its greatest handicap is in the number who can be trained. Such close personal fellowship, instruction and supervision is not possible with large groups. In addition, this personalized training makes the pupil into the image of his teacher. In the case of Jesus this is ideal. In the case of an individual missionary it may be far from ideal. It also presents problems of support, since it is the tendency to expect everything from the "rich" missionary. Yet we could doubtless use this type of training much more than we do.

b. *Short-term Bible institutes.* There is a variety of schools, lasting from one to several weeks at a time, that come under this title. They are very unpretentious, call for very little equipment and staff and have a number of other advantages. Such schools can be held in almost any central location at a time of the year that is convenient for laymen to attend. Since the period is short, those who come can be asked to cover their own personal expenses.

Ordinary members of the church and volunteer workers profit from these institutes, and they build up the general level of Biblical knowledge of the whole church. The social problems that afflict the deans in a full-time school are minimized here. Records, too, can be very simple. Of course older people can attend, and people with weak academic backgrounds, so the instruction has to be on a simple level.

There is no problem of full-time teaching personnel, unless the mission has a team going from place to place to hold such institutes. Ordinarily they are held by the missionaries on the station involved, with occasional help from visiting missionaries or nationals. The curriculum usually stresses simple Bible and doctrinal studies, Christian living, and methods of Christian work.

The simplicity of teaching necessary for some of these short-term institutes is revealed in the following words from Brazil:

> It would make your heart ache to see the way in which four or five of our Indian fellows had to struggle to do the studying. Yet they were hungry to learn more of the Word and how to help their fellow Christians. So they bit their tongues and gritted their teeth and determined to keep up with the others in most of the subjects. One fellow said, as he handed in his exam paper with only half of the answers, "It's all I could do. I'm sorry. But this is the first time I've ever really tried to learn anything.

From southwest China a missionary wrote:

> They are mostly farm boys, not accustomed to sitting still and using their heads. They smile anxiously up at Ma-Ma (they *do* want to please her), but when it comes to requiring brain work they are flabbergasted. "What is the difference between mourning for one's sin and mourning for the result of one's sin?" asks Ma-Ma for instance. Such a question leveled at a newcomer simply stuns him. His jaw drops, his eyes stare, he looks as if he had been hypnotized. One of the old students, face alit with delight at a real thinking question, will call out a suggested answer from his seat, and the questioned one will gasp with relief that is very audible. I never expect the one I question to answer; I know he will be stunned. But I ask him to awaken him and everyone else.

c. *Full-term Bible institutes.* The term "Bible institute" in the United States indicates a school that stresses the study of the Bible in English and does not require college graduation for entrance. Originally such schools aimed primarily at the training of lay workers and evangelists. They had no intention of competing with the seminaries, which were the recognized training schools for the ministry. But as more and more Bible institute graduates entered the ministry, the schools found themselves obliged to make some changes in their program to meet the situation.

We face a somewhat similar situation on the foreign mission field. There, too, Bible institutes have often been started to train lay workers. But since in many places seminaries were nonexistent, the Bible institutes soon found themselves carrying on the only preparation for Christian service. This was all the more natural in fields where the general educational level is low. Often there are very few qualified candidates for seminary training as we understand it. And the few who do get it are by that very training separated from the people to whom they expect to minister.

As a result, the over-all picture is very confusing. There are seminaries equal to those in the homeland, and many others whose work is on a lower level than that of our Bible institutes. There are Bible institutes that are preparing men for the ministry with considerable success, and there are others that are more like Sunday School classes. There is little uniformity in the use of the names, and none at all in the kind of work they carry on. Of course it is only in recent years that the American Bible institutes have moved toward some standardization of their work.

What often happens is this. A missionary feels led to start a school for the training of national workers. The mission gives its approval. At times it may even offer help with the finances and personnel. But the planning is up to the leader. He has an interest, but no special training for this work. Neither is he in a position to consult with experienced men in the field. So he does the best he can. He draws on his remembrance of the schools he attended at home. He modifies the pattern somewhat to fit the local conditions. And then he goes ahead, making other changes along the way as he grows in experience. Unfortunately, the mistakes he makes are being duplicated by countless others in other fields.

For this reason we want to give a brief orientation in some of the basic principles in Bible institute work. The field is too large to cover in much detail. But these principles should be of help to those who have known Bible institutes only as students or onlookers.

(1) *Objectives.* The objectives of the Bible institute will to a large extent determine its program. But you are going to find that they are not easy to define. Do you plan to prepare young people for full- or part-time service? Will it be as lay workers or ordained ministers or both? Just what types of ministry do you have in mind? Will your training be terminal? That is, will those who complete it go directly into the work, or will they need further preparation? Do you aim to train workers for your own work alone, or also for others? You need to know where you are going before you can plot your course.

(2) *Potential students.* What are your prospects for students? One mission leader has remarked that some missionaries start Bible institutes, not because they see a real need, but because that is the kind of life to which they are accustomed. They have spent most of their life in school. A missionary in Japan has written that there are enough Bible institutes in that land to meet the needs of a Christian population many times the size of the one that actually exists. Do you have a Christian constituency large enough to call for such a school? Will the school really help the basic work of evangelism? Or will it hinder it by removing too many workers from that job?

How many students can you reasonably expect? How many graduates will the work be able to utilize and support, year after year? It is never wise to accept everyone who wants to come. You must have some standards of acceptance and hold to them. It only takes one maladjusted student to disrupt a whole school. Does the prospective student have a serious Christian purpose? Has he already given evidence of usefulness in the Lord's service? Do his own people have confidence in him? Would they be willing to sponsor him?

Of course any school is likely to do a certain amount of recruiting. The way you do that recruiting, however, will have a great deal to do with the success of the school. Are you recruiting primarily for the school? Or are you recruiting for the work, with the school as a means for getting ready to do that work? There is an important difference here.

And when you get your students, it is just as important that you understand them as it is that you understand the subjects you are going to teach. This is one of the basic laws of teaching. It is a mistake to presume that a program that is satisfactory for the United States will also be satisfactory in other lands. The students are different. The difference is not so much one of capacity as it is of background. You must know that background. It is the basis on which you are to build. It also gives you the keys to their ways of thinking. This is why no missionary should be assigned to Bible institute work who has not already had experience with the people in the more normal environment of their homes.

A further question. Will you accept only men as students? If so, should they be married and come with their families? Married men are usually more stable and serious in purpose. But their duties to their families take quite a bit of their time, and there are problems of housing and provisions. On the other hand, is it right to keep a man away from his wife and family for months at a time? And if the whole family comes, what provision should you make for the teaching of the wives?

It might seem easier to teach unmarried men. But the problems of discipline are greater. And of course they will one day get married. How will their wives fit into the ministry for which you are preparing them? Will they have any preparation? Will they be a help or a hindrance to their husbands? A wife can make or break a man's ministry.

At home we have coeducational schools. In some mission fields the same thing is possible. In others it may seem to the people quite improper to have both men and women in the same classes. Besides, are you prepared to face the social problems such a school presents, especially if the students live at the school?

(3) *Faculty.* The question of the faculty is usually settled by finding out who is available and willing to teach. Many of our failures may be laid to this fact. Until we are ready to *make* available our best teachers, and until they accept this responsibility as the most important ministry they can perform for the Lord, our Bible institutes will be inferior. This is not a romantic work. It is very demanding. It is especially so when the teacher must also do a half dozen other jobs and live right in the midst of the students. But the work can be richly rewarding to the one who undertakes it with real devotion. And it is vitally important in the growth of the church.

Those who have themselves attended Bible institute usually fit in best. This is because they are familiar with the practical, simple, direct approach that characterizes the Bible institute movement. Those whose training in the Bible has been exclusively in the seminary do not fit in so well. They find it hard to adjust their thinking and teaching to the needs and abilities of Bible institute students.

The mission itself sets the requirements for the teachers it provides. But it makes a serious mistake when it is lax in the matter. These teachers may not be much in the limelight, but they have a tremendous influence on the future of the work. They are the ones who are developing the future leaders. It is important that they be not only good teachers but also good spiritual guides. In fact, their lives are likely to mean more than the subjects they teach.

One further note. Missionary personnel is usually limited and the Bible institutes are chronically understaffed. Yet so far as possible we ought to see that the students get their teaching from more than just one or two individuals during their course. This may not be easy to accomplish, especially if all the teaching is done by full-time workers. But it is important to avoid lopsidedness. There are several possible ways of doing it, through the careful use of part-time teachers, or the occasional rotation of teachers, or by other means. Perhaps best of all is when two or more missions find it possible to co-operate in the school, with each one providing part of the staff.

What we have said about the faculty applies to both missionaries and nationals. At the beginning the teaching is of course done by the missionaries. But at the earliest possible time they should invite capable nationals to have a part in this ministry. And the mission should be planning for the day when nationals will occupy the key positions and bear the major responsibility for this work. Of course, just as we have already said that the missionary teachers should have had experience in the work first, so also the nationals should be men of experience.

(4) *Housing and equipment.* It is possible to hold a Bible institute without special buildings or elaborate equipment. It can be done but it is hard to do it well. Many have tried it. A good faculty can always do a better job with adequate facilities.

Classrooms are a "must." But they don't have to be elaborate. What they need is to be well lighted and ventilated and to have desks or tables at which the students can work. Simple and inexpensive blackboards have sometimes been produced by coating a section of a mud wall with smooth cement, which was then painted with blackboard paint.

Most Bible institute students live on the grounds or nearby. This is valuable because it allows for some supervision of the home life and integrates the student into a program that involves more than just classroom work. In some places the school provides dormitories, roughly similar to those in the United States. In others there may be a Bible institute village, a village composed of houses for the institute students and their families. Sometimes the students are required to build their own houses. Sometimes the churches or the mission do the building. In the Bible institute village each family prepares its own food, but the dormitory calls for a common kitchen as well as a dining room and storeroom.

When a mission Bible institute erects its own building, it is usually quite a simple structure. Besides one or more classrooms, it usually has a central office and supply room, and sometimes a library or study hall. The need for a library depends on the field. In many fields the total literature in the local language is exceedingly meager. A small shelf would hold it all. This is one of the major problems in the work. But little as it is, the library plays an important part in the training of students.

(5) *Financing.* Perhaps there is no greater variation in any phase of the Bible institute work than in the plans of financing. The simplest, but the least advisable, is for the mission to cover all expenses, including room and board and textbooks for the students. There are even places where the students get a monthly cash allowance for personal expenses. It doesn't take much discernment to see the weakness of such a plan. But where it has been followed for years it is not easy to change it.

At the other extreme it is probably unreasonable ever to expect that any institute will be able to support itself by tuition and fees charged to the students. Even in the United States, where nearly all the accredited Bible institutes are now charging tuition, these charges cover only a part of the expenses. The rest is covered by contributions from interested Christians, churches, etc. On the mission field it is a rare institute that makes any tuition charge to its students.

We can divide the expenses for running an institute roughly into three classes. There are the salaries of the teaching and supervisory personnel. Then there are the expenses incident to the teaching, including the necessary supplies, buildings and upkeep. Finally there are the expenses that pertain to the individual student, such as room, board, textbooks and other materials, etc. If ever the church is to become completely indigenous, it must take over the administration and support of its own schools, including these expenses. But it cannot do so at the beginning.

From the experience of some missions, we would say that it is possible, even while the church is small, for the student to cover his own personal expenses with the help of the church. This leaves the other two kinds of expenses. It will be hard to get the church to see any responsibility for them so long as the mission keeps the teaching and administration entirely in its own hands. However, when the church is brought into the administration, and especially when it is given a dominant voice, it may be expected to assume greater financial responsibility. In other words, authority and responsibility go together. In any case, as long as there are missionaries on the staff, their salaries will be provided from abroad.

Even for the third class of expenses, those that pertain to the individual student, various plans are in operation. Often the school itself hires the students for certain jobs that need to be done. Sometimes the school raises a part of its own food on institute lands so as to reduce expenses. Or it may allot a piece of ground to each family to cultivate its own food. We do well to remember that those plans that call for someone to supervise and keep accounts for each student are likely to be the least efficient. Sometimes the missionaries spend so much time on such things that their teaching suffers.

(6) *Curriculum.* We said that those who start Bible institutes on the mission field often pattern them after what they remember of their own Bible institute experience. They even tend to copy the curriculum of their alma mater. Usually this is because they have had no experience in drawing up a curriculum, and so they don't realize its problems.

For example, many schools used to list a class in Bible Synthesis, following the ideas of the late Dr. James M. Gray, of Moody Bible Institute. This is a rapid survey of the whole Bible, calling for repeated reading of entire books of the Bible before they are treated in class. Dr. Gray used to demand two and a half hours of reading in preparation for each fifty-minute class period. Good as the plan was for American students, it broke down when missionaries tried to use it with people who had difficulty in reading at all. Some of them had never before attempted so much as a single solid hour of reading.

In general there are three factors that determine curriculum. They are: the capabilities of the students, the aims and objectives of the educational program, and the time and means at the disposal of the instructional staff. For example, under the best of circumstances a Bible institute in a backward country cannot expect to accomplish in three years what we accomplish in a three-year course in the U.S. The background of the students is too limited. Even so, a number of Bible institutes have found it necessary to introduce what they call a preliminary course. This is a course of one or two years for those whose educational background is lower than the average. This preliminary course tries to prepare students to take the regular Bible institute course later. It provides special emphasis on such things as reading, writing, grammar and simple Bible studies.

Curriculum development brings us back to our objectives of the institute. Are we going to use it, at least temporarily, to provide pastors for the church? Then we need to determine what a pastor ought to know and be and do. Should his qualifications be the same as for a pastorate in the U.S.? Then in the more primitive areas you are going to face the problem of a greatly extended period of training, and you will have good reason to complain, as some are doing, of the shortage of suitable candidates for the ministry. On the other hand, it is possible for you to lower the standards so much that the ministry loses the respect that it ought to have. You will find this especially true today when educational standards in most countries are rising so rapidly.

When we have decided on our objectives, we need to consider how best to reach them. This means the planning of subjects and courses. But don't let yourself be too much influenced by names. It is the content of a course that counts.

Obviously in a Bible institute our principal concern is the teaching of the Bible itself. Presuming that the whole Bible is available in the language, we want to seek the best means of familiarizing the students with it. We don't need to think of dealing with all parts of the Bible in detail. A complete analysis of the Bible is usually out of the question. However, a good bird's-eye view, showing the relationship of the various parts to each other, such as Dr. Gray intended in his Synthetic Bible Studies, is important. It is up to the planner to figure out how to accomplish it. There should also be analytic studies of certain parts of the Bible, both because of their own importance and so as to acquaint the student with the principles of such analysis. Hermeneutics, or the basic principles of Bible interpretation, is a very important subject, whether taught separately or in connection with some other subject. And of course a systematic study of the great teachings of the Scriptures is indispensable.

While a knowledge of the Scriptures is essential, there must also be an ability to communicate that knowledge to others. Frequently this involves giving the students instruction in the use of their own language, including its grammar. The art of speaking in public, and especially of preaching the gospel, deserves special attention. Students also need to be trained in teaching. And of course the simplest and most common means of communicating the gospel to others is through what we call personal evangelism. This also leads us into the field of apologetics, a reasoned defense of the Christian faith against the arguments most commonly brought against it by unbelievers.

The broad field of methods should also be included in the curriculum. How to organize and conduct a Sunday School; how to conduct a business meeting in the church; how to use a flannelgraph or other visual aids effectively; these and many other things may be taught according to your purpose and your observation of their usefulness in the work. But remember that methods are always secondary; they are always subordinate to a mastery of Bible content.

Several other factors will affect the number and nature of subjects your school offers: the size of your faculty and their qualifications, the length of the school year, and the load that any student can properly be expected to handle during a term. Sometimes subjects must be given in alternate years if at all. You will probably not have to be concerned about the possible transfer of credits to other schools, therefore, your program need not conform to what others are doing. Your curriculum may be considered valid as long as it accomplishes the purposes for which you have planned it. But keep reviewing to see if it is meeting the need.

(7) *Methods of teaching.* There is no one best method of teaching. Different subjects, different pupils, different circumstances, may call for different methods. The teacher is much more important than the method, but a good teacher is at his best only when using the best methods.

One of the most commonly used methods is the least effective—the straight lecture system. The teacher lectures for the full period and the students try to grasp the material as best they can, making notes to aid their memories in recalling what was presented. The system has some advantages or it would not be used so much in this country. It enables the teacher to cover a set amount of material within the allotted time, without any disturbing digressions. It is especially useful in large classes when the size of the class makes individual recitation impractical. It is useful, too, when there are no printed materials covering the subject. With an alert and interested class and an exceptional lecturer it gives reasonably good results.

But the lecture method has serious weaknesses. The student finds it exceedingly difficult to follow the thoughts of the lecturer and at the same time get down the notes he will need to aid his memory. Since he doesn't get down the whole lecture, the only thing he can study is his own note summary of what he heard the lecturer say. It takes practice to make good notes, even among people who can write rapidly. On many mission fields the lecture method is out of the question, since the people write with such difficulty.

We shall not go into the other methods of teaching that require a greater amount of participation on the part of the class. Some work best with one type of subject, some with another. But a few things need emphasis. First, we should not take it for granted that a class has grasped a thought simply because we have presented it. Good teaching involves repetition, even when a few in the class may not need it. Second, we need to aim at the greatest simplicity and clearness of expression. There is not nearly so much need of impressing the class with our scholarliness as there is of helping it to comprehend and master the basic things. Third, the failure of a considerable portion of the class is usually as much the teacher's fault as that of the students. Fourth, don't be afraid to experiment with new methods if you think they can increase the effectiveness of your teaching.

The problem of textbooks is a serious one. In very few fields are there textbooks adequate for the needs. Sometimes not even the whole Bible is available in a language students understand. Under such circumstances the teachers themselves prepare notes for their classes and have them duplicated. But many teachers soon find that preparing such notes is a real task. Then they are often tempted to try to simplify their task by making translations of English texts. But before long they find out that such translations don't quite fit their needs. Moreover, the job of translation is not as easy as it looks.

Of course textbooks are needed principally for the students to study outside of class. In those places where previous education has been very little, students are not accustomed to studying from books. As a result you can't expect much in the way of study. It is better to spend more time in class, going over the material until it is mastered. So the lack of textbooks is not so keenly felt as it might be.

Tests and examinations serve a twofold purpose. They measure the student's mastery of the subject, and they also prompt him to review what has already been covered so as to fix it more firmly in his mind. When we use tests for measuring, the question we want answered is not, "Has the student gained a perfect command of the subject?" That is asking too much. The real question is, "Has he accomplished as much as we can reasonably expect of him?"

Percentage grades are very deceptive. The mark of 100 should indicate perfection. Actually it only shows that the student answered correctly *the questions that were asked.* Most testing is merely a sampling. If the samples are all taken from an area that the student knows well, he can get 100 without knowing the rest of the subject. The samples, to be accurate, must show a reasonable coverage of the field. Again, it is possible to give a fairly comprehensive examination, but make the questions so easy that anyone can score 100, or so difficult that most of the class will fail. If the examination is too easy it fails as a measurement; if it is too hard it discourages the students.

(8) *Co-curricular activities.* There are a number of student activities that are not directly related to classroom work. Yet they do

play an important part in the student's training. Since they are not entirely outside the training program of the school, we call them co-curricular activities.

The most important of these activities are in the field of what we call practical Christian work. In other words, they are the putting into practice of what is learned in the classroom. From the beginning this has been an important part of the Bible institute plan. It endeavors to give its students experience in Christian work as well as teaching about it.

During their course of study students are given certain practical Christian work "assignments." The nature of these assignments may vary according to the location of the school. But generally there is a strong emphasis on personal witnessing, visitation, preaching, and the teaching of small groups such as Sunday School classes, children's classes and the like. The experience is always useful, but it is most effective when well supervised.

This sort of activity is not always limited to the time the students are in school. In some places the students must do some Christian work during a part of their vacation period. On occasion this may be an evangelistic tour in company with a teacher. In any case it should be planned. There are also schools that require the student, before he enters the last year of classes, to spend a year or more in a full-time Christian ministry. This makes his last year of studies much more meaningful because he has learned through experience some of his needs.

Besides these activities, no well-balanced school program will completely disregard the social needs of the students. It is true that our American schools often overemphasize social activities. In other lands the pressure is not nearly so great to have such activities. But there is a need for something of the sort that we do not always recognize. A balanced social program in the schools that prepare church leaders will lead to a balanced program in the churches themselves.

(9) *Discipline.* Discipline is often a major problem. Lack of discipline can be a greater danger than poor teaching. Yet many of those who come to Bible institutes are not used to discipline. Here is where the foreign missionary needs to walk with caution and have a good understanding of the people. This is one reason why he must have had some experience among them before he is assigned to the school.

He must maintain discipline, but he doesn't want to drive the students away or cause them a serious loss of "face." Perhaps his best safeguard is to have a board composed partly of nationals who will deal with the more serious cases.

d. *Seminaries.* Many of the statements we have made about Bible institutes apply also to seminaries. Of course we need to realize that while in the United States a seminary is a graduate school of religion, in some mission fields there are seminaries not on the graduate level. In Formosa, for example, graduation from senior high school qualifies a student for entrance. This naturally affects the program.

The seminary is normally considered to be the training school for ordained ministers. By some missions it is the only school that is seriously considered in this way. Such a view under present circumstances in many mission fields is very unrealistic. We may prefer to have our ordained ministers seminary-trained. There is certainly nothing wrong in aiming at that ideal. But in reality the present seminaries in these fields are utterly incapable of providing the pastors now needed, much less those who will be needed if the work expands very much. The rector of a seminary in Brazil estimated a few years ago that only two per cent of the population of that country was being touched by seminary graduates. And Brazil is in a much more favorable situation than many other lands.

When a seminary does require liberal arts training for entrance, it enjoys several advantages. Its objectives are usually pretty well defined. It aims to provide qualified workers for the full-time ministry of the church. Its training is terminal; that is, its graduates usually go directly into the ministry. And the background of the students who come to it is more nearly alike than that of the Bible institute students.

However, a seminary is much more likely to be tied down to a traditional curriculum that the denomination has commonly used. Its characteristic emphasis on the theoretical, the philosophical, the scholarly, is more likely on a mission field to divorce its students from the realities of common life than it is here in the United States.

Yet there are some trends toward more instruction in the practical field. A recent conference in East Asia recommended that theological schools give attention to the teaching of Christian marriage and family life. This is a matter of practical importance to every pastor who is called on to counsel. There have also been recommendations that the theological training should be more closely related to rural life. Not only in East Asia but in many other mission fields society is predominantly rural, though our theological training has generally prepared men for the city churches.

Just this further statement about curriculum. In many places, because of the lack of theological literature in the local language, the teaching is done in English, which all students must learn. Of course this does make available to the student all the wealth of literature available in English. Theoretically this is pure gain. Actually, however, it is likely to handicap the graduate in his ministry among his own people. He has mastered the teachings of the church in English, but he has not necessarily translated them into the thoughts and words of his own tongue. He has *learned* an English theology, but it is often not *his* theology because it is not in his language. Anyone who has had much experience with other languages can see how this is true. The thoughts that do not come to one in his own language are at the very best "fuzzy" in their connotations. However, because of the scarcity of good translations, commentaries, and word studies, there is more reason for the study of the Biblical languages in mission seminaries than there is at home. And many of our students in mission lands are much better linguists than American students.

The seminary, partly because of its higher requirements and consequently smaller student body, is more likely to call for inter-mission co-operation than is the Bible institute. This presents problems, when there are differences of theology involved. But the problems are just as serious in trying to run a separate school so small that it cannot be staffed properly and there are too few students for inspiring fellowship or stimulating competition.

e. *Correspondence courses.* The possibility of using correspondence courses in part for the training of our church leaders is something that very few missions are exploiting to any significant degree. We grant that alone they are inadequate. But the many successful correspondence schools in this country and the recognition that most colleges and universities are willing to give to a certain amount of correspondence work show that it does have a real value.

Correspondence courses are based on the fact that many individuals would like to study the subjects involved, but because of lack of funds or the pressure of other responsibilities they cannot do their study in residence. In a field where tuition, board and room are provided for all theological students, lack of funds may be a minor consideration. But many times a man has serious responsibilities that he cannot easily lay down to attend school. He can give a part of his time to studying, but not abandon his home. There are also many already in the ministry who could profit by additional instruction if they could get it without leaving their work. This is especially true where they are trying to raise the standards of ministerial preparation, which in earlier days may have been low.

Correspondence work presupposes an ability to read and write with reasonable fluency, to comprehend printed texts and follow instructions. It also presupposes that such texts are available, that there will be provision for tests and examinations and competent examiners, and that there is fairly regular postal service. Two items here are the most difficult to care for. Often there are no texts available until they are specially written. In a classroom a teacher may be able to get along without a textbook; by correspondence he can't. And the problem of testing without the direct oversight of the teacher is not an easy one, even if you have reliable examiners who will correct papers promptly after they are received.

There is a great deal of record-keeping in connection with correspondence courses, so no one should jump into the work without counting the cost. Results, however, will readily repay all that is expended.

f. *Training of women.* We are becoming increasingly aware of the need for training women as well as men. Not only will some of these women do full-time work as Bible women, teachers, etc., but a pastor's wife also needs to have training to be the helpmate that she should be to her husband. For this reason, even in schools where single young women are not accepted, there is provision made for the teaching of wives of men students. Sometimes this has to be done in special classes because the women do not have the needed background and must receive simpler instruction. Sometimes both can be put in some of the same classes. In most cases there will be differences in the curriculum because of differences in prospective ministry. Also, where there is a home and family to care for, the women can take only a limited amount of class work.

AUXILIARY TEACHING

In the work of missions, direct indoctrination is of course primary. However, there are other types of teaching that also contribute to the accomplishing of the missionary aim. To keep them in their proper relation to the rest of the work, perhaps we ought to call them auxiliary teaching.

1. *The need for auxiliary teaching.* There are various reasons for the missionary's entering into these other types of teaching.

First of all, we need to recognize that it is impossible to separate spiritual life entirely from all other phases of life. Man is an individual, which means that he cannot be divided up into his constituent elements and still remain a man. We can talk of his spiritual life and of his economic life and his social life as if they were separate, but actually they are so interrelated that what happens to the one must of necessity affect the others. To pretend that we can divorce the spiritual from the physical and the intellectual is to deceive ourselves and to deny our own experience.

Though in some sense we can provide training for a man's spirit without delving deeply into the other aspects of education, yet we are always touching them at one point or another. The only question is whether we shall provide Christian training for the whole man, or whether we shall leave some parts of his training to non-Christian, or at best sub-Christian instruction, or else to the haphazard gleanings of his own unguided experience.

There is a question, though, as to what proportion of the missionary staff should be assigned to this educational work. Man is not all spirit, but neither is he all mind or all body. Educational work has a tendency to absorb more and more of the missionary staff, until very few missionaries are directly concerned with the church or evangelism. This can be a dangerous situation, unless the national church itself is well established and is aggressively carrying on the evangelistic work.

Some of the needs for this auxiliary teaching are so fundamental and so readily recognized by most people that they rouse little discussion. For example, in order that those who are converted to Christ may be able to nourish their spiritual life through the reading of the Scriptures, it is necessary that they know how to read. So the teaching of reading by missionaries is seldom questioned. By an extension of the same principle we might say that we ought to teach arithmetic. Our churches cannot be indigenous until they have people in them capable of handling the church accounts. This is all presuming that such instruction is not already provided in other ways outside of the church or mission.

Then there is some teaching that is demanded by the physical or economic distress of the people. We seldom question the duty of the missionary to treat the illnesses of the people if he can. Neither should we question our responsibility to train some of them to perform this same ministry, as we are able. Whatever is right for a missionary to do it is right for him to teach someone else to do.

But the physical infirmities of a people are often closely tied up with their economic situation. They are ill simply because they don't have the means to keep well. If we can show them how it is possible to keep well, should we refuse to do it? And if that means helping them to establish their life on a better economic plane, should we withhold our help? If James says that a living faith will "give . . . those things that are needful to the body" (James 2:16), will it be any less ready to help the needy brother provide them for himself?

Some will object that this leads to all kinds of social service, to the neglect of the basic spiritual aim of missions. And such a thing can happen; in fact, it has happened. But it has happened where the social service became an end in itself and was not really just an expression of the life that the missionary had in Christ. It is always possible to emphasize the material at the expense of the spiritual. But it is also possible to emphasize the spiritual to the complete exclusion of the material. James shows us how unreasonable it is to try to divorce the two. And there is many a missionary whose spiritual ministry is practically sterile because the people cannot see how the faith he preaches has any relation to life.

And there is some teaching that we have to do because all other instruction is in the hands of those who are antagonistic to the gospel of Christ. It is strange that so many American Christians seem completely unaware of this situation in other countries. They seem not to realize how completely a single religion, a single church can dominate the public education of a country.

For this reason many oppose their missionaries entering into the field of "secular" education. Yet some of these same objectors are the stanchest supporters of the "Christian school" movement in this country. They pay substantial fees in addition to their taxes so that their children may be taught by Christian teachers, though there is no religious discrimination in our public schools. Yet they object to Christian schools for other people in lands where discrimination against the Christian minority is openly practiced.

Even so-called "lay" schools may be inimical to what the mission stands for. Recently some Presbyterian missionaries in the Congo advocated the sending of Christian children to such schools. They wanted a de-emphasis of education in the mission's program and a greater emphasis on evangelism. Perhaps they were right. Education does have a way of usurping the first place. But one Christian mother soon transferred her children back to the mission school. The liberal and materialistic philosophy of the lay school had no place for basic Christian teachings.

There is also some teaching done to secure openings for the gospel. Many people today are eager to learn the English language. Where people are not otherwise open to the presentation of the gospel, the missionary sometimes takes advantage of the opportunity to start an English class so as to reach them. He may even use the Bible as a text. Sometimes there is a similar opportunity in the teaching of music.

This teaching is not as fruitful as you might suppose, though. The pupils come already on their guard and are not easy to influence. Also, not many missionaries have the qualities that enable them to make effective use of such opportunities.

We should not overlook the fact that the government may require the mission to engage in education as a condition of its continuance in the country. This is the case in Liberia and Angola, where all missions must conduct schools.

Then, too, there is the need to provide a well-prepared leadership for the church. It was to meet this need that a number of our earliest colleges in the United States were begun. The church, to be strong, must have good leadership. It is not enough to give them the specialized training in Bible institutes and seminaries. The level of instruction in those schools is often distressingly low because the students do not have a good foundation of general education on which to build. In this country our Bible institutes commonly require graduation from high school for entrance. We do not need to provide that high school training in church schools, because it is readily available in the public school system. But in some other lands, though the educational level of the people is rising rapidly, there is no such state-supported system as ours.

One feature that gets far less attention than it should is that schools, especially primary schools, give an excellent opportunity for evangelism and solid Christian teaching. A missionary in South America once told me,

> Every school day, for an hour a day, I have a large class of girls for Bible study. Many of them are not believers, and some come from the best families in the city. They would never be seen in our Sunday School. Can you think of a better opportunity for presenting the gospel?

A missionary teacher from Africa wrote,

> Personally, after almost twenty-seven years in Africa, largely among its native people, I do not know of any work which is more directly spiritual. Truly, we cannot teach Scripture all day long. They could not take it in if we did. But neither could we gather together hundreds of children to hear the story of Jesus and His love daily in any other way. In no other way could we give them such consecutive and constructive teaching in the things of God.

2. General types of auxiliary teaching.

a. *Literacy campaigns.* Generally speaking, this is one of the types of auxiliary teaching about which there is little question on the part of missionaries and their supporters. The reason is that our Protestant Christian faith depends so largely on the Bible. Not only do we believe that the Bible is our final authority; we also believe that it is the privilege and responsibility of each one to read the Bible for himself. Our missionaries spend a great deal of time and energy in translating the Bible into the languages of the people. They want to make available to them the Word of God in terms that they can understand. And then they try to encourage the people to read it for themselves.

But what good is it to make the Bible available, if the people can't read it? The most perfect translation is useless in the hands of a man who has never learned to read. He is like a blind man. He must trust others to lead him. But when most of the others are in a similar state, who will direct their steps?

We talk about the indigenous church. It is an ideal toward which we aim. Yet no church can become truly indigenous and strong in the faith so long as its people cannot feed themselves on the Word of God. One of the greatest hindrances to church progress in some areas is the illiteracy of the people. Usually the Christians have a somewhat higher literacy rate than the people around them. But except where there is a definite program for stimulating literacy, the difference is quite small. For this reason in some places they have made it a condition for church membership that one should be able to read.

In recent years the world has become very conscious of the problems that illiteracy presents. Governments have taken up the challenge and have set up literacy programs on a large scale. In some cases they have taken desperate measures, even threatening with arrest those who did not learn to read. The immense progress made in Russia is specially notable. To aid them in their task, the governments have often called on missionaries. In Liberia, for example, a missionary was asked to head the literacy program.

But useful as these government programs are, they do not completely relieve the missionary of responsibility. There are too many places where the work is scarcely more than begun. To wait for the government to do the job is to be content with a weak, dependent church for years to come. And there are places where the languages are not yet reduced satisfactorily to written form. Moreover, literacy teaching provides the missionary with an unexcelled opportunity. This opportunity lies not only in teaching others to read but in providing those who are becoming literate with material to read. Under the government program literature will be strictly secular at best. But the missionary can make use of the Bible itself, or of specially prepared Christian works based on the Bible. The newly literate are anxious to read—to read anything—and the one who provides their reading material is the one who will guide their thinking.

As we have mentioned, the government sometimes welcomes the help of the missionary in setting up and conducting a literacy program. Should he take the opportunity or not? The answer may be either yes or no. He has to weigh carefully the possible advantages to his over-all purpose if he accepts such a responsibility. Will it give him some needed favor with the officials if he co-operates, favor that will help other parts of the work? Just how important is this? Will it give him greater acceptance with the people as they see him unselfishly trying to help them? May this open more doors for the gospel? Will he be limited in the choice of reading materials that he uses? Even if not permitted to use direct religious propaganda materials or the Bible, is the choice otherwise left up to him? Is it likely that most of his time will be spent in administrative work, without much chance to touch the people? These and other questions he will want to have answered before he makes his decision.[1]

What can the missionary or the church do apart from any government program? There are several things. In the first place, if he has the time, the help and the supplies, he can set up a full scale campaign of his own. Or the mission or church can set aside someone to take charge of such a program. This is the sort of plan that works best when one mission has the sole responsibility for an area or a tribe.

But even without such a large scale plan, much can be done. For example, one of the problems in combating illiteracy is motivation. The people often are not interested in learning to read, for they can see little advantage to it. Half of the battle would be won if they had a real desire to learn. We have already mentioned one way of stirring up such a desire. There are churches that require all candidates for admission to church membership to know how to read. Sometimes they make exceptions in the case of very elderly people. But it has been demonstrated that age is really not a serious handicap in this matter. Both the desire for church membership and the desire to be able to read God's Word provide good motivation.

In the case of a large church, this plan might seem to call for a regular reading class, perhaps in connection with the catechumens' classes.

[1]For detailed instructions in the setting up of such a large campaign, see Frank C. Laubach, *Teaching the World to Read* (New York: Friendship Press, 1947).

The class idea does have some values, especially since it calls for attendance at a regular time. For children it works out well. But for adults it is not so satisfactory. Adults seem to learn to read best one at a time.

Another incentive for learning to read is the provision of literature that everyone will want to be able to read. We have already mentioned the Bible. But there are other things as well. This is why often in connection with a literacy campaign there will be a little periodical published in simple language. It will contain news items, helpful hints, stories and a variety of other things specially attractive to the people for whom it is prepared. The idea is that those who are learning need interesting material on which to practice, and those who have not yet started need to be enticed.

To help the people develop facility in reading, it is good to make use of reading in concert whenever possible. You can often do it in church services or Sunday School classes. What does it matter if the people do stumble? Your aim is not a smooth service but a meaningful one. And even apart from its teaching values, this procedure allows the people to have a greater part in the service.

Individual reading can be encouraged, also. The old Sunday School plan of having the pupils read aloud in rotation the verses of the lesson has its value. In addition, household prayers, where everyone in the house is expected to gather and take part in the reading, provides another opportunity. I have known of at least one case where a servant in the house learned to read entirely through the instruction he received in family prayers.

Of course what we have said presumes that there is no opposition to the people's learning to read the language that they use in everyday life. It may be the official language of a country, as Spanish in Venezuela, or the language of a single group, as Kikamba in Kenya, East Africa. In either case the government encourages literacy in their own language.

The situation is different in some other places, as Ethiopia. There the official language is Amharic, the language of the ruling group. But a large part of the people do not speak nor understand Amharic. They have their own languages, such as the Galla. In order to promote unity in the country, however, the government is trying to make Amharic the national language for all its people. Schools must be conducted in

Amharic. Only literature produced in Amharic may be circulated. Even the translation of the Bible into other languages is not permitted. So apart from the Amharas themselves, any literacy campaign becomes not a literacy campaign but a campaign to teach another language in both its spoken and written forms. This multiplies the problems for the missionary.

Another situation is faced where there is a difference between the literary language and the language used in common speech. Often the Bible has been translated into the literary language, which only the scholars understand. Here the missionary must make a choice, either to try to teach the people a different language from what they commonly use, or to produce reading material, including perhaps a new version of the Bible, in their common tongue. Either one is a tremendous task.

Showing what can be done for new literates, Dr. Laubach has recently produced the New Testament story in an extremely simplified form of English. Actually this world campaign for literacy calls for the production of a different kind of literature, a literature geared to the newly literate.

The task of teaching adults to read, we must understand, is different from that of teaching children. In some ways it is easier for adults with their greater maturity and experience. They already know how to use the language and can progress more rapidly.

Yet in some other ways teaching adults to read is more difficult than teaching children. Perhaps a major difference is that most adults take up the matter of learning to read voluntarily. Many times you have to entice them even to try. And at the slightest discouragement they are ready to quit. Children will study what they are told to study without knowing its purpose; but adults have to see what they will get out of it. Then, too, adults are much more embarrassed to have others see their ignorance than are children.

There are several principles that apply in teaching adults to read:

(1) *Concentrate on the individual before you.* We have already said that it is usually best to teach adults individually. One reason is that you can gear your teaching to the one person and not worry about discouraging another. No matter what anyone else can do, you are going to help *this* man to learn.

(2) *Make it simple.* No matter how slow an illiterate may be,

he has to feel that he has accomplished something at each lesson. Plan the course so he can.

(3) *Build on what he already knows.* This is always a sound principle of teaching. Dr. Laubach's reading charts are based on it. In choosing a key word to teach, he finds an object whose shape is somewhat similar to the initial letter of its name, or the action it represents. (Of course the word must contain only the letters he is interested in at the time. This is the big problem in preparing the charts. It takes a great deal of research to find suitable words and objects.) An artist prepares an easily recognizable picture of the object. Alongside it is a duplicate of the picture, with the lines that correspond to the letter highlighted. Then the letter alone. In this way the learner associates what he is to learn with some very familiar objects.

The same principle of building on what he already knows is used in the progression of the charts and lessons. New letters are introduced in connection with those that have already been learned.

(4) *Commend him.* No matter how little progress he may have made, for him it may have been a great deal. Praise him for it. In fact, it is good to praise him for every forward step he makes during the lesson. One of the illiterate's greatest needs is for encouragement. With it he can go ahead, even though slowly. Without it he is lost.

(5) *Have him teach someone else.* "Each one teach one" has become the very familiar motto of the literacy movement. It not only multiplies those who are able to read, it is in itself a valuable learning procedure. We never really master a subject until we can teach it to someone else. The very act of teaching helps to fix it firmly in our minds. Don't wait until the end. If you can, have the pupil teach someone each lesson as he learns it. Among other things it will vastly improve his own morale.

b. *Primary and "bush" schools.* With today's great increase in education in all fields, the "bush" school no longer has as large a place in the missionary picture as it once did. By "bush" school we mean a very elementary school in a native village conducted by an evangelist-teacher. Many in recent years have been very critical of these "bush" schools because as schools their standard of achievement was very low. The teachers themselves had very little training for their task. Yet in many places, notably in Africa, this was for a long time the only education available for most of the people. Without the "bush" schools, inefficient as they were, the people would have had no education at all. The "bush" schools made a real contribution and the teachers made up in part for their lack of training in the earnest devotion they brought to the task.

"Bush" schools should be considered a temporary expedient when there are multitudes of people to be given the rudiments of education on a Christian basis, and when there is no possibility of getting enough trained teachers for the job. In one way they have an advantage over the present situation in many places—in that the pastor was also the intellectual leader of the community. Today the teacher, supported as he often is by government grants, may earn a much larger salary than the pastor and the pastorate has fallen in the esteem of the people.

The missions provide primary schools in many fields. In some places, as in the Belgian Congo, the government prefers to have the missions do this work and offers its co-operation. In other places the government is more or less neutral.

There are several principles that we do well to bear in mind. First, there is a growing tendency throughout the world to hold that the education of its citizens is the responsibility of the state. This being true, the day will come, even in those areas where the mission schools are now welcomed, when the government will insist on taking over that responsibility. South Africa has already done so. In view of this we should consider the mission schools as a temporary arrangement that will one day have to give way to something more permanent.

Second, even if Christian schools are allowed to continue, and in many cases it may be wise for them to do so, they should ultimately become the responsibility of the church rather than the mission. Again we come back to the essentially temporary character of the mission. It should not plan to be a permanent institution. It is needed for the beginnings, but it should always be planning for its own withdrawal. The sooner the schools can be placed under the church or a church-supported board, the better.

Third, in view of this, the use of missionaries in the schools will change from time to time. Within a comparatively short time there should be no missionaries teaching on the elementary levels. The national teachers will earliest be prepared for this service. For supervisory work the missionary will be needed somewhat longer, though perhaps not nearly so long as we might think. For supervising the work of whole districts the need may be longer.

Fourth, the financing of the schools will always be a problem. There is always the danger that they will consume a disproportionate amount of the funds available for the work. It is right here that many sincere critics of mission schools find the justification for their objections. If the schools are financed entirely by mission funds, we must realize that this places a definite limit on the amount that can be done. Missionary giving will never be adequate to cover a comprehensive school program for a whole field. It will only allow for a small amount of such work. Government subsidies often seem to be the way to overcome this handicap. They don't cover the whole cost but they do make a much more extensive ministry possible. However, there is a subtle danger here. The government is usually more able to supply money for the schools than the mission is to man and operate them. The government urges the mission to extend its work with the promise of new favors, though the mission can hardly do so without subtracting from other important parts of its ministry. Of course if the church itself can come to the place of supporting the school program, it is on a much sounder basis. But this is easier said than done. It is particularly hard to get the people to see the need when they long have been accustomed to having others do such things for them.

Fifth, the schools must justify their existence by their products. This is not to say that the schools have failed if not all of their students become dedicated Christians. We need to know the school's aims before we can judge how well it is reaching those aims. Unfortunately many schools are very foggy about their aims. If you were to ask, "For what are you training these young people?" they would either be puzzled to know what to answer, or they would respond in generalities that leave the answer still vague. If a school says that one of its aims is to inculcate Christian character, and the vast majority of its students never become Christians, it has failed. If it claims as its aim to provide an educated leadership for the church, and very few of its graduates ever enter the service of the church, it has failed. Even if it responds with that irritating generality, "We are preparing them for life," and the only life for which its graduates seem equipped is that of a government clerk, we could hardly call it a success. Schools, like individuals, need goals, and we need constantly to be surveying our progress toward attaining those goals.

Sixth, any training must be related as closely as possible to the life of the people. This seems like an obvious principle, and yet it is often not observed. The missionary in school work sometimes knows all too little about the real life of the people. Yet he thinks he knows a great deal. He is acquainted with some of the superficial aspects but not the basic forces. Even so, the teaching he gives may bear little relation to what he does know of the life of the people. His problem does not involve merely the use of sheep in an arithmetic problem, where the people have never seen a sheep. It is much more basic. The teacher's entire orientation is probably western. If he is teaching history in the Far East, does his teaching have a Western European orientation? To many of us Westerners history begins with Greece and Rome, and we know next to nothing about the other great nations of antiquity. Even in the modern period we are almost as lopsided. It may be well enough for us in American society, but should we teach that way in the Orient?

We are not teaching young people to live in our American society, but to live in their own lands and among their own people. And as a result of our teaching they should be able to find a place in their own society where they can live and serve and show forth the power of Christ to meet the needs that their own people have.

c. *Subsidies and their problems.* We have already mentioned the government's willingness to subsidize schools in certain places. There is quite a difference of opinion among missions and missionaries as to whether it is good policy to accept such subsidies. The principal argument against them is this: If the government pays the bills (except possibly for missionaries' salaries) it has the right to dictate what shall be taught. Whether or not the government at present is availing itself of that right is immaterial. It eventually will do so, and then those who have built up such an extensive work on the basis of government aid will feel obliged to compromise rather than sacrifice their work. Opponents point to the recent situation in Egypt, where mission schools were required to teach Islam to Mohammedan students.

It is useless to point out that if the government wants to dictate what shall be taught in the schools, it can do so even where it doesn't provide subsidies. The fact is that the likelihood is much greater where the government pays the bills. This argument is valid and it needs to be faced.

On the other side a typical argument could be drawn from the Belgian Congo. Here all the missions at present are given full liberty in their teaching of religion, and their schools can qualify for government subsidies if they meet the academic standards. Those who favor the subsidies would argue somewhat as follows: the money comes from taxes, so all the people are entitled to the benefits from its use. It is not a gift from the outside. The schools are conducted practically the same as they would be if completely supported by the mission. But because the government provides the funds, many more students can be given Christian education than would otherwise be possible. Also, because such schools are accredited with the government, their graduates are recognized and can go on to further studies in government institutions. If the day comes when the government imposes conditions that are not acceptable, then the schools can be closed, as the Presbyterians did in Korea under the Japanese.

We have presented these two arguments only briefly. There are also one or two other considerations that we ought to mention. One is the matter of "red tape." Anyone who has ever had dealings with a government knows how much paper work is involved. This is particularly true of schools. It takes a vast amount of time to prepare all the forms and reports that the government insists on having. And of course there are formalities that you have to go through in securing the subsidies.

A second question recently came up in the Congo. The economic recession had forced the government to cut down on some of its subsidies. When you have built up an extensive educational work on the basis of government subsidies, what do you do when those subsidies are suddenly reduced or withdrawn? It is a serious problem.

On the other hand we need to recognize that in order to get government recognition and qualify for subsidies, many mission schools have had to raise their standards. This means that they are doing better work than before. They are also able to pay their teachers more. But then this in itself may hamper the church work, as we have said, since teaching will offer a surer and better income than preaching.

d. *Educational systems and languages used.* Where schools are accredited or subsidized by the government, we need to conform to the educational pattern in vogue in that country. In British colonies, for example, even American missionaries follow the British system. There are a few exceptions, however. There are a few places where American mission schools, using American methods, are so superior to other local schools that they have gained recognition in spite of their partial non-conformity.

In this connection we ought to mention the importance of getting schools of any sort recognized by the government if possible. It is more than a matter of complying with requirements and meeting standards. In some places it is entirely possible for unrecognized schools to carry on their work without official opposition. They may even do it on the highest of standards. But then their graduates find it impossible to enter more advanced schools because their diplomas are not recognized. And those who have received specialized training, as teachers and nurses, may not be able to find employment except in the mission that trained them.

When it comes to the languages used in teaching, the situation varies from country to country. As a general rule the schools use the local language in the lower grades. But in colonial areas, or places where the national language is not the same as the local language, this may not hold good. Sometimes the government insists that all instruction must be given in the official language. At other times it will simply recommend that instruction in the official language should begin quite early. When the people don't already know the official language this complicates the missionary's job. But he has very little choice in the matter.

e. *Industrial and agricultural schools.* Somehow the trade school has never enjoyed the same prestige as schools of a more academic sort. It may be because in some places those who have to work with their hands are looked down on by those who do not need to do physical labor. Or it may be at times that the people are simply mimicking the attitude of the missionaries. Most missionaries get academic training, so they naturally look at it as the highest type of training. Yet in many fields the training of mind *and* hand at the same time is the more profit-able for the people. And it in no way detracts from their spirituality. It is strange how easily we lose sight of the fact that our Lord Himself was a carpenter.

As for agriculture, a large part of the people to whom we go live in an agricultural society. Here the missionary who was born and reared in the city is at a disadvantage. He doesn't have the farmer's point of view. Neither does he understand his problems nor the best ways to counsel him. Yet even our American farm boys do not usually have the same reverence for the soil that we find among some other peoples. We use or abuse the soil without any thought that it is more than an impersonal possession to do with as we will.

Someone has suggested that our relationship to the soil ought to be the same as our relationship to our bodies. Like our bodies, it is important to our earthly existence. Like them, it should be considered the temple of God, which we should respect and care for with all diligence. But some go even farther and say that it is only a possession in trust. It is our responsibility to hand it on to the next generation with its richness unimpaired.

A missionary in Africa writes that mission stations and schools are often great offenders against the soil. "For they frequently obtain new station sites in valuable bush-land and, in their zeal, immediately fell every tree and clear every bit of grass and leave the soil bare and exposed to sun and rain." The same writer adds: "Many people feel that the farmer requires no more knowledge than tradition can provide, no more training than the primitive village offers. That is the error which has put a veil upon the eyes of the farmer and limited his development. There is no occupation under the sun which requires more skill and more learning for its successful performance, than that of being the steward of God's earth." But "the hidden secrets of the earth and the interpretation of the mighty forces with which the farmer deals cannot be fully revealed by those who have no knowledge of the Creator Himself."

One problem that we face in agricultural and industrial training is the fact that so few missionaries are really qualified to give it. It is not like academic training. There we merely transfer the major part of our teaching directly from the homeland. It may not be the best idea, but we do it. And the missionary who is qualified to teach at home finds very few changes to make in the content of his teaching. But the teaching of such things as handicrafts is different. The teacher has to adjust his program to the local situation. He has to find out what materials are available. He has to know the culture of the people.

It is useless to teach men how to build with wood if timber supplies are scarce but stone is abundant. In some places it is the men who need to know how to make clothes, for they are the ones who do it. And while certain principles of agriculture are valid everywhere, different climates, soils, crops, etc., as well as the equipment available, can make a vast difference in methods. So we need teachers who have training in the principles as well as some experience at home, but who also will learn on the field how best to apply those principles in the situation that they face.

Unfortunately, the governments themselves do not always recognize the value of industrial schools. For this reason they hesitate to give them the same support they give other schools. However, in recent years there has been great improvement along this line.

f. *Secondary schools.* Some missions have recognized for a long time the importance of secondary schools in their program. Others more recently have come to that realization. In one of the Latin American countries a national leader spoke to me very earnestly. "We need an evangelical secondary school. It is the greatest need we have today. We are losing our young people. The cry everywhere is for more education. But when our evangelical young people want to go on beyond the primary grades they have to go to schools where their faith is attacked and undermined. Where are we going to get our Christian leaders if we don't do something about it?"

It is true that the educational level is rising in most countries. In some cases the changes are almost spectacular. Even in lands where the secondary school today is still something of a rarity, it will soon be demanded. We face again the same problem of how far we can go in the educational work without getting top-heavy on that side and neglecting our primary task. The answer is not easy. The state-operated secondary school, without religious discrimination, is what we might like to see. We have it in the United States. But it is not common in our mission fields. And even here there are many Christian parents who want and are willing to pay for distinctively Christian high schools. When will the younger churches in the mission fields be able to maintain such schools?

The secondary school, though in some fields it has a number of adults, normally deals with teen-agers. This means that the problems of discipline are much greater than in the primary school. Yet this is also the period of life when a dedicated teacher may have a tremendous influence on the students.

The head of the Student Christian Movement in China once stated that "It is an established fact that 85 per cent of the Christians who are educated were all converted in the middle school." From a survey of Christian students they learned that the most decisive factor in securing decisions for Christ among the students was the Christian character of the teachers. Second came Christian literature, and then preaching.

Decisions affecting the whole course of one's life are commonly made in early adolescence. And youth are more readily attracted to ideals than are their disillusioned elders.

Some have suggested that secondary education on the mission field should be provided only for Christian students or those who are preparing for Christian service. In 1925 the Bible Churchmen's Missionary Society of England adopted this resolution:

> This Society shall under no circumstances provide secular education above the primary stage for non-Christians; but it is willing to offer education to Christian boys and girls as occasion may arise, and in so far as it is able to do so. In all cases the teaching shall be given only by those who have signed the B.C.M.S. basis.

This was clearly an attempt to avoid some of the pitfalls that had entangled some of the older missions in their educational programs.

Of course the secondary school is more expensive than the primary school. It is also more difficult to get qualified teachers for this ministry from among the people. Then there are problems of accreditation, for those who graduate may want to go on to colleges or other schools in their own country or abroad. Yet it is not easy to keep the standards as high as they should be. It may be easier, however, than it is at home, where attendance is compulsory and the pressures on a teacher to pass a poor student are often tremendous.

g. *Colleges and universities.* The next logical step beyond the secondary school is the college. Yet here a variety of new problems present themselves. Here, too, it is much more difficult to justify the costs in money and man power for missions. As an evangelistic medium we know from experience that the college is very seldom effective. Very few of its students who are not Christian when they enter become Christians during their course of study. This has led to the common accusation that the mission colleges are producing mostly educated heathen. On the other hand, the defenders of the colleges say that while they do not produce many converts, they do create a more favorable attitude toward Christianity on the part of the people.

Actually the issue has not been settled in our own country. There are numerous church-related colleges that are partly supported by church funds, as well as some independent Christian colleges that also depend partly on the donations of interested Christians. Most of them are having a hard time in competition with the state schools and some of the heavily endowed private institutions. Fees paid for tuition never cover the full cost. But there are many who believe that a Christian college is an important asset and they are willing to contribute to its support.

Colleges are expensive. Libraries, laboratories, and other equipment necessarily go far beyond what we have in the lower schools. In addition more teachers in proportion to students, and more highly trained teachers, are needed. Of course missionary salaries are usually the same regardless of the work done, but it is only at the beginning that all the teachers are missionaries.

The establishment and operation of a college is usually too large a task for a single mission. It calls for co-operation. The direction of the school may be in the hands of a separate board, but with the missions or churches having the right to select members for the board. The missions may also contribute the services of some missionaries for the staff. This co-operation means a broader basis for the school, both for financing, securing students and giving a better rounded education.

One of the major problems for the college is its staff. Usually a missionary college will start out with a Christian faculty. Inevitably there comes a time when it is difficult to fill a vacancy on the faculty. Neither a Christian national nor a missionary is available. Yet the subject must be taught. As a temporary measure a non-Christian who is willing to teach in a Christian school is hired. However, temporary measures have a way of developing permanence. And then the same situation may be faced in another vacancy and the same expedient is used again. In this way some missionary colleges have come to the place where a majority of the faculty is non-Christian. Then what becomes of its missionary purpose? Of course the situation is not much better when the home board sends out teachers who are academically qualified but lacking in missionary motivation.

To some, the college problem would seem to be best answered by sending the few candidates they have to the homeland for training. It would certainly be less expensive than to operate a college for a handful of students. In fact, the people at home are generally interested enough in the foreign students to provide rather liberally for their education. But this in itself is a problem. We know from experience that some who have enjoyed the "fleshpots" of the United States for a season are quite hesitant about returning to their own land and the more difficult conditions there. Others, although they do return, continue to look to their American friends for their personal support. And they even rebel against the direction of the mission or church, confident that much of that support will continue even if they become independent of any authority. The more co-operative, too, after some years abroad find it very difficult to readjust to life in their own land. Their training as well as their manner of living abroad has not prepared them for work in their own society, since it was geared to the needs of American students. One African leader studying in the United States remarked that for the African, studying in another country is not only a question of taking a particular course but of absorbing an entirely new culture. No student should be sent abroad without taking into consideration these possibilities. For service within their own country, training within the native environment is the ideal, if it can possibly be worked out.

Where secular colleges are available, especially state-supported schools, they often provide a satisfactory solution. The major problem, of course, is the fact that they may attack or undermine the faith of the Christian minority. It is just here that the student Christian organizations show their great value. If the Christian minority has a focal point for fellowship, encouragement and development of the Christian life and witness, it can not only maintain its faith but actually strengthen it. Christianity often thrives under opposition. For this reason in our own land young people with a good Christian background are often encouraged to attend state colleges and universities. They have to face misunderstanding and opposition, especially among their fellow students; but if their faith is real this may serve to strengthen it and also to give them an opportunity for a Christian witness among unbelievers. They will not, however, be getting definitely Christian instruction, and they will need encouragement. On the mission field the sponsoring of a student Christian group is a special phase of missionary work that deserves serious attention.

h. *Teacher training.* The field of missionary education is greatest in the most backward areas. However, even here the missionary teacher should be anticipating the day when his services will no longer be needed. The nationals should be taking over the work, whether under the mission, the church, or ultimately under the state. But this presupposes a body of trained teachers. Who will train them?

There are places where the government conducts teacher-training programs and trained Christian teachers are available for mission schools. However, there are many other places where the missions, if they are to have national teachers, must do the training themselves. In some areas the government is glad to co-operate with them in this task, because it is for the good of the country. In its long-range results this training of teachers is far more important than the conducting of schools. The missionary who trains others to teach is multiplying his ministry. However, not all are qualified to do a good job here.

Perhaps it goes without saying that teacher training schools must be in places where there are schools in which they can get practice. Practice teaching is a very important part of the training.

Another thing that may be too much taken for granted is the spiritual training that should be given. For missionary purposes it is not enough that our teacher training students should be taught to teach. Neither is it enough that we give them special instruction in the Bible and Christian doctrine. We must try to inspire them with the challenge of teaching as a Christian ministry. They must come to see in it an opportunity to serve the Lord as well as their people. We need teachers with a sense of calling. This sort of training can be given in the classroom only insofar as the students see it exemplified in the ones who teach them. The ones who teach in a teacher training school need not only to be qualified pedagogues but also real missionaries.

One of the major problems in many of our mission schools is the teaching staff. It is not enough that our teachers should be professing Christians. As one missionary educator has written, "Better no religious instruction at all in a school than to have it given in a formal and life-less manner by teachers who do not attempt to practice even the little they teach." Our mission schools are sometimes plagued by teachers to whom teaching is only a good way to earn a living.

i. *Medical training.* It is always a marvel to me that the chronically overburdened missionary doctor or nurse finds time to train others. Perhaps it is because he is so desperate for help and knows that he will never get enough for his needs from the homeland. At any rate this matter of training others is an important part of the work of the medical missionary.

How it is done differs from place to place. There are some things that can be quickly and easily taught so as to relieve the doctor from some routine jobs. However, he soon finds out that he needs to keep checking to make sure that the job is done right. Relatively untrained people seldom realize how important details can be. They think the foreigner is simply "finicky." If they can get away with it they will let some things slide.

Where there is a hospital, formal instruction is frequently given by the doctor or nurses. The plan is similar to that for training nurses at home, instruction coupled with a great deal of practical experience. Full medical training, at least for doctors, is seldom provided by the mission, except where joint colleges are set up, as at Vellore or Ludhiana, in India.

There is some medical training that is very elementary and yet very important. This involves classes held in hygiene, child care, community health, etc. Even in areas where other medical services of a missionary sort are not welcomed, these classes are usually accepted.

CHAPTER TWENTY-TWO

HEALING

The Place of Healing in Christian Missions

DOES HEALING HAVE ANY PROPER PLACE in missionary service? If so, what is that place? Is it only auxiliary to the main task? Those who are engaged in it don't think so. Their opinion was well expressed in a report they presented to the great Edinburgh Conference of 1910: "That medical missions should be recognized as an integral and essential part of the missionary work of the Christian Church."

1. *The place given by Christ and His apostles.* The healings that Christ performed play a very important part in the gospel narratives. Preaching and healing went hand in hand. Furthermore, when Christ sent out the Twelve, "He sent them to preach the kingdom of God, and to heal the sick" (Luke 9:2). Later, when He sent out the Seventy He commanded them, "Heal the sick . . . and say unto them, The kingdom of God is come nigh unto you" (Luke 10:9).

When we come to the accounts of the Great Commission, it is true that four out of the five make no mention of healing. And in the only one that does, the account in Mark, it is given a secondary place. But the apostles didn't understand this to mean that they should omit healing. As a matter of fact they continued a ministry of healing after Christ's ascension. And Paul goes so far as to list gifts of healing as provided by the Holy Spirit for the ministry of the *Church*. The method of healing they used is not important. The fact that they took healing to be a part of their Christian labors is important.

2. *Two mistaken ideas.* There are two false ideas about missionary medical work that are sometimes held by one or another group in the

285

Christian church. They are seldom held by the medical workers themselves.

a. *That the ministry of healing is only bait to attract men to the
gospel.* Quite often their opponents accuse the missionaries of holding
such an idea. They heal only because it is an effective way to win converts. Sometimes even the supporters of missions give expression to the
same idea. Medicine is only a means to an end.

Now we are not going to argue the ethics of using healing in such a
way. All we need to say is that the Scriptures give us no basis for such a
view. Christ Himself did not use His healings as bait. It is true that
they attracted people. But there is an important difference. He did not
lure people to accept the gospel simply by healing them. In fact He
seems to have been careful to avoid using His healings that way. If His
experience with the ten lepers was typical, much of His healing didn't
even earn Him a word of thanks. Yet He healed those who came, without any discrimination.

Notice the difference between using healing as bait and taking advantage of its drawing power to evangelize those who come. Dr. Paul
Roberts of Ecuador refers to this drawing power when he writes of
"Medicine, the Magnet." He means that the prospect of healing will
draw the people from many a corner where the missionary would never
reach. They will come in greater variety and larger numbers than he
could ever seek out individually. What else could make a witch doctor
forget his enmity and come to the missionary with his sick wife whom
his own remedies had failed to help?

But though the prospect of healing draws people, the medical worker
does not use it as a means to secure their conversion. It simply gives
him an opportunity to present the gospel to multitudes who otherwise
might not hear it. They are still free to accept it or reject it. Again referring to the example of Christ, we read that the chief reason the
multitudes followed Him was the healings He performed. (See John
6:2.) He knew this, and He took advantage of the opportunities it
gave Him to teach them. But He never used it as a lever to make them
become His disciples.

There is also a difference between using healing as a bait and using
it to break down suspicion and prejudice. This has been one of its great
values in the difficult Moslem fields. No amount of talking, no intense

sincerity of purpose, no exemplary manner of living can succeed in removing the suspicion with which many of these people view the missionary. But in a time of physical distress some of them in desperation will go to the Christian medical missionary. The unselfish, friendly care that they receive helps to break down suspicion and makes them more willing to listen to the message.

b. *That the healing ministry should have nothing to do with religion.* There are those that say it is wrong to take advantage of a man's illness to preach the gospel to him. Some of those who argue this way would like to have the medical services of missions, but they don't want the gospel. We can understand their point of view. But unfortunately it is also the view of some who, as Christians, would presumably be in favor of the gospel. Perhaps the real basis for their view is that their Christianity is not vitally important to them. It is not a life-and-death affair. The whole matter is like a game. You have to be on one side or the other. You naturally want your side to win, but you must be careful not to take unfair advantage of the other side. It isn't sporting. Such people would also object to presenting the gospel to those who have been recently bereaved. You must not sow the seed while the ground is broken up.

This view also is far from scriptural. Again we say that in the ministry of Christ, healing and the presentation of the gospel went hand in hand. The same was true with His apostles. The people often are inclined to identify illness with sin, with an offense against the gods. According to Christ this may at times be true, as it apparently was in the case of the palsied man. But at other times it is far from true, as in the case of the man born blind. Yet Christ presented healing for the body and healing for the spirit together, with no more obligation to accept the one than the other.

3. *The proper place.* What place should healing have in missions? To answer, let us get back to the fundamentals. What is the great aim of missions? What do we expect to accomplish through them? When we have answered this question, then we are in a position to say what place healing should have in the program.

The primary aim of missions should be evangelistic. It involves winning people to a new life in Jesus Christ, followed by the establishing of the church as a community of the redeemed. To this one great aim

every activity of missions should point. From it they get their significance. Healing, then, must contribute to this evangelistic aim.

But healing is more than just a means to that greatest of all aims.
It is that, of course. But it is also an expression of the life that we have
in Christ. It is a demonstration of Christian concern for man, that he
may be made whole in every way. Just as Christ Himself had com-
passion on the sick, so do we. As He healed without discrimination, so
do we. But as He constantly associated His spiritual ministry with His
healing and emphasized the superiority of the spirit over the flesh, so
also do we.

We do not heal simply to win converts. Neither do we heal simply
to be healing. We heal because as Christians we cannot be indifferent
to human distress when we have the means of relieving it. But also
as Christians, and especially as Christian missionaries, we take advantage of the opportunity we have in healing to present the Great
Physician of the soul. Often this may be our only opportunity of presenting Christ to the one who comes.

Our medical missionary work can only justify itself in the measure
in which it reaches its objective. If, as Dr. Thomas Cochrane observed
some thirty years ago, it "is becoming more merely medical and less
missionary," it has lost its aim. It may be making a valuable medical
contribution to world health. But there is no evidence that a healthy
world is any more inclined toward God and righteous living than one
where physical disease is common. When medical missions lose their
aim, they forfeit their place in the missionary enterprise.

In the early days of Christian missions, and in some places today,
the missionaries offered the only reliable means of healing from disease.
To the amazement of the people, they offered their help gladly to all
who came, not expecting any reward. Most non-Christian religions
have never been concerned about the welfare of mankind except in
those few cases where they have learned it from Christianity. In Islam
illness is only a part of the all-embracing will of God, which we cannot
resist. In Hinduism it is the result of offenses committed in a previous
incarnation. Besides, each one is concerned for himself alone, and for
his family. Only Christians seemed to care about others.

But today a different factor has entered the situation. Governments
have become concerned about the health of their people. They have

built hospitals and set up dispensaries. They have allocated large sums
to combat the most prevalent diseases. They set up free clinics and
dispense free medicines, milk, and other helps. They have vastly greater resources for such a ministry than have the missions. It is very
unequal competition. But should it be competition at all? Should missions try to compete with government agencies for patients? In such a
competitive atmosphere can they effectively carry out their primary
purpose?

There are still many places where the missionary hospital has a place
of most effective ministry, especially in the more primitive and remote
areas. There are places where it is welcomed, or at least accepted, because the government is unable to provide for the needs. But as governments increase their own facilities, more and more restrictions are
placed on the missionaries. They must use only local doctors, sometimes without the power to choose which ones. And finally there comes
a time when they are forbidden to evangelize in the hospital. So they
become just another hospital. They differ only in two ways from the
others. The government does not have to pay for their operation; missionary funds take care of that; and a different spirit seems to pervade
the place. Yet they are not allowed to explain the source of that spirit.

When a hospital has reached this last stage, is there any longer a
reason to consider it a missionary work? It may well be a work of
benevolence, but is it missionary? It is a gesture of friendship and
good will, but what does it have to do with missions? Perhaps it should
be kept in operation, but should it consume the funds that are given
for Christian missionary work and the dedicated personnel that aspires
to make Christ known among the heathen?

We need to face this problem honestly. We need to re-evaluate our
medical work from time to time to see if it is really accomplishing its
purpose. We carry it on at a high cost, both in man power and money.
Do the results justify the expenditure? If so, let us give the work our
wholehearted support. If not, let us see if it can be improved. We are
God's stewards. Let us give good account of our stewardship.

We have treated this ministry of healing as if it were the concern
of the foreign missionary alone. This is far from true. At the beginning
it may be so, for the missionary may be the only one qualified to carry
it on. But it should not continue that way indefinitely. As with the

work of evangelization, the missionary may be the initiator, but he should always be aiming for the day when another will take his place. The mission society may inaugurate the work or build the hospital, but always with the view that some day the national church will take over. Even medical work should not be kept in the hands of the foreigners any longer than is absolutely necessary.

For this reason it is unwise to build elaborate plants furnished with all the most modern equipment, even if it were possible. (Usually it isn't.) For this reason also the medical work must be made to pay part of its own way. No hospital is ever fully self-supporting. But we do wrong to put the work on a basis that makes it impossible for the growing church ever to think of taking it over. We have the choice: either to provide simple medical care for a great many, on a basis that makes it possible one day for national Christians to take it over; or to provide top facilities and treatment for a much smaller number, with the knowledge that when the funds fail or the missionary must withdraw, the work will cease or else the government will take it over.

This is no excuse for careless, inefficient work. Neither is it an excuse for following antiquated procedures or failing to make use of the best of the modern drugs. Missionary medical workers should give the best that is in them and inspire the nationals to do likewise. This sort of dedication has put some of them in the forefront of their profession. But at the same time it is amazing to see with what primitive equipment they have had to do their work. They are great improvisers, and they have taught others how to do a great deal with only a little.

Dr. J. P. Crozier of India tells this story:

> In one of our mountain villages I had been preaching well into the night to a group of lovable Maratha farmers. At the close, as I pleaded with them to give their hearts to Christ, I noticed an old man listening intently. As I prepared to leave he came forward and, commenting on the slides of the life of our Lord which he had just been shown, he said, "I know Him. I have seen Him. And He was just as you described Him, full of love for us, helping us. Yes, I have seen Him. He operated on me at the mission hospital at Wai." The doctor to whom he referred was Dr. Lester H. Beals of the American Board.

We must mention one other place that healing has in missions. This is the caring for those who are already Christians. While medical help is increasing in many lands, it is still far from enough for all the needs. In many places the people will get no help at all if there is no missionary to give it. But even beyond this, when an evangelical Christian is ill in some countries he faces a difficult problem. There may be a hospital available, but he knows he would not be welcome in it. Or if he were received, he would be neglected or even mistreated. At the best he would be subjected to constant pressure to change his faith in return for favorable treatment. It has happened over and over. Until national Christian doctors are raised up, or until treatment is sincerely offered without discrimination, the missionary doctor will be needed.

THOSE WHO HAVE A PART IN THE MEDICAL WORK

There was a time when nearly every missionary expected to do something along the line of healing. His medical knowledge might be scanty, but he used what he had to provide some relief for the people among whom he labored. In a few places such work is still going on. But increasingly medical work is being restricted to those who have special preparation for it. In some cases those who have had a limited amount of special instruction may conduct dispensaries, as at present in Nigeria. But in others the medical workers must be fully qualified doctors or nurses.

In some countries they must also meet special requirements for licensing by the government. In British areas in East Africa, for example, it is permissible for nurses to conduct dispensaries. But they must be properly enrolled in the government program either in nursing or midwifery. In addition the mission doctor must make a monthly visit to each dispensary. But in a number of fields it is impossible, or next to impossible, for foreign doctors to practice, or else the local medical profession may be reasonably adequate. If you are thinking of a medical ministry, be sure you know the conditions in the area you have in mind.

SPECIAL RISKS IN MEDICAL WORK

1. *Risk of the death of a patient.* No doctor can save all of his patients. He knows that some will die under his care. He can't avoid it. But his great concern is that it should never be through any fault of

his. We understand this in our own country and would seldom blame the doctor in case of the death of a loved one. Our doctors, through many years of devoted service, have built up a reservoir of good will on the part of the general public. We have learned to trust them.

The situation is different in some mission fields. There the mission doctor is not only a foreigner. He may also be something new and unfamiliar to the people. They are not acquainted with doctors of his sort. So he faces the long and tedious process of winning their confidence. A few remarkable cures at the beginning will help to build up his reputation. But let him be blamed for a single death, and he is in serious trouble. The least he can expect is that the people will shun him. But sometimes there are reprisals of a more serious sort.

It is not long since Dr. Scheel of Ethiopia had to defend himself against a lawsuit growing out of the death of a patient. The family wanted indemnity. Dr. Hume, who established the Yale-in-China Hospital, learned at the beginning that it would not be wise to accept a patient who might die. The death of a patient in the hospital might lead to its being boycotted. Its ministry would end before it had a chance to build up confidence. In another hospital at Lanchow, China, a man who appeared to be a Tibetan brought his dying son to be operated on. Only after he died did they discover that the man was really Chinese and they should have taken greater precautions in getting permission to operate. The relatives stirred up a serious case.

This must be one of the calculated risks in a work of healing in missions. And along with it must go a realization that often, even when you are successful, there may be little gratitude expressed.

2. *Risk of going beyond ability.* There are times when every doctor has to take a chance. But usually the extent of his training and experience will keep him from making any glaring errors. It is the untrained or partially trained worker who needs to be warned of the danger of going beyond his knowledge and ability in the treatment of illness. There may come a time, as with the doctor, when he will have to take a calculated risk and do something to try to save a life. But overcaution is usually wiser than overboldness. Much depends on the personality of the missionary. Some are by nature very cautious, while others are too much given to taking chances.

3. *Risk of spiritual sterility.* The pressure of medical work in most

fields is very great. Often the medical worker finds himself pushed into it before he has a good chance to get to know the people or their language. And if he lets it, the medical work can occupy all his time and strength to the exclusion, not only of any spiritual ministry, but also of the upkeep of his own spiritual life. It is easy to see this danger, and most missionary doctors are aware of it. It is not so easy to avoid it.

Perhaps most of all this problem calls for a clear view of the spiritual objectives of our medical ministry. It is not enough to be a doctor— a good doctor. It is not enough to be a Christian doctor. If our medical work is to justify itself as a part of Christian missions, it must make its contribution to the basic missionary purpose. It must have a spiritual direction. It cannot be entirely occupied with the physical. If it is a ministry of missions it must in some way be tied in with the ministry of the church. Yet we know that there are times when the medical work has no relation to the church. Even more, it may actually hinder the church's development.[1]

In a way, the whole problem is a matter of priority. In this it is like many other missionary ministries. There is more to be done than you can possibly do. Some things will have to be postponed or remain undone. Which will they be? From his medical training the doctor has gained a sense of his obligation to do all that he can to relieve human suffering. But as a Christian he has assented to the primacy of the things of the Spirit. In case of a conflict, which will win out? With Jesus Himself the Spirit took precedence, though His power to heal was infinite. Many missionary doctors have followed in His steps. But it isn't easy. The conflict causes a testing of the reality of their dedication.

OTHER DIFFICULTIES

1. *Language.* We have already mentioned that often doctors are put to work before they have had a chance to learn the language of the people. Usually this is not by their own choice. It is the doctors themselves who have complained about it. Of course we can sympathize with the mission's viewpoint. It is in desperate need of the doc-

[1] See Dr. F. Lake, "The Realignment of Medical Missions," *International Review of Missions*, April, 1949.

tor's services. There is much that he can do even without the language.
So why delay the beginning of his ministry?

But this is a place where often "haste makes waste." The doctor may
not need to know the language as well as the evangelistic missionary.
And there may be some ailments that he can diagnose without talking
with the patient. But if he has to question the patient through an interpreter, who himself may not understand the doctor's questions, he
works under a serious handicap. He needs to be given an opportunity
to study the language *before* he begins his medical ministry. Usually
it should be in a place different from the one where he is to work.
That is the only way he can be reasonably sure of having time to study.

2. *The people.* Closely associated with the need to learn the language is the need to know the people. One missionary doctor speaks
of it as "learning the native point of view." Many of the people in
mission lands are not familiar with our western medicine. They are
willing to try it—up to a point. If it conflicts with some of their cher-
ished ideas they will reject it or misapply it. Dr. Hume tells of the
first Chinese official who came to him as a patient. In only a short time
the man walked out in a huff. The doctor had taken his pulse in one
wrist but not the other. Everyone knows you can't tell what is wrong
unless you take the pulse in both wrists at six different points. The
doctor wasn't thorough.

And the doctor needs to realize that in many places you can't give
a patient a bottle of medicine and expect him to take it according to
directions. If a teaspoonful each hour will finally make you well, why
not hurry up the process and take it all in one dose? This is also one
of the trials the nurse faces. How can she get patients to do what she
says? How can she get them to understand the importance of cleanliness? How can she keep them from mixing up the doctor's remedy
with the cures offered by friends and neighbors? It all takes a knowledge of the people as well as a knowledge of medicine.

Perhaps one of the most exasperating things is the nonco-operation
of the people in answering questions. The doctor is supposed to tell
them what is wrong with them. That is what he is for. Why should
they have to tell *him?*

3. *Lack of equipment.* Modern medical practice calls for more and
more in the way of expensive equipment. In the United States much

of this equipment is centered in the hospitals or medical laboratories, to which the doctor can take or refer his patient. Only such centers can afford to purchase some of this equipment. Even so, and in spite of the high fees they charge, our hospitals still have to cover a part of their costs by public subscription.

On the mission field the mission hospitals are usually very small affairs trying to meet an overwhelming need. The fees they charge are based more on the ability of the people to pay than on the real costs of their care. Consequently the mission hospital is likely to carry on its work with inadequate or homemade equipment. The missionary doctor becomes a master of improvisation. Dr. Seagrave of Burma wrote a well-known book on his "waste-basket surgery," surgery performed with discarded instruments from an American hospital. Many other missionary doctors have had similar experiences. They learn to make the most of a little, realizing that mission boards just don't have the money it takes to provide enough topnotch equipment.

4. *Need to be a builder and handyman.* Occasionally a mission may have a full-time builder on its staff. There are also places where they can secure reliable contractors to erect the buildings they need for the medical work. But there are all too many times when the doctor, if he is to have such structures, must be both architect and builder. This means he needs to know something about costs and materials, be able to keep accounts and also to supervise the workmen. In some places he will install an electric generating plant and see that it is kept in working order. At the same time he will be continuing his medical work.

5. *Relation to other local doctors.* Native medical practice in some areas is exceedingly primitive. Much of it is based on superstition. So it may be possible for the missionary doctor there to ignore its practitioners or even to oppose them. However, it is a mistake to assume that all native medicine is a fraud and that there is nothing we can learn from it. Even in primitive areas the natives may have useful knowledge of local plants. And there are more advanced areas where local medical practice, though different from our own, may have a number of things to teach us. There is missionary medical work going on, too, in areas where there are other doctors practicing. Here the problem of professional relationships calls for real tact. The typical American

attitude of looking down our noses at other people is definitely out of place.

6. *Nurses taking the place of doctors.* There are numerous places where the only medical worker is a nurse. Obviously she will have to assume more responsibility in the treatment of illness than is generally considered proper in the United States. The same principle applies here as in the case of others who take the risk of going beyond their training and knowledge. Level-headed judgment and a proper attitude of caution will avoid any serious difficulties when it is necessary to overstep the usual bounds.

In many places nurses carry on dispensary work when there is no resident doctor. In Kenya, for example, the only requirements made by the government are that each dispensary be visited by the mission doctor at least once a month, and that the nurses in charge must be properly enrolled in the British nursing system, either in nursing or midwifery.

TYPES OF WORK USUALLY CARRIED ON

1. *Dispensaries.* We mention this first because it is the most elementary and the most widespread. There are still some places where nonmedical missionaries are allowed to dispense medicines and treat minor ailments. Doctors also do some of this work, especially when they are making a tour of their district. But more and more it is being handled by nurses under the general supervision of the doctor. In tropical Africa a high proportion of mission stations have dispensaries. In India, where the major problem of rural health continues, mobile clinics have proved very useful.

2. *Hospitals.* It is generally recognized that when a mission secures the services of a qualified missionary doctor, it should be ready to provide him with a hospital. Only so can he fully carry out his ministry. The doctor who has no facilities for surgery, for example, not only is greatly limited but may tend to lose some of his skill in that line of work.

Mission hospitals are often quite crude, as compared with the mammoth institutions in this country. Buildings may be of one story, constructed of such materials as are available locally. Beds for inpatients are always a problem and sometimes are only the cheapest of cots.

Often the hospital must have its own electric generating plant to provide light for the operating room, power for the X-ray machine if there is one, etc. Often, too, it must make its own provision for a safe and adequate water supply. There is no drug supply house near at hand, so provision has to be made for the safe storage of fairly large quantities of medical supplies. In some places provision has to be made even for the family of the sick man, who may accompany him and need a place to sleep, cook meals, etc. It may be necessary also to provide living quarters for the native nurses or medical assistants and their families.

One mission in China stated it as its policy to have hospitals of about sixty-bed capacity, as well staffed and well equipped as possible, with laboratory, X rays and nursing school. It is strongly recommended that there should be at least two doctors to a hospital, plus a hospital administrator to look after the nonprofessional end to co-ordinate the medical and evangelistic work. This is in addition to the nurses needed, both missionary and national. However, in practice a single doctor has often had to carry on with a limited nursing staff.

While the doctor or nurse does have opportunity to speak a word in season, and his testimony has special force, it is generally considered best to have a worker specially designated for the spiritual ministry in the hospital. The medical personnel may have an active part in the program, but should not be burdened with the whole program in all its details.

The program, of course, needs to be carefully planned and consistently carried out. A hospital in Egypt has a daily Bible lesson given in rooms and wards. The sequence of lessons covers the whole plan of salvation in fifteen days. (This is the average stay of a patient.) Four fifteen-day periods are planned, using different Bible readings each time. So the one who has an unusually long stay of two months in the hospital will have heard the gospel plan four times, but with different Scriptures. Another hospital in Congo has a unique set of symbols put on the patient's card that indicate at a glance his spiritual status. This is of help to the worker who comes to talk with him. And there are many other plans. Of course in no case is any undue pressure brought to bear on the patient to become a Christian.

3. *Leprosaria.* Much of the progress in the study and treatment of

Hansen's disease, or leprosy, has come from the work of missionaries. For many years the Mission to Lepers, in England, and American Leprosy Missions, in the United States, have solicited support for this work and in other ways have helped to meet the need. In recent years governments also have been more actively concerned.

A great deal of progress has been made, and it is now possible to discharge many patients each year as "symptom-free." This means that the disease has been arrested and that they can return to society without fear of infecting someone else. In active cases, however, it is still the general practice to isolate the sufferer from others in leper colonies, or leprosaria. This is in spite of the fact that in some areas of high incidence there is a trend toward treating the patients in their own villages or having them make periodic visits to the leprosy centers for treatment.

Many of the leprosaria are conducted by the missions, with aid from the government. In others, the missions are given the opportunity of carrying on a spiritual work among the people. One of the great problems with leprosy sufferers is to maintain their morale, when they must be separated from the rest of society. It is here that the non-medical missionary often finds a place of service. Not only can he minister spiritually, but he can set the patients to work at tasks that they can do to keep them from feeling utterly helpless and hopeless.

One of the other problems of the leprosarium is what to do with the untainted children of leprous parents. They usually must be kept separate from the parents so as not to subject them to contamination. But this means a children's home, conducted very much as if it were an orphanage.

4. *Dental work.* For some reason, there are very few dentists in full-time missionary service. Comparatively few doctors and nurses have had special training in this line. Yet missionaries as well as nationals need dental attention at times. So sometimes the medical workers turn their hands to simple extractions. But dentures or more serious cases are generally either passed by or referred to the larger centers where competent help is available.

5. *Preventive measures.* What often troubles the missionary is that so many illnesses are unnecessary. They could have been prevented. Some are the result of ignorance. Some come from the unsanitary con-

ditions in which people live. Some are closely related to the poverty of the people. Whatever the source, he knows that he can do greater good by helping them to avoid the illness than by trying to cure it after it is well established.

So today preventive medicine is getting increasing attention on the mission field as well as at home. And together with it goes a concern for community health. Many of the problems of sanitation, a pure water supply, etc., are broader than the interests of the individual. Yet the individuals must see their necessity.

The types of preventive work that are possible depend largely on the co-operation of the people and their government. This is one area in which the government becomes rather closely involved. Missionary efforts commonly involve classes in hygiene and prenatal clinics. Nurses as well as doctors may conduct these. Added to this there is the missionary's constant insistence on cleanliness. He can teach more by example than in any other way if he is careful to show how it is possible for the people themselves to do the same things. Otherwise they are likely to think that only a person with the missionary's wealth has the means to keep well.

CHAPTER TWENTY-THREE

LITERATURE

THE GREAT VALUE OF LITERARY WORK

WHEN WE THINK OF MISSIONARY WORK we are most likely to think of the oral preaching of the gospel. The spoken word is indeed basic in the evangelizing of other people. Unquestionably, too, more missionaries will use this means than any other for making known the good news.

But as we mentioned in discussing evangelism, the spoken word does have its limitations. It is a highly perishable commodity. If it is not appropriated at the moment it is spoken it must be repeated or it is gone forever. And so from very ancient times men have sought the means of giving greater permanence to their words. Sometimes they have put them in poetic form or set them to music so that others could more easily memorize them and repeat them to others. This did have its value. In fact it is still more valuable than we today are ready to recognize. We find it difficult to understand how some people, depending entirely on oral tradition, have been able to hand down with remarkable accuracy from generation to generation such things as tribal history, and genealogy.

But the most valuable means of giving permanence to a message is writing. Writing fixes the message in a reasonably permanent form. In addition it makes it possible for the message to go where the living messenger cannot. Anyone who learns the method of writing and knows the language cannot only read the message but he can read it repeatedly. He can study it carefully; he can compare it with messages from others; he can, if he wants, copy it and hand it on to others.

300

Many different means of writing have been invented. One is the pictograph, a crude pictorial representation of objects and actions. But pictures take a long time to draw. So there is always the tendency to simplify them, to fix a certain pattern of lines that others will recognize as the representation of the idea, even though they are not true pictures. The "stick figures" so commonly used in chalk illustrations show the beginnings of this tendency. When it is more fully developed it becomes a complex system something like the characters used in Chinese writing. These characters, as you know, represent ideas rather than sounds. This is why there are so many thousands of them.

It was a tremendous advance when alphabetic writing was invented. The alphabet deals not with ideas but with sounds. It ties writing in with the spoken language. There are uncounted thousands of ideas. But we manage to express them in speech with a limited number of sounds and sound combinations. In English, for example, we get along with less than forty meaningfully different sounds. Those few sounds, arranged in an infinite variety of patterns, are adequate to express all of our ideas. New words, new phrases, new patterns are constantly appearing, but they all make use of the same set of sounds. Even the foreign words that we adopt are modified so that they can be pronounced with this same set of sounds.

The idea of the alphabet is to have one symbol—one letter—represent a single meaningful sound or group of sounds. Then a person who learns that basic group of letters will be able to record visibly everything that he can express orally. Not only so, but he will also be able to read orally whatever anyone else has written in the same system. He can even read the words without understanding the ideas they represent, for he is dealing only with sounds.

I suppose someone will object that we don't have anywhere near forty letters in our English alphabet. This is perfectly true. It is also true that you can't always tell how an English word is pronounced by seeing how it is spelled. This presents a terrific hurdle to those of other lands who try to learn English. It also explains why so many of our own citizens are such poor spellers. Through the centuries English has made a number of changes in its spoken form. But while these changes were going on, the written form remained largely static. In speech the "gh" in such words as "thought" is no longer pronounced. Yet we continue to write it as in the days when it was pronounced. So English has departed from the alphabetic ideal.

But in spite of imperfections, the alphabet has made it possible for men to dream of world literacy. Nearly everyone can learn an alphabet with its comparatively few letters. It isn't the intellectual feat that it would be to learn thousands, or even hundreds, of characters. The type of alphabet is almost immaterial. Many languages use the Latin alphabet, with some modifications. But the Russian alphabet is no more difficult to learn. Nor is any other alphabet that may be used. With a good alphabet anyone who already speaks a language can soon learn to read it. And from reading, it is only a step further to writing.

And world literacy is on the way. There was a time when only a few were pushing the subject. For years there was a modest but unspectacular gain in literacy rates, especially in lands where missionaries were serving. But in the past twenty or twenty-five years the gain has been tremendous. Part of this has been due to new methods of teaching literacy, such as that developed by a missionary, Dr. Frank Laubach. But even more decisive has been the attitude of the governments. They have found that an illiterate country is a weak country. In addition they have found out that a governing minority needs some large-scale means of swaying the thinking of the people if they are to continue in power. And literacy followed up by an ample supply of suitable literature provides that means. New millions have learned to read in the past few years. A new avenue has been opened to their minds, to a large extent because their governments have wanted to reach them and so have pushed their literacy. Even older adults have been obliged to learn to read.

This highlights the importance of a literature ministry in missions today. Important as it was in the beginning, and men like Carey recognized that importance, its importance is multiplied today. Where once it had to be used mainly with the literati, the cultured class, it now has a vast ministry even among the lowest classes. Where once you could communicate the gospel to most people only in an oral way, today the highway of print is available. The oral message has not been superseded. Instead it has been supplemented. But it is a supplement with such vast potential that it can be compared to the use of air power in modern warfare. It may not do the job alone, but it is invaluable in opening the way and in supporting the foot soldier.

Perhaps we ought to mention right here five distinctive values in a literary work. Potentially your audience has no limit, except the number who speak and read the language. No other means of communicating the message can compare with it in scope. We have to presume, of course, that you will find a way to circulate the literature and that people will want to read it.

People can read the message over and over until it is assimilated. The printed message is not imperishable but it is very durable. Even on cheap paper it will stand a number of readings. And even though one copy is silenced, there are many more that can take its place. It is the most inexpensive of missionaries, and it always says the same thing. It never tires of repeating its message.

The printed word can penetrate where the living messenger cannot. In older days it was an easier job to keep Tyndale out of England than it was to keep out the printed Bible. Today authoritarian governments like those of Spain and Russia may have some success against clandestine printing presses inside the country. But they never are able completely to shut off the flow of literature that is smuggled into the country from the outside.

Through literature the reader can have more than one teacher. Each author is a different teacher. Each one views the truth from a slightly different angle. And when we put these different perspectives together they add depth to the picture. The one who learns from a single teacher will usually adopt the bias of that teacher. The one who learns from a variety of teachers is more likely to come to his own conclusions.

Literature lays the foundation for a stable church. It does not of itself guarantee that the church will continue to exist. Recently a missionary visited an Indian tribe in Central America who once had the Gospel of John in their language. Yet today there is not a single believer among them.[1] But literature does make it more likely that the church will continue. And even more important, it opens the way for Christians to secure spiritual nourishment that they need for growth, even in the absence of a missionary, pastor, evangelist or Bible teacher.

[1] William H. Walker, in *The Central American Bulletin*, Dec. 1958.

HIGH REQUIREMENTS

A literature ministry is exceedingly valuable. In missions it is one of the greatest challenges that face us today. But we must not conclude that it is a ministry for everyone. Far from it. It is a specialized field in which only a small proportion of missionaries qualify for full-time service. Yet it is also a ministry that touches nearly every other phase of missionary work. So every missionary has a stake in the literature work and can contribute something to it.

In dealing here with the requirements, however, we are thinking of the one who is in charge of such work, or the one who gives the major part of his time to the creative end of it. We are not dealing with the printer or with the distributor, important as their work is. We are concerned rather with the one who decides what should be produced and how, the one who plans the program as well as the one who writes the manuscript, who does the translation or the editing.

In the first place he faces the knowledge that if he does a poor job it may bring reproach on the gospel. You see, when the living missionary speaks to the people, he himself is the embodiment of his message. Whatever his personality, he makes use of it in trying to get a favorable response. In literature, however, the living messenger is absent. The same message may be there, but it is not clothed in human form. The impression it makes depends first on the outward appearance—its format—and then on the message itself and the way it is presented. Its form is fixed. It cannot be changed to fit the circumstances. And the reader will usually associate the content with the form. If the literature is shoddily prepared, the message it contains cannot be of any great consequence. If it is well prepared, there must be some value in it. If the language is stilted and foreign-sounding and the mistakes of grammar and spelling are numerous, who will waste his time on it? Such a handicap is hard to overcome, even for the most vital message.

A ministry in missionary literature demands someone who knows what it is to express himself clearly and accurately. It may not call for finesse, but it does call for readability. And this is not something that we can develop in another language if we have not been able to develop it in our own. Clear expression calls for clear thinking. And

---

the one who has learned to think clearly and express himself clearly in his own language will carry that trait over into any other language that he learns. Even if his job is only to edit the writing of others, he will try his best to make it readable. It is amazing how obscure some otherwise able people can be in their writing.

A third requirement is a sufficient mastery of the native tongue to write correctly, clearly, and accurately. This is one reason why few first-term missionaries can be used in a literary ministry. They need time and experience to master the language. This applies even in editorial work. It is just as important for the editor as for the writer to know what is good writing. It is true that in some places where there is very little literature the inferior compositions of missionaries may find some acceptance. But with the rapid increase of literacy and the production of literature in so many languages, only the better works will receive attention.

Then it is also necessary to know native patterns of thought as well as the language. The two are quite closely related. What subjects should be dealt with in our Christian publications? How should they be presented so as to interest people and move them to action? All our writing presumes some background knowledge on the part of the reader. What knowledge do they have? Unless we know these things, no matter how diligently we work, we are going to clutter our stockrooms with works that cannot be sold, works that are incapable of promoting our cause.

Almost inevitably the missionary will turn to translation as the means of solving some of his problems. There is a wealth of valuable material in English. Why not simply translate this material, making adaptations wherever it is necessary? In many cases we can do this, at least as a temporary measure. It is one way of producing a quantity of literature before there are writers capable of doing the needed creative writing. But we need to remind ourselves that good translation is in some ways more demanding than original writing. Besides knowing the language from which he is translating and the language into which he is translating, the translator must also be familiar with the subject matter and be able to interpret the author's meaning. Take, for example, the question, "What are you going to do?" Is it a true question, or is it an expression of frustration? To translate it you will have to know what the author meant.

A final requirement has to do with hymns and other poetry. Their original writing called for some understanding of poetical principles in that language. If they are to be translated, the translator must also know something about poetry of the language into which he is translating. And if he is dealing with hymns, he must also have musical knowledge.

WORK AMONG NONLITERATES

The vast majority of the world's inhabitants use languages that have a written form. Only a small percentage do not. Yet even though the percentage is small, there are still some millions of these nonliterate people, using many hundreds of different languages. What should we do for them?

1. *Providing a written language.* The obvious answer seems to be that their languages should be reduced to writing. Then we can give them the Scriptures in their own tongue. But the obvious answer is not always the wise answer. Writing has the effect of perpetuating a tongue. And not all languages should be thus perpetuated. When should a written language be provided?

The answer to this question is still a matter of argument among missionary leaders. But it seems to me that we can state the matter fairly in the form of five "ifs." We would do well to provide a written language—

If no other language that has a written form is generally understood. Spanish, for example, is the official language of Bolivia, but a large part of the people understand it imperfectly if at all. The missionaries are right in wanting the Quichua in written form.

If it seems unlikely that another language will soon supplant the one in question. An argument published against the work of the Wycliffe Bible Translators in Mexico was that they were perpetuating languages that for the unity of the country ought to be allowed to disappear. When, however, after four hundred years of Spanish dominance some of these languages show very little sign of disappearing, the argument loses much of its force.

If there are enough speakers of the language to warrant the vast amount of work required. Reducing a language to writing is not the work of a year or two. We would not presume to question the call of the man who believes he should spend his life among half a hundred Indians. But we would question the judgment that would lead him to spend his time in reducing their language to writing and trying to produce a literature in it. They are too few for that job.

If the people who speak the language are not tending toward extinction or absorption into other groups. John Eliot of course could not know that one day his translation of the Scriptures would have no one to read it. But in view of the many small tribes that have disappeared in the past few years, we are foolish to disregard this factor. Several years ago a missionary to Brazil told me of a tribe he had contacted when he first went to the field. It numbered about fifty. Before he left, after one term of service, he had seen the last man of that tribe die.

If there is no serious government opposition. There are some governments that encourage linguistic work among their peoples. There are others that are definitely opposed. Often their idea is that they want to unify the people by obliging them all to use a single language—the official language. This is true, for example, in Ethiopia. Of course the missionary in such a situation has very little choice. The government's policy may be open to question, but he is not in a position to have it changed.

This matter of reducing a language to writing always brings up the question of trade languages. What part do they play in the work?

Here we need to distinguish between two types of trade languages. A trade language in general is a language that is used by people of two or more different tongues so that they can deal with each other, especially in matters of trade and political relations. Sometimes it is the actual language of a dominant group, such as the French in Vietnam or the English in Nigeria. At other times it is an artificial language made up of elements from more than one language, such as Swahili in East Africa or Pidjin in the South Pacific. Sometimes Pidjin is called "Pidjin English" because the words it uses are largely drawn from English, but the structure is quite different.

The missionary soon finds that there are several advantages in using a trade language in his work. First of all, such languages are usually widely understood. Swahili, for example, can be understood by people of a great many tribes in East Africa. That means you can reach a multitude of people through the medium of one language.

In the second place, if the people of a large area ever do get together on a common tongue or official language, the likelihood is that it will be one of these trade languages. In Kenya, for example, the language may be English or Swahili, but it is not likely to be Kikuyu, Kikamba, Masai or the language of any other one tribe. Many Filipinos would like to have Tagalog as the official language of the country, but up to the present the trade language, English, has all the advantage.

Finally, when the missionary adopts and uses these languages for his literary efforts, it helps to unify the people and to create a better understanding between them. A common language is always a bond of unity.

However, there are also some weaknesses in the use of trade languages for missionary work. This is why the subject often arouses warm debate among missionaries.

The greatest weakness is that, while the message may be understood in a trade language, it always has a foreign sound to the one being evangelized until it comes in the language that he considers his own. Many Nigerians understand English for practical purposes; but the gospel message in English doesn't mean nearly so much to them as it would if it came in Yoruba, Efik or Hausa. To get closest to a man's heart, you must speak to him in his native tongue.

A second weakness is that trade languages of the second type are often weak in vocabulary that doesn't have to do with commerce and government. They were not developed as vehicles for religious truth. Of course in time they can develop such a vocabulary and some have done so.

A third weakness is that there are always large segments of the population who do not learn the trade language. Yet they do deserve to hear the gospel. If they are to be reached it will probably have to be in their own vernacular.

Some would point to another supposed weakness. They contend that the second type of trade language is really a hybrid, a sort of improvisation to meet a need, but not a respectable language. A somewhat similar argument was once brought against English and French and

Italian. Actually these trade languages do develop a regular grammatical system and, with usage, come to be as rich as any other language.

Reducing languages to writing is a very specialized missionary activity. For this reason those who engage in it should get special linguistic training. Such training will enable them to work much more quickly and with greater accuracy. Even so, we should not despise the accomplishments of those missionaries who, without the benefit of special training, have shown an amazing aptitude in this sort of work.

At the risk of being somewhat less than scientifically accurate, we want to give here some idea of the studies that are involved in language reduction. First is the matter of phonetics and phonemics. Both of these have to do with the sounds of a language. Phonetics is a study and description of the sounds used in speaking the language. Since we are eager not only to recognize but to reproduce the sounds, we describe them in terms of the organs we use to produce them (vocal cords, tongue, lips, etc.) and the manner of their production. There are many hundreds of possible sounds that are distinguishable from one another. English uses only a fraction of these sounds, so we must learn to recognize others when they appear. No other language will use precisely the same sounds that we have in English.

But while any one language may use scores of different sounds, the differences between them are not always meaningful. In English there is a difference between the "l" sound in "lay" and the "l" sound in "play," but we are not conscious of it. The difference is not meaningful. No matter which sound we use for either word, the sense is the same. On the other hand we are very careful to distinguish between the vowel sounds in "bed" and "bad," though they are very close together and other people find it hard to hear the difference. The reason is that to us even that slight change in sound means a change of meaning, while in other languages it doesn't. The study that tries to find out what differences of sound are meaningful and what ones are only meaningless variations, we call phonemics. Phonemics is the basis of the alphabet that we adopt. There is no use having two letters for the "l" sounds if the difference between them doesn't mean anything.

In developing an alphabet the following things can well be kept in mind: (1) the letters of the alphabet should equal and not exceed the phonemes; (2) it is standard procedure to use Latin letters as far as possible, so as to facilitate transfer from one language to another; (3) where there are others dealing with the same language, it is advisable to consult and co-operate; (4) you may have to conform to the orthography of the official language in some countries (for example, using the "qu" for the "k" sound in a Spanish-speaking country); and (5) before going too far with the work, consult the Bible societies so as to have the value of their wide experience. Remember that they do most of the Bible publishing and they have definite standards for the translations they will accept.

The words of a language, its lexicon, also engage our attention. Without going into detail, there are just three practical suggestions we want to make. (1) Get the meanings as accurately and as fully as you can, *including the connotations.* For example, in English we seldom use the word "propaganda" any more about publicity that we approve. It is almost always associated with things that we condemn. (2) Many words have widely different meanings according to their usage, so get both the word and the context, or setting. This is one reason why good linguists like to get extended stories, or texts, from the people instead of just individual words. (3) If you find two words that appear to mean the same thing, make sure that they are always synonymous. Barbrooke Grubb, in his work among the Paraguay Indians, found several words that seemed to mean "to bring." For some time he used the simplest and most common of these words for the bringing of all sorts of things, including horses and people. Then he found out that the word really means "to carry here in the hands."

To many Americans the very name of grammar is anathema. Yet every language has its grammar. Grammar is simply the pattern of the language. It describes how the words of a language are used. Grammar rules are not inventions of the grammarians. Instead they are descriptions of the way in which acceptable speakers of the language actually use it.

We must understand that each language has its own distinctive grammar. So we must not think that the principles of English grammar will have their counterparts in other languages. It just isn't so. Some European languages do have similarities to English in their structure, but other languages are built on entirely different principles. Only careful and extended observation can discover how people actually use their language.

When we analyze a language we discover that the smallest meaningful unit is not the word. It is what we call the "morpheme." Sometimes a word is composed of a single morpheme, as our English word "can." But many times it has several morphemes, as the word "unanimously," which has four: un/anim/ous/ly, literally "one/spirit/of/manner," or "in the manner of one who has one spirit." The study of these basic units and how they are used we call "morphology."

But we also study the larger units of meaning: the words, their relationship to each other and the way they are grouped into complete expressions or sentences. This is the study of syntax.

If all languages were completely orderly and logical we should not have to go further. But we find that not all the things we observe in a language can be reduced to fixed rules or scientific description. Grammar represents the science, the laws of the language; diction is the art. A statement that conforms entirely to grammatical principles may still be poor diction, since "we don't say it that way." Take, for example, the statement that came in a letter from Spain: "What a great many of American papers are to be had here everywhere." The expression is understandable but seems awkward to us.

Furthermore, in any language there are combinations of words that have meanings different from what you would get from a strictly grammatical interpretation. These irregularities we call idioms. When we say, "His house and all his possessions went up in smoke," we mean that these things were destroyed by fire. "Went up in smoke" is an American idiom. To understand a language you must also understand these idioms.

2. *Providing literature.* Reducing a language to written form is not an end in itself. It is like opening a path. The path is only useful if it leads you somewhere that you want to go. And then there must be enough traffic to keep it open. Otherwise it will soon be overgrown and lost to sight. In the same way, the reduction of a language to writing has only an academic interest if it does not result in literature and in literacy on the part of the people. Some languages have been put in written form, but no one learned to read them. There was no large-scale effort to teach the people to read, and there was next to nothing

for them to read if they did learn. So the writing of their language had little if any effect on them. The path that was opened with a great deal of labor was soon forgotten.

a. *Bible translation.* When a missionary opens the path of literacy, it is for the purpose of giving people access to the Word of God. Protestants have always laid great stress on the Bible. They hold it to be the norm of faith and practice. So Protestant missionaries are far in the lead in promoting translations of the Bible and the literacy that makes it possible for people to use them. The total number of translations of the Bible, in whole or in part, long ago passed the thousand mark. Yet there is still a great deal to do.

A word of warning is in order for the new missionary who may be tempted to think that Bible translation is an easy task. It isn't. It is a tremendous job that can well occupy the major part of a lifetime. In fact, it is usually done best by a committee of experts, people who are thoroughly familiar with the language and also with the Scriptures. It is the most exacting kind of translation because of the extreme importance of the message. Even minor details are important in such a task.

In such a book as this we cannot hope to give adequate instruction for such a specialized task.[2] All we can do is point out several features that deserve attention. Then those who may find it wise to begin the task without special preparation will at least have a few landmarks to go by.

(1) *Parts to be translated first.* You will find a wide difference of opinion among missionary linguists in this matter. Partly this arises because of differences in people and in circumstances. Generally, however, they will choose some part of the New Testament, because its message is basic for Christians. Of the Gospels, Mark is chosen more than others because it is short, clear and incisive. John, on the other hand, is often avoided at the beginning. Its highly figurative language makes it more difficult to translate well, and many people find it hard to understand without interpretation.

It is not necessary, however, to take a whole book at a time. The missionary may want to give as much of the basic gospel message as he can in the shortest possible space and time, and with the greatest clearness. Then he will confine his translation to a few well-chosen selections.

[2]An excellent comprehensive treatment of the subject is the book by Eugene A. Nida, *Bible Translating,* American Bible Society, 1947.

Selected Portions from the Word of God, published by the Bible House
of Los Angeles in various languages, shows what can be done in this
line. The whole plan of redemption is presented in quotations from
Scripture within a reasonably condensed space.

Of a somewhat different nature is Dr. Laubach's simplified version of
the New Testament. This is an attempt to simplify the language of
Scripture for the benefit of illiterate or semiliterate people around the
world. Long sentences are broken up into short sentences. Common
words or phrases are used to replace words of low frequency. In a few
cases transition phrases or sentences are introduced to help the reader
follow the thought. Technically this is an adaptation of the Bible rather
than a translation. Yet it comes closer to the Scripture than the usual
Bible storybook and is intended for adults. Its usefulness is based on
the idea that many people, even if they learn to read, will find the language of the Bible difficult to understand at first. They need this transi-
tional stage.

(2) *Versions to be used.* There is no question that the best
work requires translation from the original languages. Translating
from a translation always multiplies the possibility of errors or misunderstanding. But there are not many missionaries who have the needed
familiarity with the original languages. Very few have had more than
two or three years' study of Greek, and even less of Hebrew. Many
have not had this much.

Even so, there is no reason why a fairly good translation may not be
made from the English version. That is, you can do it with care. The
American Standard Version of 1901 probably represents the closest ap-
proximation in English to the original. Using it as a basis, but consulting other versions and even commentaries to get a clearer and broader
understanding of the text, you can produce an acceptable translation.
That is, you can if you know the language into which you are translating well enough.

(3) *Procedure.* The missionary seldom knows the language
as well as he thinks he does. So he is very likely to follow some unsound
procedures in his translation work. Some years ago I knew a missionary to Africa who had begun to translate the Bible during his first term
of service. Furlough interrupted the work, but he brought it home with
him. Then during furlough, far from anyone who used the language,

he continued his translation, to the admiration of many of his Christian friends. Both he and they presumed that he knew the language well enough to do the job without help. But it wasn't so.

The only sound procedure is to work on the translation with the help of reliable native speakers of the language. Even so, you cannot always be sure. Your helper may agree with you too readily. Or he may not understand what it is you want. Or he may not know the answer but will tell you something anyway, just so he won't appear ignorant. So you need constantly to check the translation with others so as to make sure they get the right understanding from it. The Bible Society is glad to help you in this matter of procedures by sending you its guide for translators and also by consulting with you on the problems you face.

(4) *Problems.* Problems in translation are legion. For example, what word are you going to use for God? The words that the people use are all based on their own ideas. They may have no concept of a God such as we worship. And if they don't have the concept they won't have a word for it. You will either have to find a roughly similar term and infuse it with new meaning, or you will have to introduce a new name to identify the new God whom you preach.

And how will you express spiritual truths like grace, love, mercy, etc., where these concepts are not found in native society? Men have words only for those things that they experience or think about. New ideas, new inventions, new experiences, all call for new ways of expression, or else a change in the meaning of old terms. In English, during the Second World War, we adopted the word "blitz" from the German "blitzkrieg" to mean a sudden attack without warning. It is now a new word in our language, used both as a verb and a noun. On the other hand, when the Spanish-speaking people in South America wanted a word for a different kind of hammock, made not of woven cloth but of a sort of network of cords, they simply took the word for a certain kind of fishing net, *chinchorro,* and gave it this new meaning.

Then, too, how are you going to deal with a passage such as that on the Good Shepherd in an area like the islands of the South Pacific? The people there have never seen a sheep. Should you use "leopard" for "wolf" in Central Africa? And how will you interpret a hundred other customs that were common in ancient Palestine but are unheard-of

among your people? These and many other problems face the missionary translator of the Bible. But he persists in the work, knowing that it
is fundamental to the establishment and growth of the church.

b. *Hymn writing.* Even before you translate the Bible, you may
find it wise to prepare some hymns for the people to sing. Christianity
is a singing religion. Singing is often one of the best ways of fixing the
teachings of the faith in the minds of the people.

But there are not many missionaries who combine in themselves the
talents of both poet and musician. Often they don't have much talent
for either. But they know the importance of gospel music. So they
do what they can.

This means the writing of some sort of hymn or gospel song, or else
the translation of one from the English. Very rarely is a new tune composed for the verse. Usually the missionary adopts one that is already
known in English. He is likely to do it in one of two ways. Either he
decides to translate an English hymn and use it with the same music, or
else he prepares his verse first and then looks for a tune that will fit
the meter. Many hymn books have a metrical index that helps to find
music with the appropriate meter.

Translation of hymns is a difficult task. It is even more difficult, and
sometimes almost impossible, if you try to fit the translation to the
same music. Can you express the same thought in another language
with words that have the same number of syllables? Can you make the
accents come in the same places? Remember that some languages, like
French, tend to stress the last syllable of a word. Others, like Spanish,
stress most of their words on next to the last syllable. Some, like English, have a great many words of one syllable. Others have mostly words
of several syllables. Add to these problems the fact that some languages
are tonal. That is, the same word means different things each time you
change the tone.

A hymn should be singable, but it should also make good sense. A
few years ago a missionary wanted to get some of his translations of
hymns and choruses published. The editor criticized a few of the translations as ungrammatical and lacking in meaning. The missionary, de-
fending one of the songs, said, "Why, our people have been singing
that song for a long time! They love to sing it! It is one of their favor-
ites!" The editor was unimpressed. He knew that people will often

sing nonsense if it has a catchy tune. But it doesn't have any real value to them. It is much more important to make sense than it is to make rhymes.

Hymns are used for adoration and praise, but they are also used for testimonies and to teach doctrine. In any of these cases the principles are much the same. They must bear the marks of good sense, sincerity and simplicity. And then the people must find them singable. If they meet these tests they don't have to be great poetry or great music to accomplish the missionary's purpose. Eventually national poets and musicians will do the better job.

c. *Periodical literature.* For the newly literate it is wise to provide periodicals of a simple sort from the very beginning. The reason is that they need stimulation to continue the use of their new skill. They need something not too long, that is adapted to their abilities, and that has enough current interest so that people will want to know what it says. Such a periodical may be little more than a single mimeographed sheet, but it has an important ministry. Like hymn writing, it is something that should not wait for the translation of the whole Bible.

d. *Devotional, inspirational and other works.* Just how much literature we should provide for new literates depends on several factors. There are the immediate practical questions, such as the personnel and time available and the money on hand to do the work. Then there is the long-range question of just how extensive the literature should be in a language that comparatively few people use. It is likely that the practical considerations will be the most decisive.

3. *Literacy campaigns.* Readers without literature and literature without readers are equally undesirable. We need the literacy campaign both for newly literate peoples and for the many illiterates in countries that already have a written language. (See pp. 267-272.)

WORK AMONG THOSE WHO HAVE A LITERATURE

While a great deal of missionary work is carried on among pre-literate peoples, or those who are just entering into literacy, it is probable that most missionaries are dealing with people who have had a written language for many years. They do have a literature, even though little of it may be Christian, and though only part of the population are able to read it.

1. *Where the literary language differs from the spoken.* It is probably true that in most languages literary style differs from the spoken style. But in English and some other languages the difference is almost altogether a matter of style. It doesn't have much to do with understanding. In some languages, though, the literary or classical form differs widely from the colloquial. It is almost as if they were two separate languages. The man in the street would have just as much difficulty understanding the literary language as the ordinary American would have in reading Chaucer.

There are a number of languages like this, including Chinese and Arabic. And in most such cases only a small proportion of the people are literate, though there is often a great veneration for the written word.

a. *How much should we do in this language?* This is a moot point. There are some who insist that the gospel gains in prestige by being presented in the most elegant literary style. However, there are others who remind us that the New Testament itself was not written in the literary Greek but in the Greek of everyday conversation. Do we want the recognition of the scholars, or do we prefer to reach the understanding of the man in the street? If it is the message itself that has greatest importance, then we ought to concentrate on the language that most people understand. However, in many cases we may want to be able to use the literary language so as to reach those who would not otherwise pay attention to our message. And we know that sometimes the people themselves have a prejudice against seeing their spoken language in print. They don't think that it is respectable enough for that.

b. *Should we teach the people the literary language?* This is a tremendous task for the missionary, even where he knows the language well enough to teach it. It is almost the same, in some cases, as teaching a new language. And we know that the number who will be able to read the literature we produce in this language will always be small. The trend today, spurred on by the desire for universal literacy, is all in the other direction.

2. *Where the spoken and written languages are practically the same.*

a. *Become familiar with both forms.* Here the missionary has some pretty clear responsibilities. First, you should familiarize yourself with the language in its written form as well as its spoken form. You will probably do this. In fact some missionaries complain that in language school too much attention is paid to reading the language and not enough to speaking it. But even where the conversational approach is used, it is not likely that reading will be omitted. This may be the most difficult part of the course in nonalphabetic languages.

b. *Learn about important literature.* But you should not content yourself with a limited ability to read some things in the language. If it has a literature, you ought to get acquainted with some of the best-known works. They not only help you to know the language better, they also help you to know the people.

c. *Discover what Christian works are available.* Find out also what Christian literature is already available. There is no use in your duplicating what someone else has already done. Yet missionaries sometimes do this. Usually it is because they don't check first. Or it may be that the one who did the work first did not publicize it so that others would know. In some fields inter-mission organizations are performing a real service by publishing lists of what is available and keeping in touch with new projects. For it has happened that three missionaries were engaged in the translation of the same book, each one unaware of what the other was doing.

d. *Push distribution of available works.* Then, knowing what is available and usable, push its distribution. Some of us seem to think that books will sell themselves. We presume that if people really want them they will seek out the place where they are sold and buy them. This is only true to a very limited extent. You may feel that you don't want to commercialize your missionary calling. But if you have to exert yourself to get a hearing for your spoken word, you are going to have to work just as hard to get people to take the written word. And you will probably find that selling a book to a man is in the long run more profitable than preaching a sermon to him.

There are some who feel that the bottleneck in the missionary literature enterprise today is the lack of distribution. If so, it is because so few missionaries have concerned themselves with distribution. We are not thinking of those few who give their full time to such a work. We are thinking rather of the many missionaries who in their public meetings and private conversations have the chance to promote the

circulation of literature if they will. The main problem is to get them
to see the importance of such an effort for their own work.

(1) *Colportage.* Colportage, or the distribution of literature
by selling it from house to house, is perhaps the most valuable way of
distributing Christian literature. It reaches the people where they are.
It does not wait for them to come into a bookstore or mission station.
It also gives an opportunity to talk with people about the message the
literature contains. So it is in itself an evangelistic medium.

But don't expect colportage to be economically profitable. It isn't.
It usually has to be subsidized in one way or another. The greatest expense is the colporteur himself. So if he is in a position to donate his
time as a missionary service, that may take care of the matter. But for
full-time colportage the mission may have to underwrite the salaries
of the colporteurs and their expenses. Or else they may offer books to
a colporteur at a price below cost and allow him to keep the difference
between that and the sales price.

Colportage is a work that can be carried out either by a missionary
or by a national with a modest amount of training. In some cases it
may be advisable for two or more to go together. They are a help and
stimulus to one another.

Transporting and caring for sizable quantities of literature, which is
always heavy, does present problems. Still, at least one mission in India
has succeeded in fitting up bicycles for colportage purposes. And a number of missions have transformed trucks into "bookmobiles." These
have the advantage that they cannot only transport books but can be
turned into traveling bookstores. By connecting up a public address
system they can advertise their presence and their wares. They can even
be used to conduct open air services.

Three practical hints for missionary colporteurs may be of help.
First, it is a good idea to interest people in a book before you offer it for
sale. This means that you yourself have to know what is in it. Some
have found that by reading a carefully chosen portion or two they can
arouse interest. Then, although it is all right to give away tracts freely,
books should always be sold or traded. The question is not whether
you can afford to give them away. Perhaps in some cases you can. But
people are not likely to esteem very highly a book that costs them nothing. If they pay for it they are always more likely to read it and to

preserve it. Finally, make every sale for cash instead of credit and avoid any later unpleasantness. Of course when we say cash we don't rule out the possibility that you may at times want to accept goods or services in place of cash.

(2) *Bookstores.* Setting up and operating a bookstore is too complex a matter to deal with in detail here. Its ministry, however, can be exceedingly important. There are a few principles that we ought to mention.

The objective, of course, is to get good Christian literature into the hands of the people. This may have an evangelistic aim. People will often buy a book and read it who would not enter a gospel service. Or it may aim chiefly at supplying the growing church. It will take a good-sized church to support such a store. Or else the store will have to serve a fairly large region. Perhaps most stores combine both aims. Some may add to the store a reading room.

Ideally the operation of such a store should be a full-time job. Nor should anyone think that this is not "real missionary work." It may lack in romance, but it is far from lacking in effectiveness as a missionary tool. Yet actually many missionary bookstores have only the part-time services of a missionary. In some cases he may employ a national as a clerk. But he only gives this work a part of his own attention. And in many cases the missionary does not have a formal bookstore. Instead he has a stock of books in his own home that he sells as he has time and opportunity. This is only a stop-gap measure, but a very useful one where there is no store.

Whether as a missionary you think of running a bookstore or only selling books as a sideline, you need to take a hard look at the financial end of the matter. Here is where many make their most serious errors. The missionary who sells a few books from his home as a service to the people has the fewest problems. The supply house may not give him much of a discount, if any. But if he can sell the books for what they cost him, he may come out all right. His operation is small, and he can absorb most of the expense personally. His own salary is cared for, his rent is paid, and while he may have quite a bit of capital tied up in stock, the other expenses are likely to be low enough so that he can care for them personally. This amounts to a personal subsidy of the work. Some missionaries can afford it. Others can't.

But these tiny personal enterprises will never meet the need. And few individual missionaries would be able to finance a real bookstore. With capable management, after the first several years, it may possibly be able to pay its own way. Especially if it has a missionary in charge, whose salary comes from outside. But for those first years it will have to be subsidized. And we should always have in mind the importance of training nationals to take it over. So putting it on a pay-as-you-go basis as soon as possible is sound policy.

Here are a few of the expenses and problems you will face. There are some fairly heavy initial expenditures, including such things as stock and store fixtures. The stock problem is a big one. If you don't have enough you will discourage customers. But if you have too much it ties up your capital, takes up valuable space and deteriorates. At the beginning it is safest to go slowly until you learn what will sell well. One trouble in foreign fields is that you are a long way from your source of supply. Items ordered today may not reach you for some months.

Then there are the fixed overhead expenses: salaries, rent, light, upkeep, license fees, etc. These expenses go on month by month, without regard to the quantity of your sales. Suppose your overhead runs to $300 per month and your margin on sales averages about 30 per cent. That average sounds good, doesn't it? But just do a quick calculation. In order to break even you are going to have to sell at least $1,000 worth of books every month. That means at full price and for cash. Everyone who gives any credit at all will have some accounts that he can't collect. To make good for every dollar that is uncollectable he will have to sell more than $3.33 extra. And to balance a 10 per cent discount you would have to show a 50 per cent increase in your volume of sales.

We have presented these simplified facts only to impress you with the need of making careful plans and operating on sound business principles. Unless you have had experience yourself, get the best counsel you can. And then follow it! Otherwise your much-needed bookstore will be another missionary casualty.[3]

(3) *Libraries and reading rooms.* Many a missionary has made a practice of lending books to nationals. Even though some of these

[3]Missionaries considering opening bookstores will do well to get in touch with Evangelical Literature Overseas, Wheaton, Illinois, for advice.

books never get back to their owner, he feels that it is a good investment. When a person asks to borrow a book he is likely to read it. It
is a comparatively inexpensive way of giving out the message. Of course
it involves some labor to keep track of the books that are loaned. So
some missionaries set up a simplified library system. However, if
there is a church and the church is willing to take the responsibility, this
is a better plan. Whether the missionary lends or donates the books or
the church buys them, they are for the good of the church. So the
church can well appoint a librarian to take charge of them.

As we have mentioned previously, the possibilities of good reading
rooms have not been exploited in many fields. Perhaps the major difficulties in the way are the finding of a suitable place and getting someone to man it. Ideally it should be a part of the library.

In some fields there are already secular libraries in existence. Some
of them have welcomed gifts of Christian books for their shelves. Such
gifts may be a wise investment. Often these Christian books are the
most used ones in the library.

e. *Prepare new material.* Here we run into two critical problems.
The first is the matter of translation. How much use should we make
of translations from English? And how should translating be done?
The second has to do with missionary writing. Is the missionary ever
qualified to write acceptable works in the language of another people?
What else can we do?

(1) *Translation.* There is little question that missionaries depend too much on translations from English. But it isn't altogether
their own choice. Many of them do fail to realize the inherent weakness
in translations. They don't understand that a book written for Americans may not fit the people of Japan, for example, even though it is put
into their language. Imagine the confusion of a Japanese on reading
that one woman was giving a shower to another before her wedding!
Did she need to have her friends bathe her?

But even though he realizes these and other difficulties, the missionary
still feels the need to use translations. There are probably three main
reasons for it. First, he is a busy man. If it depends on him, he doesn't
see how he can take the time to write an original work. Translation
looks easier. Second, he isn't a writer anyway. He has had no experience in writing books in his own language. How can he do it in an-

other? It is better, he reasons, to translate a book that he knows is well written. Third, some books, such as reference works, he doesn't have enough knowledge to write. They took a lot of research in English. Why not make use of the results rather than try to duplicate all that labor?

These arguments are perfectly valid. They do justify *some* use of translations. But we carry them too far. *Good* translations take time and work. In all our haste we try to "get by" with many that are done very poorly. And while most of us are not experienced writers, there is no reason why we shouldn't attempt more than we do. Our greatest need in most mission fields is for simple, readable books. Polished style is not important. Clearness and simplicity are. And while it is perfectly true that reference books often ought to be translated, why should we depend on translations for our devotional books, Bible storybooks and the like? There may be some of them that are so excellent that they can stand the loss that always comes with translation. But most of them are less effective than a more mediocre work written originally in the language.

Still, as we have said, there will continue to be a need for translation, even after the nationals themselves are able to produce useful works. So for the day when you will try your hand at the job, let us state a few principles and make several suggestions.

(a) *Principles.* Any language is a set of arbitrary symbols that we use to express or convey thoughts and emotions. The symbols in a spoken language are the sounds or combinations of sounds that we make with our vocal apparatus. In a written language we ordinarily take those same sounds and represent them on paper with a system of marks that we call letters.

Most of us are likely to think that differences of language are simply differences of words and differences of letters for writing those words. These differences do exist, but they are the easiest differences to overcome. There are two others that are more basic and more difficult. They are differences of ideas and differences in the way of expressing an idea. For example, workers among the Lisu of southwest China found that they had a word for "curse" but not for "bless." Evidently the idea was foreign to them. But even if the idea were a familiar one, as the idea of disappointment, they wouldn't say as we do in English, "His countenance fell."

What we do in translation is try to take the ideas expressed in the symbols of one language and re-express them in symbols that a person of another language will understand. If we could do a perfect job, he would not only get the same thoughts but also all the implications of the original and it would produce in him the same emotions. But this never happens. There are several reasons why it doesn't. Not only are the ideas different in the two languages; even words that are close to one another in meaning seldom correspond entirely. Words represent areas of meaning, not just points. The English word *go* and the Spanish *ir* are roughly equivalent. But for *go up* you use *subir,* for *go down, bajar, go in* is *entrar* and *go out* is *salir,* and if you are talking about a motor going the word is *andar.* On the other hand this last word *andar* not only means in English *go* but *walk, run* (as a clock), *behave, get along,* and even *ride* (in an automobile).

Add to this the fact that words and phrases always gather connotations from their use by one people that the equivalent word does not have among another. The word *propaganda* in English, for example, has come to have a bad connotation that it did not have originally and that it still does not have in Spanish. So we can say that at the very best, our translations are only approximations.

There are four marks of a good translation: (1) It is true to the sense of the original; (2) it is readily understandable; (3) its grammar and diction are true to the language into which it is made, not awkward or "foreign"; and (4) its effect on the reader is similar to that of the original.

There are also four qualifications for a good translator: (1) He must be a master of the language from which he is translating; (2) he must be a master of the language into which he is translating; (3) he must be familiar with the subject treated in the work; and (4) he must himself be a capable writer.

Many people overlook this last qualification. Yet it is very important. Here is what one Spanish writer says on the subject:

It is not sufficient and neither is it necessary for one to be a Castillian to write our language well, whether originally or translating into it the writings of others; but, having that language as his own, he needs also to possess the abilities and talents of a writer. That is the only prime requisite for making good translations: that the one who does it should be a writer.[4]

(b) *Practice.* Suppose you have definitely decided to undertake a work of translation. What procedure should you follow? Experienced translators will agree that the following seven steps are all important.

1. *Acquaint yourself with the work to be translated.* Is it really just what you want? Even though the main message is what you want, are there illustrations and other references in it that your people wouldn't understand? How much would you have to omit or change? Would it be better to adapt it rather than translate it outright?

2. *Decide how literal you should make the translation, whether you ought to make some change in the style, or whether some other modification is needed.* Free translation is best for stories, where details are unimportant. Stories ought to be given in a smooth, idiomatic style. But in dealing with a theological study you have to be careful with the details. For example, one translator of a survey of doctrine used the word meaning "pardon" to translate "acquittal." This was a serious error, since pardon implies guilt while acquittal is a declaration of innocence.

Changes in the style of writing should be made with caution. Some years ago a certain missionary got the idea that good Spanish style called for long, ponderous sentences. At the time he was engaged in translating a book whose American author tended to use brief, pithy, direct sentences. The translator tried to do what he could under the circumstances. He ran two or three sentences together with a liberal use of conjunctions. But he succeeded only in muddling the translation. Some of the sentences were not related to one another. He was mistaken in his ideas of what constituted good Spanish style.

The most acceptable change in style is usually that which makes the writing simpler, easier to understand. In most of our mission fields we are dealing with people who do not find it easy to read or study. We want to make it as easy as possible for them to read and understand what we have to present.

3. *Have at hand as many helps as possible.* This means espe-

[4]Francisco Ayala, in *El escritor en la sociedad de masas*, p. 145. Mexico, Obregon (1956).

cially dictionaries and grammars, but also other helps according to the nature of what you are translating.

4. *Pray, and then begin.*

5. *As you go along, take time occasionally to read over to yourself or to someone else what you have translated.* Do it entirely apart from the original version, so you can check the translation for smoothness, sense, idiom, etc.

6. *When you have finished, go through the work as a whole for any necessary revisions.* This is especially important for finding inconsistencies. One translator actually used a different name for a main character in his book in the second part of his translation.

7. *Always check your work with others, preferably native speakers of the language.* You may have to encourage them to be critical. Often they are too polite to mention the errors that they see. At other times they may not know just how to explain what is wrong. But if they do make any adverse comments, don't disregard them. They may be wrong. It sometimes happens. But if you decide to reject a criticism that they make, be sure that you have a good substantial reason for it.

The process we have outlined is practically the same whether the translation is done by the missionary or by a national. Some think that only nationals should do the translating. But this is not always true. The one advantage that the national has is his intimate knowledge of his own language and people. But just how extensive is that knowledge? How many Americans can do a good job of translation into English? As Ayala remarks[5], the fact that we know the language of everyday experience doesn't confer on us the ability to go beyond those limits to the expression of realities, ideas or feelings that are not common to that experience. In other words, if the national is to be a better translator than the missionary, he must equal him in the other three qualifications of the translator. That is, he must have a mastery of the language from which he is translating, he must know the subject which is being treated in the book, and he must be a qualified writer.

There is a story that Dr. Malcolm, of Natal University College, and a native Zulu were both asked to translate a government notice. When the translations were compared, some educated Zulus said it was obvious that one of the translations had been made by a Zulu. But the one they

[5]*Ibid.*

selected was actually the one made by Dr. Malcolm. While such instances may not be common, I have personally seen enough poor translations made by nationals to be wary of them. Don't take it for granted that any national can do a better job than any missionary.

(2) *Original writing.* Original compositions avoid some of the problems that are common to translations. For example, you don't face the problem of understanding precisely what the author meant to say. You are the author. If any statement doesn't seem to be clear, you can change it to suit yourself. You don't have to worry about misinterpreting the author's meaning.

Also in an original composition you are not likely to use many words taken from the dictionary about whose exact meaning you may have some doubt. You use your own vocabulary, not that of another. Also you are likely to use your own style of writing. You don't have to try to follow a style that is too complex or flowery or ponderous for your own abilities.

As a result, original writings are almost always clearer, smoother and more idiomatic than translations. Added to this, they are also written for the particular people among whom they are to be distributed. A translation takes a work that was prepared for one people and tries to fit it to another. In that sense it is like a secondhand suit. You can take it in here and let it out there, but it will never be a perfect fit. An original writing is tailor-made.

Of course original writing calls for creativity. For this reason it often takes more time than translation. And it calls for a certain measure of ability. The translator, as we have said, has just as great need to have the skills of a writer as a creative writer in order to do a good job. But he does not have to do creative thinking. He merely follows the thoughts of others. But even one who is not specially gifted in this matter of creativity can take the thoughts of others, modify them, rearrange them and re-express them in his own words. Every writer depends to some extent on the thoughts of others. None of us is entirely original. The adapter simply depends to a larger degree than others on the work of a single author.

(3) *Types of literature needed.* The Bible of course is foundational. For believers it should also be accompanied by the hymn book. Among literate peoples, however, propaganda literature such as tracts

may well precede even these important works. Devotional works and commentaries, Sunday School literature, and other types will follow. Their order of production will depend on the local needs and on the interests and abilities of those who do the writing. The following are suggestive, not exhaustive:

(a) *Hymnal.* All hymn books are collations. Be careful not to include hymns whose message is inaccurate or is devoid of meaning. Many assume the hymn book to be on a par with the Bible in doctrinal truth. The message is essential; the music and poetic form are auxiliary. Don't let attractive melodies govern your choice. Presuming that you have enough songs for a choice, include various types on a variety of subjects. Pay attention to the ones the people themselves love to sing.

(b) *Propaganda literature.* The word "propaganda" is used here in its good sense. This is literature to interest unbelievers and is usually distributed free.

i. Tracts.—The most common type. They are best prepared specially for the field where they are to be used, and they may be also printed there. Tracts should carry an address to which the reader may go for further information. The address may be printed in the tract or added with a rubber stamp. Translated tracts are usually inferior, even though they may be sent to you without cost. The quality of paper you use depends on the amount and quality of printed material available in the country. The main purpose is to secure attention and attract reading. Pictures are a help. Poor grammar is bad advertising.

ii. Posters, Texts, Cartoons.—These are for public display. Even where the display is limited to the inside walls of a house, they give out their message to visitors and to the curious who peer in.

iii. Newspaper items.—Many small newspapers welcome articles contributed by readers if they are of some interest, well written and not too controversial. They will also print letters from their readers. Where the newspapers are widely read, it may be profitable to buy advertising space for a gospel message.

iv. Periodicals.—Many mission periodicals on the field are largely evangelistic and are distributed free in limited quantities. They are not an individual concern but are usually supervised by the mission. Sometimes several missions co-operate.

(c) *Devotional literature.* This kind of literature usually speaks a universal language, so it can well be translated if the illustrations are changed. Don't overlook the need of helps for family devotions also.

(d) *Doctrinal.* Catechisms, or brief surveys of Christian doctrine, are useful from the beginning, and especially for baptismal classes. There is a need for full doctrinal treatises after Bible training schools are started. Treatises on individual subjects are often needed at a very early period. Such would be the case, for example, when one of the sects begins to invade the field and the Christians need to know what the Bible teaches about their strange doctrines.

(e) *Commentaries—Bible study helps.* Simple helps and expositions of individual books or passages are the earliest needs. The simple, popular type is the most useful. Complete commentaries are as yet available in very few languages. Here is an outstanding need.

(f) *Sunday School literature.* Sunday School papers for the pupils are often too great an expense for an infant church. Books or quarterlies for the teachers, however, are a real need, since so few are trained for the work.

(g) *Bible story books—juveniles.* Books for children, like all work for children, can produce rich results. Many children's books get a wide reading even among adults.

(h) *Christian fiction.* A useful form because of its interest. But judging by the quality of most Christian fiction in English there are not many missionaries prepared to do it well.

(i) *Helps for preachers.* These are more needed abroad than at home. This is an important way to help build the indigenous church. The preachers themselves usually need and want such helps. Volunteer workers especially welcome them. However, they need to be prepared in simple, practical form, with ample detail.

(j) *Periodicals.* This is treated in part under propaganda. When the church is well established, though, it needs instruction of the sort that is not usual in the evangelistic paper. In a large field you should also consider the need for a magazine for preachers.

(k) *Correspondence courses.* Here is where the literature and teaching ministries join hands. The one who prepares the courses must be a teacher, but he must also know how to write. This is not a glamorous ministry but it is an increasingly important one.

(4) *Co-operation.* Missionary time and effort are too valuable for you to waste in duplicating the efforts of someone else. Before you begin a work of translation or composition, make as sure as you can that no one else has already undertaken the same task. Here is one place where our literature committees and inter-mission literature organizations have a real ministry. They try to keep in touch with the situation. And they are usually glad to counsel with the individual missionary. But many missionaries jump into the work on their own, without seeking anyone's counsel. This complicates the matter.

Each mission needs a literature committee on the field. To be useful it should be more than just another committee. It should be composed only of those who have a real interest and ability in literary work. At the same time it needs to realize that it can carry on an effective work only as it enjoys the confidence and co-operation of individual missionaries. So the committee must not be dictatorial. To try to dictate to any missionary what he can or cannot do is fatal. The committee should not discourage initiative, rather it should encourage initiative and help channel it into the most productive areas.

Suppose, for example, that missionary M. decides that he would like to translate for his people a well-known book of children's Bible stories. The literature committee gets word of his project. They have no objection to the project, but they know that someone else has already started a similar work in the same language. Should they try to stop M.? Not at all. Try to make use of his interest and initiative. Write to him that missionary A. is also at work on the same problem. Why don't they get together and make it a joint project? Working together they can get it done much more rapidly, and the joint product will have a much wider use. Of course if M. doesn't want to work with A. you can always suggest another needed work that no one is engaged in producing. But try to present it to him in a challenging way.

Literature is one area where we soon recognize that our limited resources, both in talent and in funds, make it necessary for us to have broad co-operation. Missions that are not co-operating with others in any other way often take part in inter-mission literature conferences and programs. Co-operation is especially important where a number of missions are working in the same language. So important is it that several years ago, when the home board of a certain mission refused to seek membership in such an inter-mission organization, some of the missionaries on the field raised the necessary fee so that they could have representation in it.

CHAPTER TWENTY-FOUR

MUSIC AND ART

MUSIC AND ART have always played a large part in the expression of the Christian faith. This is true in every country to which the faith has been carried. So, though it is seldom that a missionary is ever set aside for this particular ministry, it is a ministry that to some degree is included in the work of every mission. Music, in particular, has claimed some attention from a majority of the missionaries.

WHICH FORM?

The problem that we immediately face in both music and art is whether to use the forms familiar to the missionary or to find and adapt native forms. Or is there a possibility that the nationals, with encouragement, may develop some new and different forms? This whole thing is a moot question. All we can do is present some of the facts that influence both missionaries and nationals in their varying decisions.

First, these things are only partly an expression of our faith. Even more they are an expression of our own emotional reaction to the faith. Different people will react in different ways, even though their faith is similar. For example, in any local congregation in our Western Christian society there is likely to be a wide diversity of tastes in the music used for worship. Between people of different races and cultures the diversity is even greater. Our music seems strange to others, and theirs seems peculiar to us. There may be a question as to whether there is a moral or immoral quality in certain types of music, but there is no question that in those types that no one would find basically objectionable there is room for a wide diversity of forms. The nature of the music is determined fully as much by personal characteristics as by the nature of the faith.

Second, in many places there are already some well-developed forms of music and art that the people are accustomed to and seem to prefer. When they accept the Christian faith, they are also willing to accept expressions of it in the forms that the missionaries bring to them, but they always have a feeling that these things are foreign.[1] If they are left for a time on their own, even after having learned these new forms, they often revert to the more familiar ones or to an adaptation of them. Missionaries have sometimes taught the people a song and have then gone away for a time. On their return they have found the people singing the song, but with unfamiliar music. They have usually blamed the people for inability to remember the music; but as often as not the cause has been that the people unconsciously modified the music to fit a more familiar pattern. This is particularly true where people commonly use the pentatonic scale rather than the octave.

But, though it might generally seem advisable to have the people use their own forms of expression, there are some drawbacks. Often these forms are associated in the minds of the people with heathen worship or immoral practices. For this reason a group of East African pastors threw up their hands in horror when I asked if they ever used drums in their services or as a call to worship. They insisted that the drums to them meant heathen dances, and they should not be used in the worship of God. Yet in other parts of Africa, as in Nigeria, they are so used, and with great acceptance by church leaders.

Also, there are places where the people prefer to learn Western forms of music, perhaps because their own form is so poorly developed. Or having begun with Western forms in their church services, they identify the two so closely that they don't want to make any change. But some with much more training in musical matters would take a different point of view. One educated Nigerian stated that the African "must have the aid of foreign music to some extent—just as we benefit from foreign culture, bringing it and applying it to our own." His idea was that through the study of Western music the African would learn

[1]In a recent issue of the *African Challenge* (May, 1958), a Nigerian pastor was answering questions about the use of Western music in the churches. On the whole he believed that it had had a good influence. "Western spiritual music tones you down, it gives discipline; yes, it is very good." But when he was asked if he preferred Western music to indigenous in the church, he replied, "Actually, Western music is good only to the literate. Africans cannot really appreciate Western hymns—even we literates sense that they are foreign."

to appreciate what is good in his own. He himself was studying Western classical music "particularly with the idea of improving our own music."

As for art, though many missionaries have not developed an appreciation for native art, yet they seldom voice any serious objections to it. Some indeed have made a sympathetic study of it. And of course in some lands, as Japan, art is highly developed and admired by western students. The one place where Western art patterns make themselves most prominently felt is in architecture. The architecture of many mission churches is definitely western and utilitarian. It is not so much that the missionaries object to anything else as that they are not familiar with anything else. And it is sometimes claimed as a weakness of our Protestant building that we are too severely utilitarian and pay too little regard to the aesthetic, the artistic.

HYMNS, GOSPEL SONGS AND CHORUSES

The songs sung in our churches are the product of hundreds of individuals over a long period of time. New songs are constantly appearing, of which only a few will be well enough received to find their way into our regular song books, and fewer still will continue in use a number of years from now. In lands where the gospel is comparatively new, we cannot expect to have this same wealth of material. It will take years to build it up, years to develop the song writers and composers with the necessary spiritual experience and technical ability and preparation, years to let the songs pass through the crucible of Christian acceptance. Meantime the missionaries do what they can. They really need to be poets and musicians, but few of them are. So most of them give their attention to producing more or less acceptable translations of the English songs with which they are familar, employing the same music with minor modifications.

Sometimes the missionary is able to produce an acceptable piece of poetry in the native tongue that can be used as a devotional hymn. But he is not a musician. Never mind. If the language is not a tonal one he has an alternative to writing his own music. He can make use of a metrical index of English hymn tunes. After finding one or more that fit the meter of his composition, he can try them out and see if any of them suit its spirit also. He can be encouraged in his task by realizing that many of the hymn tunes we use today were not composed for the hymns with which they are now used.

INSTRUMENTS

A great variety of musical instruments have been used in Christian services. The only limitation seems to be that the instruments should not be closely associated with things that are contrary to Christianity. In India, for example, instruments are used that are peculiar to that country.

Missionaries have often introduced the portable organ or piano. In some places they have introduced brass wind instruments and have taught many of the people to play them. Such inexpensive and extremely portable instruments can have a great effect on the music of the people. In places where the people are not already used to the octave they help to keep them on key. Such instruments, too, because they have considerable carrying power, are useful for attracting a crowd.

CHAPTER TWENTY-FIVE

SUPERVISING AND COUNSELING

G ENERALLY MISSIONARY WORK passes through three stages. First there is the pioneer stage, when the missionary does all the work. Then there is the stage when the nationals are brought into association with him and do an increasing amount of the work, but he keeps the responsibility and exercises supervision. Finally there is the stage where responsibility is turned over to the church, and the missionary stays on as helper and counselor. Actually these stages are not at all sharply defined. In the same general area work in all three stages may be observed. Also there is a great deal of helping and counseling in the second stage, just as sometimes the missionary may be given a certain amount of supervision in the third. However, in general this is the picture. Today a great portion of the work of missions is in the second or third stages. This calls for particular attention to the matter of supervising and counseling.

Both of these matters require a broad understanding, both of Christian work and of people. The missionary must know what needs to be done and have some workable ideas as to how to reach the objectives. In addition, since he is not to do all the work himself, he must know what can be expected of his workers and how to get them to exert themselves fully and wisely. If he isn't decisive in his planning, he will lose his leadership and flounder badly. If he doesn't know the people, he may demand too much or too little, antagonize them unnecessarily or get to be known as an easy mark, create discouragement with impossible goals or set the standards so low that they fail to offer any challenge. For this reason missions usually want as candidates young people who have reasonable maturity, who have had some experience in the work of the church and have occupied places of responsibility and leadership.

Supervision

Supervision cannot be exercised in absentia. There is a Spanish proverb that says, "The eye of the owner fattens the horse." You need to see what is being done if you want to be sure that it is properly done. Christian workers as well as others need to realize that their work is constantly under inspection, both for approval and disapproval.

But the supervisor cannot be everywhere at the same time, nor watch every detail of what is done. Neither is it good for the worker not to place any confidence in him. There is nothing so irritating as to know that the boss is watching every move you make. Trust the worker and let him know that you are trusting him and in most cases he will try to merit your trust. But don't fail to check up at a convenient time, so that any failure can be promptly corrected.

For this reason the supervisor not only needs to visit the work but he needs to have his eyes open and know what to look for. Poor workmanship is seldom left out in the open. We need not be overly suspicious, but neither should we be gullible. A good worker will fail now and then. Let him know that you realize this and that you want to help him, not to criticize him. Then he will not be so anxious to hide his failures from you. Men appreciate a boss who "knows the score" and insists on good work, if he is fair. They don't respect him if they can easily put things over on him.

A good supervisor oversees but doesn't do the work himself. He probably can do the work much better. But while he is doing the work of one he can't oversee the work of many. There is always a temptation to put his own hand in, but if he does so the worker won't learn. This is sometimes the hardest part of supervision, to get another to do acceptably a job that you could do much better yourself. But in an emergency the supervisor should always be willing to help out. Only don't make your emergency classification too broad.

Good supervision calls for sympathetic understanding, but also for frankness. If a man's work is not satisfactory, let him know it. It is usually possible to do this without making him "lose face." Sometimes Americans are too blunt and outspoken in their criticisms; but I have also known American missionaries who would speak to everyone else about a man's faults other than the man himself, even though he was under their supervision. Don't be too critical, but when correction is clearly needed, don't be afraid to apply it. Only so can you fulfill your responsibility.

Have clear plans and give definite instructions. We do not hesitate to repeat this counsel. In our own thinking we may have many tentative ideas. We may want to change our course of action according to the circumstances or problems that arise. But in directing others we need to be precise. We need to give clear instructions according to our best understanding of the situation at the time. If later we need to change, we should just as clearly revise our instructions. The worker needs to know what he is to do; he cannot enter into all the mazes of our thinking.

Consult freely. A supervisor who loses personal contact with those directly under him is bound to do faulty work. A suggestion box may be a good idea, but it doesn't take the place of a personal conversation. You need to know what those under your direction are thinking. It may or may not influence your actions, but you should know it. You need also to allow them to express their opinions. Some of them may be of real help to you. At any rate they should be heard. Remember that those whom you now supervise will one day themselves be responsible for the work.

COUNSELING

There is no part of a missionary's work that takes more time than counseling. On the other hand there is no part of his work that enables him to exercise more real spiritual leadership than counseling. It is one of the first jobs that faces him as soon as he can understand and make himself understood in the language. It is the last job he will have to relinquish when the work has reached its full maturity. It faces him in every phase of the work. And it does not always bear a direct relation to his official position. Some in high position are seldom sought out for counsel, while those of humbler rank attract many.

In general we may say that there are two types of counseling in which the missionary engages. They might be called personal counseling and group counseling. That is, there is a sort of counseling where you deal only with one or two individuals. Their problems may be personal or they may relate to the work. At any rate their personal attitudes and actions are concerned. But there is another kind of counseling where you deal with a larger group: a committee, a board, a church, etc. Their problems deal with the society, the organization, or the work it is to accomplish. There is to be group action.

1. *Personal counseling.* There is no end to the variety of subjects on which people will seek the counsel of the missionary. Of course he expects that people will consult him about their personal spiritual problems. And they do, much more than they will consult the pastor here in the United States. They do it especially if the missionary is the one who first brought them the gospel. He should know all the answers. But they don't stop with spiritual problems. They also ask for counsel about family relationships and about other social relationships. They want the missionary to advise them on health matters and economic affairs. They often embarrass him with their questions, for he cannot possibly know all that he is expected to know. Yet he must give some sort of an answer.

What should a missionary do when his counsel is sought? The following suggestions may be of help.

a. *Be accessible.* This means not only to be physically where the one who wants counsel can find you, but show an approachable spirit. There are always times when those of us who are called on to counsel groan inwardly as we see another person come in with a problem. It is then that we need to remind ourselves of the scriptural injunction, "Bear ye one another's burdens, and so fulfill the law of Christ" (Gal. 6:2). But it is only as we show ourselves willing to listen that people will come to us for the counsel they need. Be a good listener.

b. *Allow the person to state his case fully.* This can sometimes be a tiresome proceeding, for he will often wander far away from the real issue. But you cannot give good counsel unless you know all the facts. Some impatient counselors start telling the inquirer what to do, even before he has finished telling what his problem is. This may be all right if it is a common problem and you already have a pretty good picture of it. However, I have often heard it done where the counselor obviously didn't realize the extent of the problem. In such a case the inquirer is likely to lose confidence.

c. *Ask questions to clarify any points that are not altogether clear and to secure any additional information.* Invariably the inquirer will fail to give some facts that are really pertinent, and he doesn't always know how to make himself clear. Sometimes he thinks that you can tell him just what to do on the basis of some very sketchy information. He doesn't realize how little of the background you may know. So even though it takes time, ask enough questions to get a reasonably complete picture of the problem.

d. *Try to understand the person and his situation.* We can never entirely "put ourselves in the other fellow's shoes," but we can try. We can try to see the problem from his point of view, so as to help him work out a solution. Of course that means that to some extent we will have to know him. At least we need to have come to some idea concerning his character. What we would do in a similar situation might be of no help to him because he can't do it.

e. *Restate the case in your own words to check your understanding of it.* Say, "Now, is this the situation . . .?" As often as not you will find that you have it slightly wrong.

f. *Point out the fundamental issues at stake.* This is the very heart of counseling. You need to be able to see through confusing details to what really is the issue at stake. Try to help the inquirer see it. It may be well to tell him, "This is what it will mean if you decide this way. . . ." The most important thing is not to tell him what to do but to get him to see what his action will mean.

g. *Do not attempt to dictate a decision.* Try to get the person to the place of making his own choice. If there are two or more possible choices, state the advantages of each one, but leave the decision to him. After all, he is the one who will be most affected by the decision. Also, deciding is what builds character. If you make the decision and if, for any reason it doesn't work out well, he can always blame you. Let him assume the responsibility, for it belongs to him. What is desired from you is counsel.

h. *Make good use of prayer.* It is an open acknowledgment of your dependence on God. And you do need Him in this work fully as much as in your public preaching. It may be well to pray with the inquirer as soon as he has stated his case and before you give any counsel. Or the prayer may come before the decision is to be made.

i. *In important spiritual matters it may be well to press for an immediate decision.* Putting off a decision merely aggravates the situation. But there are many matters that require more lengthy deliberation. Too hasty a decision in such cases may be unwise.

j. *Be absolutely certain to keep confidences.* The inquirer may not tell you that what he is saying is confidential, but he will appreciate it if he knows that you will not embarrass him by revealing it. The basis of all counseling is confidence. Yet confidence is one of our most perishable commodities. It is much more easily lost than gained.

We should also say a few words about those who need counsel but do not voluntarily seek it. There are times when everyone needs counsel. But sometimes we do not recognize our need, or by nature we are very hesitant to open our souls to others or to seek their counsel. Is there anything to be done in such cases?

Actually there is a great deal that can be done. But it depends on the counselor's knowing, or at least suspecting, that there is a need. For this reason again it is important that the missionary be in close touch with his people. He needs to be sensitive to their spiritual condition. He needs to be something like a parent who senses that something is wrong with his child even before he says a word.

You can't always ask a person to come in for counseling. But you can usually find a way to get him into a private conversation and then do a little tactful probing. If he avoids you, you may be sure there is something wrong. If in the course of the conversation you can inspire confidence in him, he may be led voluntarily to reveal his need. Don't try to drag it out of him. Counsel given to an unwilling hearer is useless.

Sometimes a counselor is asked to seek out a certain individual who is in need of help. Some refuse to do so. They say that you can't help a person who doesn't want help. To some degree they are right. Most people resent a person's trying to counsel them if they suspect that it was at someone else's suggestion. They consider it unwarranted interference in their personal affairs. However, there are some counselors that can even overcome this great handicap and so win the confidence of the one they are dealing with that he will welcome their help. And there are cases involving wrongdoing where the offender needs to be made aware that others know of his actions, and reproof should be given even if counsel is unacceptable.

Here's a special word about counseling with pastors, evangelists and teachers. Always remember that they are fellow laborers with you. If possible, avoid dictating what they *must* do. In any problem that concerns the work, solicit their ideas and then give them sincere and careful attention. They probably wouldn't be in the positions they occupy if they didn't have some worth-while ideas. In addition, they are likely to know their own people better than you do. If you don't believe their ideas will work, show them why. If you can merely give the worker the germ of an idea that he will adopt and develop until finally he brings forth a plan that he thinks is entirely his own, you will have done a superb job. What does it matter who gets the credit? "I have planted, Apollos watered, but God gave the increase" (I Cor. 3:6). And because it is God that gives the increase, be sure that both of you together seek His guidance. When you pray together you are drawn closer together.

2. *Group counseling.* From the beginning of organization in the work, the missionary is called on to do group counseling. Whether he is able to continue that counseling to the end of his missionary service depends largely on himself. In many ways he is in a position like that of a father with his sons. If he succeeds in keeping their confidence and respect during the difficult adolescent years, they will continue to look to him for counsel.

Actually there are three times when groups are likely to accept counsel. One is when they recognize the position of the counselor as entitling him to give counsel. That is, if he is the founder of the work or has succeeded to a position of responsibility they may look to him for counsel. But a missionary should not presume that simply because he is a missionary his counsel will be acceptable. I have seen some experienced missionaries resent the fact that their authority was not recognized by a group that was not well acquainted with them. They should have expected it. The fact that they called themselves missionaries meant nothing to the group. Missionaries had come and gone, both good and bad, and the group had little confidence in the title of missionary.

A group will also accept counsel, and even seek it out, from those whom they believe have knowledge and experience beyond their own. The missionary may not have all the answers. He may not even pretend to. But as long as they believe that he has more knowledge of the matter than they, they will want to get what benefit they can from his knowledge and experience. This means that he will have to gain a reputation among them for these things, whether justifiably or not. Again it is a matter of winning confidence.

A third time when groups will accept counsel is when they believe that the one who counsels them has a keener perception, a more discriminating judgment, or a deeper spirituality than they. He may not know any more facts, but he can see more clearly what those facts mean. Or he may be able to call to their attention important details or aspects of the problem that they have overlooked. In the student Missionary Union at Moody Bible Institute one time there was a critical need for funds for operating expenses. There were no dues, and donations from students were all for missionary work, not for the modest overhead expenses. The executive committee had received an offer from the Institute to advance them enough to meet the emergency, and they were inclined to accept the offer. But when they asked counsel, the suggestion was made, "Most of you are planning on missionary service, and a number will be serving under faith missions. Might this not be a good opportunity to put that faith principle to the test? Of course it is up to you." The committee simply hadn't thought of it that way before, and they unanimously turned down the offer with thanks. God honored their faith by meeting the need very shortly afterward.

When a counselor fails, it is usually because he is too dictatorial or because he is too reticent in giving counsel. Generally it is the former. He mistakes his position. He either wants to tell what action the group must take, or at least to have a vote in making the decision. He finds it easier to act than to try to influence thinking. He forgets that in a sense he is an outsider. The group does not make him one of themselves. They simply want the benefit of his knowledge, his experience, his insight; but they will make their own decision, just as they will bear the responsibility for it when it is made.

There are three "dont's" that the counselor does well to have in mind: don't talk before you have the facts; don't talk until you have had time to think through the facts; don't talk too much. You will gain greater respect for your opinions if it is obvious that you have reached them on the basis of the facts and after careful, unbiased study. In counseling your conclusion is not nearly so important as your reasons for coming to that conclusion. If those reasons led you to a certain conclusion, they ought to be good enough to lead others to the same conclusion. At least that is the attitude they will take.

Such counseling takes patience, patience to explain, to discuss, to clarify and simplify, to repeat. It also calls for tact, and even a good sense of humor.

CHAPTER TWENTY-SIX

BUILDING

To MANY PEOPLE the idea of missionary work is inseparably associated with building. This is because in so many places missions have felt obligated to construct all their own buildings. Especially is this true where there are no native buildings suitable to house the missionary or his work. But it is also true in other places where both buildings and builders are available, but where the mission for one reason or another has preferred to do its own building.

The situation varies so much from field to field that it is difficult to deal with the problem of building as a whole. There are fields where building must be done under any circumstances, as with a missionary family who have recently established a work among a hitherto unreached Indian tribe in the interior of Brazil. They are building with the help of the Indians. In the cities of that same country, though, there are buildings that can be rented. Yet renting is sometimes not so economical as building, or it may be necessary to buy or build so as to be sure of a permanent foothold, because of entrenched opposition to the work.

There are several principles that we do need to keep in mind both in buying property and building. They do not apply equally to all situations but they should be considered before a decision is made. First, missions by their very nature are supposed to be temporary. We need always to be conscious of the fact that one day our services will no longer be needed, nor even welcomed. But an extensive building program creates just the opposite impression. Buildings speak of permanency. The possession of property, especially improved property, creates a permanent vested interest that ties the mission to the country. The missionaries themselves settle down as if they would always be there.

The people of the country look at the mission as a permanent institution. They may consider it an unwelcome intruder or a beneficent source of income and aid. At any rate it is there to stay. This attitude is very likely to mitigate against the establishment of an indigenous work.

Now we must acknowledge that this argument can be carried too far. As we have said, there are times when buildings must be constructed. Also, though the missionary's work is essentially temporary, that word has a very flexible meaning. It may mean two or three years, it may mean twenty or thirty years, or it may mean two or three generations or more. It is the *attitude* of permanence that is dangerous, not the fact that the building will stand for a long time. It is always possible to build substantially with the thought of turning over the building to the nationals at the earliest feasible time. But I am afraid that while we may talk about such things we don't often actually carry them out. There is too much of our building that obviously was fitted to the peculiar needs of the American missionary.

A second consideration has to do with legal involvements. A mission seldom has reason to retain the services of a lawyer until it gets some real estate. Of course there is nothing wrong about having a lawyer, and the mission may need property to carry on its work. It is simply that it needs to count the cost, not only in money but in time and energy and worry. Sometimes a mission finds it advisable to set up a corporation within the country so as to hold and administer the properties it obtains. This involves a board of directors chosen from among the missionaries, regular meetings, and minutes kept in the language of the country so as to meet with the legal requirements. There are questions of title and boundaries that need to be settled. For construction a permit is often needed, including sometimes a special permit to cut timber, even though it is on your own land. In the cities there are zoning restrictions and building codes, even though they may not go by that name and may not be clearly published. And there are many other times when the owner of property or the builder will come in contact with the laws of the land. This is one of the reasons why many missions have a rule that individual missionaries may not own property. All property must be held in the name of the mission and all representations to the government made by the mission to avoid more complications.

There are further complications when the property on which the mission builds is not owned outright but is granted for the use of the mission by the government. There may always come a time when a new government may decide to take over the property for its own uses, including any buildings on it. The mission may or may not get some remuneration for its buildings. Even more serious is the situation when the government has provided some of the funds for the construction of such things as schools, hospitals, etc. Not only may they take them over at their pleasure, but they may insist, while the mission still operates them, that they not be used for purposes of evangelism, or that in the schools instruction in another faith be given.

Building by the mission does have some advantages at times. In some newly opened areas it brings many workers daily under the sound of the gospel who might not otherwise be reached. In other places it provides employment for needy Christians. It also trains them in work that they may be able to turn to their profit later in working for other employers.

But there is one thing that is often misleading in this as in other work that missionaries do. In calculating the costs of a building we usually fail to include the cost of the missionary. It is true that it doesn't cost any more to support him when he is building than when he is engaged in some other part of the missionary work. But when he is giving full time to the building, he cannot be doing the other work too. There are times when the missionary must be a builder, for there is no one else who can do it. But there are also times when he does the building simply because it seems cheaper than to hire someone else. His salary, indeed, may not come out of the building fund, but it is a part of the real cost of building and it may be greater than the cost of a hired worker. Always be sure to include this in your calculation of the costs.

PART FIVE

Furlough

CHAPTER TWENTY-SEVEN

FURLOUGH

W HAT IS WRONG with the young people of today?" the mission secretary asked. "Recently whenever I have talked with them about missionary work, one of the first questions they ask is, 'What kind of a furlough plan do you have?' When I went to the field we were interested in the work. We didn't worry about the furloughs."

Perhaps the secretary is right to be worried. In a day when workmen seem to be more interested in benefits, privileges, economic security, than they are in their work, it is not surprising that something of the same attitude carries over into missions.

Yet furlough has become an integral part of missionary service. And while it is not the missionary's main task, it is still something that calls for understanding and careful attention. So we ought to give it some attention in these pages.

Need

What we call furlough is a development of the modern missionary movement. It has gradually come into general use during the past century and a half. It was unknown during the earlier centuries and it has not been adopted by the Roman Catholic missions. These very reasons, plus some others that we shall mention shortly, have caused some people to question the furlough idea in Protestant circles. But there is not much likelihood of a radical change.

We should notice that the furlough idea is not restricted to Christian missions. Business houses and governments have adopted very similar measures for the benefit of their workers overseas. In fact, two or three years of service before being given a leave is much more common among them than the four or five years of the usual missionary term. Their reasons for granting such leaves are different from those of the missions, but they have found the plan generally helpful.

There are usually three reasons why the furlough idea has been questioned. All three are perfectly valid and will often find considerable support among the missionaries themselves. Yet when balanced against the reasons for the giving of furloughs, they invariably lose out.

First, it is argued that furloughs today are physically unnecessary. There was a time when the only really competent medical help was in the homeland, and the conditions of life on the field tended to break down the missionary's health. He needed the time of furlough to recover his health so as to continue his work for another term. But today conditions of living are greatly improved. In some places they are not much different from what they are at home. Even in tropical areas missionaries have refrigerators for the protection of their food, their food supplies are much more varied and ample, and many of the diseases that most commonly used to afflict them are now brought under control. Why shouldn't the missionary live out his life in the field to which the Lord has called him?

Second, furloughs are expensive. The expenses are not great when the country is nearby, but they are quite high for those who go to such places as Africa and the Orient. There is the cost of bringing the missionary all the way home from his field, together with his family, and then an equal amount to return them to the field some months later, when the furlough period is ended. Does this not increase the cost of missions unnecessarily? Wouldn't it be wiser economy to keep the missionary on the field and use that money to increase his allowance, or to send out other helpers?

Third, furloughs cause serious interruptions in the work. At times mission stations are left unmanned, because there is no one to take the furloughed missionary's place. At other times someone is assigned to the station, but he is unhappy with the assignment, partly because he realizes that he is just filling in. He cannot plan for the work as if it were to be his permanent responsibility. And the assignment of missionaries becomes complicated, for you usually don't want to move a missionary to a new place if his furlough is going to be due in a short time. And what are you going to do in the case of the man whose furlough is due, but for whose important work there just is no one else qualified to take over? There is no question that furloughs are a major headache in mission administration.

Yet we have said that there is no likelihood of a major change in the furlough situation. The reason is that furloughs are still needed. They are needed for a variety of reasons, and those reasons are sufficiently important to overweigh other considerations. We shall briefly mention some of these reasons under five headings.

First is the matter of health, *both physical and mental.* It is true that physical conditions on the mission fields are much better than they used to be. We can rejoice in this. It is this very fact that has helped to make the furlough a more common thing in missions. The day has gone in West Africa, for example, when few missionaries lived long enough to go home on furlough. Today they are able to go back for second, third and other terms of service. But we should not presume that because living conditions are improved a missionary can labor on indefinitely without a leave. Perhaps in some places, under some conditions, and doing certain types of work he can. But in many other cases he can't without grave risks to his health. Take, for example, the nurse in charge of a dispensary who has just reported handling more than 11,000 cases during the past year, nearly 95 per cent of them new cases.

But fully as important as physical health is mental health. We are not now thinking of those cases where a missionary may suffer what is commonly known as a "nervous breakdown." Such cases, though they do occur, are a minority. What we are thinking of is the missionary who through the strain of his work has become mentally and spiritually fatigued. He can still carry on, and often he does. Sometimes he himself is not aware of his condition. He thinks that he is still able to do the work, but those around him know that to a large extent he is just going through the motions. He needs freshness of outlook and renewed vigor of mind. His efficiency is impaired so much that, for this reason alone, a furlough might be a profitable investment.

A second reason for furlough and a very important one is the stimulation the missionary brings to the church at home. It is wrong to think that the missionary on furlough has nothing to do but rest. It is true that there are differences between missionaries. But to balance those who have comparatively few responsibilities during furlough, there are many others who are constantly at work. Deputation work, the constant ministry to the churches, especially when it involves long itineraries, can be exceedingly wearisome. The little boy who said his ambition was "to be a missionary on furlough" saw only part of the picture. He saw the missionary being feasted and lionized, and thought it must be a wonderful kind of life. He didn't know that sometimes the missionary wishes he could skip some of those delicious meals; they are just too much. Often the missionary would much prefer to be with his own family in some quiet spot. The constant giving of oneself, morning, noon and night can be almost as tiring at home as abroad. But the missionary does it because he knows it is an important part of his ministry. In some cases it is necessary for the securing of his support, or the renewing of interest on the part of those who are already giving. But apart from that financial consideration, he delights to make known the work that he has been doing and to inspire the church to a greater interest in its missionary task.

And the church needs that stimulation. The churches whose missionary interest and activity are at low ebb are almost invariably those that seldom see a missionary. Those that are the most active are the ones to whom missions become personalized through the living presence of the missionary. No salesman can be so effective for missions as the missionary himself, however humble he may be.

A third group of reasons for the furlough has to do with the missionary family. Most Protestant missionaries have families. In fact, some of them have rather large families. In most cases some, it not all, of the children have been born abroad. It was the missionary himself who made the choice. He chose to give his life to the Lord for service in that other land. But what about the children? Is it right to deprive them of that liberty of choice that their parents had? Even though the parents might want to exile themselves permanently from their homeland for the sake of their work, is it right to force this same exile on the children?

Often the missionary and his supporters do not think the matter through in this way. They simply take it for granted that the children of American missionaries will be Americans, and that they should have the opportunity of an American education and of fitting into American life if they should choose. So the time comes when the parents must make arrangements for leaving the children in the homeland. When they are of college age the problem is not great, for it involves only the choice of a school. But not many missionaries are able to keep their children with them on the field until that age. And it is not easy to make satisfactory arrangements for the younger children unless you see to it personally. Children are not like property that can easily be entrusted to another's care. The separation from their parents is hard on them at best. It is foolish to make it harder by *sending* them home to unfamiliar people and surroundings, when they can be *left* at home in circumstances with which they have already become familiar.

A fourth reason for furlough is the opportunity it gives for further study or additional preparation for the missionary's job. When the missionary comes home on furlough, he has a far better idea of what he needs than he had when he first went to the field. He has had the opportunity of feeling out the sort of ministry in which he may be the most useful. And it may be quite different from anything he was thinking of at the beginning of his service. Some have become interested in literary work, for example, only after they have actually seen the need and the opportunity. But they lack certain special preparation that would make them more useful in that ministry. Others have become conscious of other lacks in their training. Not a few of those who have reached the field without completing their college work have asked for extended leave to do so, because in their work they felt the need for it. Medical workers and other specialists count on furlough to allow them to learn the new developments in their field of work, or to take special training in some field that they now know will be of real help.

A fifth reason for furlough may not impress us so much as the others and it is not publicized, but it is a valid reason. Furlough provides an excellent opportunity to evaluate the missionary's service and see whether he should be returned to the field, and if so to what kind of ministry. You see, we have been dealing with "career" missionaries, those who expect to devote their lives to the service. But while the missionary may retire at almost any time if he is not satisfied with the mission, the mission does not find it quite so easy to dispose of an unsatisfactory missionary. It can always act in cases of serious misbehavior, but what about those other cases where the missionary simply "doesn't work out"? Should the fact that they once appointed him oblige them to keep him as long as he wants to stay on the field?

Furloughs provide convenient breaking points in the service of the missionary. The precise arrangements differ from mission to mission, but even the missionaries are accustomed to speak of so many "terms of service" when they are asked how long they have been on the field. Some missions recommission their missionaries after each furlough. Some ask for a recommendation from the field when the missionary comes home, to see if he should be returned. Others have no set rule.

But even where there is no question about a missionary's fitness this same idea is helpful. It has been decided that Missionary A——— is to be set aside for a new ministry. When should he begin it? Why, after furlough. He will need to be replaced in his present ministry at that time, anyway. Then he can be thinking and planning for the new ministry while he is away. He may also be able to consult with others or even get special training. If he needs special equipment he can see to its selection and purchase. Then everything will be ready to begin the new enterprise as soon as he returns.

A missionary doctor in Japan adds a variation of this reason. He says:

> I think furloughs are necessary to give us a perspective of our work. If we get away we can view it dispassionately. We can see our mistakes. Just getting away where people are not after us 24 hours a day, 365 days a year, is what we need. Some people are capable of staying here 15 years and not going home. Others need to go home in four years. This is an individual variation.[1]

TIME OF FURLOUGH

The length of a term of service on the field is determined individually by each mission. It may vary anywhere from three to seven years. Perhaps the principal factor in making the decision is the matter of health conditions. Where a three-year period is adopted, it is almost always in a very difficult tropical area. A representative of a mission in tropical Africa announced some years ago, "When we reduced the term to three years, we practically did away with having to invalid missionaries home." On the other hand, terms as long as seven years are unlikely except in

[1] *Japan Harvest*, Winter, 1957.

temperate regions. The average of all fields seems to be about five years.

Of course there are other elements that enter into the length of a term of service. Some missions use a term slightly longer than they might otherwise prefer because of the expense and other problems connected with the constant going and coming of their personnel. Yet they don't like to keep the worker on the field too long, so that his ties with the church at home are seriously weakened. Also, if he is going to get additional training after a term of service, it shouldn't be postponed too long. And of course they must always give attention to the availability of replacements. Many a missionary is asked to extend his term for another year until someone can be secured to take his place.

The exact time of furlough is usually determined on the field, in consultation with the missionary. Even when a replacement is at hand, there may be no transportation available. Or maybe the season of the year is not suitable. Missionaries from the humid tropics would prefer not to land in New York in the middle of winter. Or family interests may dictate a time that will make it possible for the children to enter school at the beginning of the school year. And of course a missionary can hardly move until there is money available, even though his furlough may have been granted.

Length of Furlough

The most common duration for furlough is one year. But when we say this, we have to be ready to note numerous exceptions. It may sometimes be eight months, unless the missionary stays on the field more than the minimum term, or unless he is assigned to do special deputation work or to take classes. Then again a missionary may be granted more than a year where his health requires it or his studies may be prolonged. In some cases his permission to re-enter the country where he has labored may expire at the end of the year. Then he has to make sure to be back within the year.

Usual Responsibilities on Furlough

Perhaps the first and most common requirement is a good medical and dental check-up. Sometimes this can be taken care of at the port of entry. But in many other cases the missionary waits until he reaches his home. This check-up is particularly important for those who have been in poor health. But even if you have enjoyed reasonably good health, don't neglect it.

Some missions instruct their missionaries not to take any meetings or get involved in any other responsibilities for a number of weeks after they reach home. The principal reason is that the missionary should be in good physical condition before he starts any strenuous deputation work or other activity. But it is also a good idea for him to get readjusted to life at home before he undertakes a public ministry. One who has been away for several years, even if he tries to keep informed, does get out of touch. Often he has forgotten just how things were before he went to the field. The churches like to get a missionary "fresh from the field." But with that freshness there often goes also a bit of crudeness, especially if he has not recently done much speaking in English. It is possible for missionaries, like meat, to be too fresh.

Of course the missionary is expected to visit and minister to his supporting church or churches. If he can settle in the community and take an active part in church affairs, he will not only bring blessing to the church but it will also bring benefit to him. He will find that there have been changes. He will get acquainted with new members who have known him only by name before. Their interest in his work will now take on a personal character. The children of the church have been growing, and some of these young people will seek him out for counsel about their life's plans. All of this is in addition to the public ministry he may have in preaching, teaching, etc.

But some have supporting churches in more than one part of the country. This involves traveling. You will not be able to stay long in any one place. (After all, the children do have to be in school.) But no excuse should keep you from renewing the contact with every one of your supporting groups. And make your visit long enough to be meaningful. Always remember that this is a part of your ministry as a missionary—"one who has been sent" by others.

Every missionary has a responsibility to minister to his supporting churches, at least in the sense of giving them a personal account of what the Lord has done through him. But most missionaries will also have other calls on their services. You will be asked to speak in churches, to young people's groups, in schools and many other places. The demands on you will depend on how well the people know you and how effective you are as a public speaker. The mission itself will sometimes ask you to take certain engagements.

Again we say, this is an opportunity for a useful ministry. From some of the meetings there may be no apparent result, except possibly an offering. In another you may perhaps touch the life of one who one day will join you on the field. In still another you may bring some needed encouragement, or inspiration, or even the word of salvation. But in every case, as with your work on the field, take it as an opportunity to minister for the Lord. In other words, the instructions we gave for your deputation work before going to the field apply fully as much here. Even the recommendation that you make much of your own experience applies. The difference is that now your experience includes service on a mission field.

Perhaps, though, we ought to say a little more about the character of the messages you give. Should they be simply stories of the work? Should they always have a text and be developed as sermons? Should they contain anything about the geography of the country and the customs of the people? What is a missionary message, anyway?

You will find a good many differences of opinion on the subject. At one extreme are those who avoid the story-teller's role and insist that as ministers of the Word they should talk only about the Bible and their Lord. At the other extreme are those whose talks are mainly travelogues, or who seem to delight mostly in amusing, shocking or otherwise entertaining their audience. How can you steer a safe middle course?

There are a few questions that will help you decide. First, what kind of meeting is it, who invited you, and what do they expect from you? If the principal of a school invites you to address an assembly of the students, you know that he doesn't expect or want a sermon such as you would give in a church. In fact, he may warn you that in a public school you are limited in what you may say of a religious nature. But even in a church service they may not want the usual sermon. One of the common complaints about missionaries is that they are invited to speak about their work and instead they give a Bible message. You don't have to accept the invitation to speak; but if you do you are obligated to fulfill the conditions. It is dishonest to accept the invitation and then not do what you were asked to do, even though you think you know better what they ought to have. If you don't know what they want, ask.

Another question to ask yourself is this, "What do I want to accomplish with this talk? Do I want to entertain, to inform, to inspire, or just what?" In other words, any talk should have an objective. Then make your talk conform to the objective. A talk doesn't become a sermon simply because you refer occasionally to a Biblical text. Neither is it any less a sermon because no specific text is read. If you do use a text, deal with it honestly. Don't use it as a pretext, a sort of pseudo-biblical basis into which you read the thoughts that you want to put across. If your thoughts don't come from the Scriptures, don't pretend that they do.

What about using slides or films in your deputation work? They will often draw a crowd much more readily than an address. People like pictures—if they are good pictures. And pictures can be made to tell the story more effectively than words alone. Here are a few suggestions for their use.

1. *Use only good clear pictures.* One of the things that have given missionary pictures a bad name is the persistence of some missionaries in using pictures that are out of focus, underexposed, overexposed, or in some other way quite faulty. Every photographer has some failures. That is why an experienced man doesn't usually content himself with just one shot of a scene. He never expects to use all the pictures he takes. He knows that he will have to throw some of them away. If missionaries would learn to weed out ruthlessly their inferior pictures, they would do themselves and their audience a favor. Remember that the same thing applies to moving pictures. Just because a picture sequence is on your roll doesn't mean that you have to show it. Good films are all edited. The original pictures are only the raw material. They need cutting, splicing, rearranging, etc.

2. *Arrange your pictures in a sequence to tell a story or to fit into a talk.* There is nothing so tiring as a succession of pictures that have no relation to one another. If they are good pictures they may hold attention for a few minutes, but not for very long. Just as in a sermon, there needs to be progress. The kind of sequence you use will depend on your purpose and on your own inventiveness. The whole idea is to

present a message with your pictures in such an orderly fashion that the audience will be interested in following through.

3. *In using slides, make the slides illustrate your talk; don't make your talk an explanation of the slides.* Too many missionaries will flash a picture on the screen, saying, "This is a picture of . . . ." Then after they have finished their explanation of that picture and the various thoughts it brings to mind, they go on to the next, "This is a typical. . . ." Pictures are either supposed to bring a message by themselves, or else to illustrate and amplify the spoken word. If they need explanation they have failed in their purpose.

4. *Plan your talk carefully so as not to hold any one slide too long.* An average of as much as one minute per slide is too much. Some slides can be held longer than others, but it is never wise to hold any one for several minutes. Any slide that is held should have sufficient interest *in itself* to hold the attention of the viewers without their tiring of it.

5. *If you have trouble keeping within the time limit, write out your talk.* It is a good idea to do this at the beginning anyway, until you get accustomed to timing yourself accurately. You can even read the talk unobtrusively with the aid of a small flashlight, since the attention of the people will be concentrated on the screen. However, if you do plan to read it, be careful that your writing is not stiff and formal. Make it sound as free and natural as if you were talking extemporaneously.

6. *Use group pictures very sparingly.* No matter how interesting the people in it may be to you, to your audience they are just a group of people. The worst thing you can possibly do is to try increasing their interest by telling the story of each person in the picture. Yet many a missionary tries it.

7. *Avoid clichés such as "This is a typical . . . ."* Expressions like this come to be meaningless. In fact, the audience sometimes wonders if they are true since the speaker obviously is just parroting an expression.

When you have been invited to show pictures in a meeting, there are several practical precautions you want to take.

1. *Make sure the proper equipment is available.* This means the proper projector (sound projector for sound films, for example), a good screen, projector stand, extension cord (if electric outlet is not close at hand). Many churches have such equipment today, but it is not always

in good condition. So check to make sure. Remember also that a bulb may burn out in the middle of a meeting. Have a spare available.

2. *If at all possible, have the machine set up and focused before the meeting.*

3. *Unless you are going to operate the projector yourself, make sure that the operator is familiar with it.*

4. *Check through your slides before each showing, unless they are in a fixed order in a slide-changer.* It is all too easy to get them mixed up during one showing so that the next time they appear on the screen out of order, which can be embarrassing. Make sure also that films are rewound.

5. *See that the operator understands the order in which the slides are to be shown.*

If you plan to be very active in deputation work, you must let people know when you will be available. Let them know well ahead of time, so they can get in touch with you and make plans if they want to. Some churches and schools have their schedules made up several months ahead of time. So when the missionary writes and says he will be in their neighborhood next week, the probability is that they won't be able to use him.

Always give an address where you can be reached on reasonably short notice. Occasionally there are unexpected openings, but the person in charge cannot wait for a letter to follow you around the country. Some missionaries have found it advisable to tell what months they are to be in what areas, giving the address of a person in each area who will have information about their schedule. If you ask that person to make engagements for you, though, be careful not to make any yourself that might conflict with something he has arranged.

When you have made an engagement, keep it. Sometimes after a missionary has made a commitment, he receives another invitation that looks more attractive. He is tempted to write and cancel the first appointment. If there is still ample time for the church to make other arrangements, he may take the chance. However, he needs to realize that his action may still give offense and that he may be canceling the opportunity of a future invitation from that same group. This is a practical consideration. The Bible principle is less flexible. The one who dwells in the house of the Lord is the one who "sweareth to his own hurt and changeth not" (Ps. 15:4). You don't have to be in haste about accepting an engagement, but once you have accepted, be sure you get there, and don't cancel out unless you have the best of reasons.

Of course those who do a great deal of deputation work find that they must plan their itinerary. It is impractical to keep darting back and forth across the country. To economize your time and energies as well as money you need to group your meetings as much as possible. The trouble is that invitations do not all come at the same time, and often there are extra openings that show up along the way. How can you plan for such things?

Remember that, no matter how careful the plans, every itinerary involves a measure of risk. Meetings you had planned on may not materialize, offerings may be smaller than you anticipated, you may have difficulty securing accommodations at a reasonable rate, or there may be unexpected delays en route. These should be calculated risks. If you are not prepared to take any chances, then don't start out.

A plan that many use is to secure first a few key appointments in the most promising places. If there are enough invitations to warrant their going ahead, then they try to fill in the vacancies without too much back-tracking. This means planning in hope far ahead of time. Often there will be invitations you can't accept. Be reconciled to it. There will also be periods without any engagement. But you don't need to be idle. Holding meetings is only a part of your ministry.

Here is a word to those missionaries who are hesitant about offering their services to pastors and churches. If your primary aim is to raise money, then I don't blame you for being hesitant. Your job is just as hard as that of the door-to-door salesmen who harass the busy housewife. You must have a fair amount of self-confidence, a manner that will impress most people favorably, and an ability to take rebuffs. Diplomacy and persistence have to be your watchwords.

But if your main desire is, as we have said before, to minister to the church, to bring to it the vision and the inspiration that are yours, to give rather than to receive, then the situation is different. You have something to offer, something that the church needs. You are not selling it. It is not a commercial transaction. It is a part of your ministry. With a true sense of humility you can approach any group and offer your services. If they accept, you can serve as unto the Lord, not unto men. Many will not accept the offer. But don't despise any opportunity that may be given you. Our standards are not those of the world. The little things that the world despises are often the key to the greater.

BIBLIOGRAPHY

THE FOLLOWING BOOKS represent a variety of points of view. Yet even those with which we disagree have something to contribute to our understanding of missionary life and work. Obviously the list is far from exhaustive. The subject is too broad. We have tried to limit ourselves mostly to books from a missionary point of view even where, as with anthropology, there is a great deal of valuable secular material.

The nine divisions we have made are for convenience. Many of the books could be listed under more than one heading. But to avoid duplications we have arbitrarily assigned each one to a single division where it seems to fit best. Some that are too broad to be listed under a specific heading are entered under "General." Dates given are those of the latest edition to which we have had access.

I. THE MISSIONARY

Adolph, Paul E. *Missionary Health Manual.* Chicago: Moody Press, 1954.

Bloomfield, Leonard. *Outline Guide for the Practical Study of Foreign Languages.* Baltimore: Linguistic Society of America, 1942.

Cable, Mildred and French, Francesca. *Ambassadors for Christ.* Chicago: Moody Press, n.d.

Calverley, Eleanor Taylor. *How to Be Healthy in Hot Climates.* New York: Thomas Y. Crowell Co., 1949.

Carmichael, Amy. *God's Missionary.* London: Society for Promoting Christian Knowledge, 1953.

Culshaw, W. J. *A Missionary Looks at His Job.* London: Student Christian Movement Press, 1937.

Cummings, Thomas Fulton. *How to Learn a Language.* New York: 1916.

Fleming, Daniel Johnson. *Living as Comrades.* New York: Agricultural Missions, 1950.

Grubb, Norman P. *Touching the Invisible.* Philadelphia: Christian Literature Crusade, 1946.

Hall, Ronald Owen. *The Missionary-Artist Looks at His Job.* New York: International Missionary Council, 1942.

Higdon, E. K. *New Missionaries for New Days.* St. Louis: The Bethany Press, 1956.

Housing in the Tropics. United Nations Publications, 1952.

Koskinen, Aarne. *Missionary Influence as a Political Factor in the Pacific Islands.* Helsinki: 1953.

Lennox, William Gordon. *The Health and Turnover of Missionaries.* New York: Foreign Missions Conference of North America, 1933.

Levai, Blaise, ed. *Revolution in Missions.* Vellore: The Popular Press, 1957.

Moyer, Kenyon E. *A Study of Missionary Motivation, Training and Withdrawal.* New York: Missionary Research Library, 1957.

Nida, Eugene Albert. *Learning a Foreign Language.* New York: Foreign Missions Conference of North America, 1950.

Price, Frank W. and Moyer, Kenyon E. *Mission Board Policies with Relation to Missionary Personnel.* New York: Missionary Research Library, 1958.

Riebe, John R. *The Romance of Language.* Brooklyn: Africa Inland Mission, 1952.

Secretary of the Committee on Missionary Personnel. *Recruiting, Selection and Training of Missionaries in North America.* New York: Division of Foreign Missions, N.C.C.C., 1957.

Smith, Edwin William. *The Shrine of a People's Soul.* London: Church Missionary Society, 1929.

Taylor, John V. *Christianity and Politics in Africa.* London: Penguin Books, 1957.

Thompson, Phyllis. *Proving God.* Philadelphia: China Inland Mission, 1956.

Warren, Mary. *On with the Job.* London: The Highway Press, 1957.

Warren, Max A.C. *Partnership.* London: Student Christian Movement, 1956.

Westermann, Diedrich and Ward, Ida C. *Practical Phonetics for Students of African Languages.* London: Oxford University Press, 1933.

Williamson, Mabel R. *"Have We No Right—."* Chicago: Moody Press, 1957.

II. THE PEOPLE

Azariah, Vadanayakam Samuel and Whitehead, Henry. *Christ in the Indian Villages.* London: Student Christian Movement, 1930.

Bhatty, E. C. *Towards Richer Life*. Mysore: Wesley Press, n.d.

Broomhall, A. J. *Strong Tower*. London: China Inland Mission, 1948.

Cormack, Margaret. *The Hindu Woman*. New York: Bureau of Publications, Teachers College, Columbia University, 1953.

Cunningham, Rosemary. *Under a Thatched Roof in a Brazilian Jungle*. Toronto, Evangelical Publishers: 1955.

Davis, John Merle. *Modern Industry and the African*. London: Macmillan, 1933.

Eakin, Paul A. *Buddhism and the Christian Approach to Buddhists in Thailand*. Bangkok: 1956.

Haldane, James. *Trekking among Moroccan Tribes*. London: Pickering & Inglis, 1948.

Harris, George K. *How to Lead Moslems to Christ*. Philadelphia: China Inland Mission, n.d.

Highbaugh, Irma. *Family Life in West China*. New York: Agricultural Missions, 1948.

Jones, L. Bevan. *Christianity Explained to Muslims*. Calcutta: Y.M.C.A. Publishing House, 1952.

Lucas, William Vincent, *et al*. *Christianity and Native Rites*. London, Central Africa House Press: 1950.

Mackay, John A. *The Other Spanish Christ*. New York: Macmillan, 1932.

Manikam, Rajah B. and Highbaugh, Irma, ed. *The Christian Family in Changing East Asia*. Manila: Philippine Federation of Christian Churches, n.d.

Nida, Eugene Albert. *Customs and Cultures*. New York: Harper & Bros., 1954.

Parrinder, Geoffrey. *African Traditional Religion*. London: Hutchinson's University Library, 1954.

——. *Religion in an African City*. London: Oxford University Press, 1953.

——. *West African Psychology*. London: Lutterworth Press, 1951.

——. *West African Religion*. London: The Epworth Press, 1949.

Phillips, Arthur, ed. *Survey of African Marriage and Family Life*. London: Oxford University Press, 1953.

Price, Thomas. *African Marriage*. London: Student Christian Movement, 1954.

Reyburn, William D. *The Toba Indians of the Argentine Chaco*. Elkhart: Mennonite Board of Missions and Charities, 1954.

Ross, Emory. *African Heritage*. New York: Friendship Press, 1952.

Rycroft, William Stanley, ed. *Indians of the High Andes*. New York: Committee on Co-operation in Latin America, 1946.

Shropshire, Denys W. T. *The Church and Primitive Peoples*. London: Society for Promoting Christian Knowledge, 1938.

Smith, Edwin William, ed. *African Ideas of God*. London: Edinburgh House Press, 1950.

Smith, Edwin William. *The Golden Stool*. London: Edinburgh House Press, 1927.

——. *Knowing the African*. London: Lutterworth Press, 1946.

Smith, Gordon Hedderly. *The Missionary and Anthropology*. Chicago: Moody Press, 1945.

——. *The Missionary and Primitive Man*. Chicago: Van Kampen Press, 1947.

Thompson, Edgar W. *The Word of the Cross to Hindus*. Madras: Christian Literature Society, 1956.

Westermann, Diedrich. *The African To-Day and To-Morrow*. London: Oxford University Press, 1949.

Westermann, Diedrich and Thurnwald, Richard. *The Missionary and Anthropological Research*. London: Oxford University Press, 1948.

Wilson, J. Christy. *The Christian Message to Islam*. New York: Fleming H. Revell Co., 1950.

Wiser, Charlotte Vial and William H. *Behind Mud Walls*. New York: Agricultural Missions, 1951.

III. EVANGELISM

Broomhall, Marshall. *The Bible in China*. Philadelphia: China Inland Mission, 1934.

Chirgwin, A. M. *The Bible in World Evangelism*. London: Student Christian Movement, 1954.

The Common Evangelistic Task of the Churches in East Asia. Prapat: East Asia Christian Conference, 1957.

Edmeston, Rhoda C. *The Protestant Youth Movement in Latin America*. New York: Committee on Co-operation in Latin America, 1954.

Pickett, Jarrell Waskom. *Christian Mass Movements in India*. New York: The Abingdon Press, 1933.

Scott, R. W. *Evangelism in India*. Nagpur: National Christian Council, 1952.

Scott, R. W., ed. *Ways of Evangelism*. Christian Literature Society, 1953.

Weber, Hans Ruedi. *The Communication of the Gospel to Illiterates*. London: Student Christian Movement, 1957.

IV. THE CHURCH

Allen, Roland. *Missionary Methods, St. Paul's or Ours?* Chicago: Moody Press, 1956.

———. *The Spontaneous Expansion of the Church.* London: World Dominion Press, 1949.

Appasamy, A. J. *The Christian Task in Independent India.* London: Society for Promoting Christian Knowledge, 1951.

Blair, Herbert E. *Stewardship in Korea.* Seoul: Christian Literature Society, 1938.

Blair, William Newton. *Gold in Korea.* New York: Presbyterian Church in the U.S.A., 1946.

Clark, Charles Allen. *The Korean Church and the Nevius Methods.* New York: Fleming H. Revell Co., 1928.

———. *The Nevius Plan for Mission Work.* Seoul: Christian Literature Society, 1937.

Clark, Sidney J. W. *The Indigenous Church.* London: World Dominion Press, 1928.

Davis, John Merle. *The Economic and Social Environment of the Younger Churches.* London: Edinburgh House Press, 1939.

———. *Mission Finance Policies and the Younger Churches.* Bangalore: Scripture Literature Press, 1938.

———. *New Buildings on Old Foundations.* New York: International Missionary Council, 1945.

Fleming, Daniel Johnson. *Devolution in Mission Administration.* New York: Fleming H. Revell Co., 1916.

Hodges, Melvin L. *On the Mission Field.* Chicago: Moody Press, 1953.

Janes, Maxwell O. *Servant of the Church.* Westminster: The Livingstone Press, 1952.

Kane, J. Herbert. *Twofold Growth.* Philadelphia: China Inland Mission, 1947.

McGavran, Donald Anderson. *The Bridges of God.* New York: Friendship Press, 1955.

Nevius, John Livingstone. *Planting and Development of Missionary Churches,* Grand Rapids: Baker Book House, 1958.

Phillips, John Bertram. *The Church under the Cross.* New York: Macmillan, 1956.

Price, Frank Wilson. *The Rural Church in China.* New York: Agricultural Missions, 1948.

Ritchie, John. *Indigenous Church Principles in Theory and Practice.* New York: Fleming H. Revell Co., 1946.

Sundkler, Bengt G. M. *Bantu Prophets in South Africa.* London: Lutterworth Press, 1948.

Thomas, Winburn T. *Indonesia and the Indonesian Church in Today's World.* New York: Missionary Research Library, 1958.

Urban Community and the Urban Church, The. Nagpur: National Christian Council, 1957.

Village Church in West Pakistan, The. Lahore, West Pakistan Christian Council, 1957.

V. EDUCATION

Anderson, George and Whitehead, Henry. *Christian Education in India.* London: Macmillan, 1932.

The Anderson-Smith Report on Theological Education in Southeast Asia. New York: Board of Founders, Nanking Theological Seminary, 1952.

Barton, James Levi. *Educational Missions.* New York: Student Volunteer Movement, 1917.

Bates, M. Searle, *et al. Survey of the Training of the Ministry in Africa,* Part II. New York: International Missionary Council, 1954.

Brockway, K. Nora. *A Larger Way for Women.* London: Oxford University Press, 1949.

Christian Education in China. New York: Committee of Reference and Counsel, Foreign Missions Conference of North America, 1922.

Commission on Christian Higher Education in India, The. *The Christian College in India.* London: Oxford University Press, 1931.

Goodall, Norman and Nielsen, Eric W. *Survey of the Training of the Ministry in Africa,* Part III. New York: International Missionary Council, 1954.

Hamilton, Floyd E. and Cochrane, Thomas. *Basic Principles in Educational and Medical Mission Work.* London: World Dominion Press, 1928.

Helser, Albert D. *Education of Primitive People.* New York: Fleming H. Revell Co., 1934.

Jones, Thomas Jesse. *Education in East Africa.* London: Edinburgh House Press, 1925.

Mulira, E. M. K. *The Vernacular in African Education.* New York: Longmans, Green and Co., 1951.

Neill, Stephen. *Survey of the Training of the Ministry in Africa,* Part I. New York: International Missionary Council, 1950.

Ranson, Charles Wesley. *The Christian Minister in India.* London: Lutterworth Press, 1946.

Ranson, Charles Wesley, *et al. Survey of the Training of the Ministry in Madagascar.* New York: International Missionary Council, 1957.

Reynhout, Hubert, Jr. *Some Problems Concerning the Preparation of the Christian Ministry on the Foreign Mission Field.* Providence: Providence-Barrington Bible College, 1955.

Sailer, T. H. P. *Christian Adult Education in Rural Asia and Africa.* New York: Friendship Press, 1943.

Scopes, Wilfred. *Training Voluntary Workers in the Service of the Christian Church in India.* Lucknow: Lucknow Publishing House, 1955.

The Use of Vernacular Languages in Education. Paris: U.N.E.S.C.O., 1953.

Van Doren, Alice Boucher. *Christian High Schools in India.* Calcutta: Y.M.C.A. Publishing House, 1936.

VI. HEALING

Adolph, Paul E. *Surgery Speaks to China.* Philadelphia: China Inland Mission, 1945.

Garlick, Phylis L. *Health and Healing.* London: Edinburgh House Press, 1948.

Harrison, Paul Wilberforce. *Doctor in Arabia.* New York: John Day Co., c. 1940.

Hume, Edward Hicks. *Doctors East, Doctors West.* New York: W. W. Norton & Co., c. 1946.

Lambuth, Walter R. *Medical Missions: The Twofold Task.* New York: Student Volunteer Movement, 1920.

MacDonald, A. B. *Can Ghosts Arise?* Glasgow: Church of Scotland Foreign Missions Committee, 1952.

Moorshead, Robert Fletcher. *The Way of the Doctor.* London: The Carey Press, n.d.

Roberts, Paul W. *Medicine, the Magnet.* Talcottville: The Voice of the Andes, 1955.

Robbins, Nancy Estelle. *Greater Is He.* London: Society for Promoting Christian Knowledge, 1952.

Ross, Emory and Phillips, Gene. *New Hearts—New Faces.* New York: Friendship Press, 1954.

Tales from the Inns of Healing. Toronto: Committee on Missionary Education, The United Church of Canada, 1942.

Thompson, Henry Paget. *Medical Missions at Work.* Westminster: The Society for the Propagation of the Gospel in Foreign Parts, 1947.

VII. Literature and Literacy

Brower, Reuben A., ed. *On Translation.* Cambridge: Harvard University Press, 1959.

Diffendorfer, Ralph E. *Christian Literature in the Mission World.* New York: International Missionary Council, 1946.

Flesch, Rudolph. *The Art of Readable Writing.* New York: Harper & Bros., 1949.

Flesch, Rudolf and Lass, Abraham Harold. *The Way to Write.* New York: McGraw-Hill Book Co., 1955.

Gudschinsky, Sarah C. *Handbook of Literacy.* Norman: Summer Institute of Linguistics, 1957.

Gunning, Robert. *The Technique of Clear Writing.* New York: McGraw-Hill Book Co., 1952.

Laubach, Frank Charles. *The Silent Billion Speak.* New York: Friendship Press, 1945.

——. *Teaching the World to Read.* New York: Friendship Press, 1947.

——. *Toward a Literate World.* New York: Foreign Missions Conference of North America, 1938.

Moody Press Personnel. *The Christian Book Shop.* Chicago: Moody Press, 1952.

Nida, Eugene Albert. *God's Word in Man's Language.* New York: Harper & Bros., 1952.

Penning, Philip. *The Christian Bookseller.* Madras: The Service Council of Christian Literature Agencies, 1954.

Shaw, Trevor and Grace. *Through Ebony Eyes.* London: Lutterworth Press, 1956.

Shepherd, Robert H. W. *Bantu Literature and Life.* Lovedale: Lovedale Press, 1955.

Ure, Ruth. *The Highway of Print.* New York: Friendship Press, 1946.

Warren, Ruth Ure. *Literacy.* London: Edinburgh House Press, 1955.

VIII. Agriculture and Other Special Services

Dancy, Harold K. *Mission Buildings.* New York: Sudan Interior Mission, 1948.

Davis, Jackson, *et al. Africa Advancing.* New York: Friendship Press, 1945.

Felton, Ralph Almon. *Church Bells in Many Tongues.* Lebanon: 1958.

——. *Hope Rises from the Land.* New York: Friendship Press, 1955.

Gillies, John. *A Primer for Christian Broadcasters.* Chicago: Moody Press, 1955.

Higginbottom, Sam. *The Gospel and the Plow*. New York: Macmillan, 1926.

Highbaugh, Irma. *We Grow in the Family*. New York: Agricultural Missions, 1953.

Jones, Clarence W. *Radio, the New Missionary*. Chicago: Moody Press, 1946.

Loveless, Wendell Phillips. *Manual of Gospel Broadcasting*. Chicago: Moody Press, 1946.

Moody Institute of Science. *Suggestions for Missionary Film Production*. Chicago: Moody Bible Institute, 1950.

Moomaw, Ira W. *Deep Furrows*. New York: Agricultural Missions, 1957.

Standley, Robert R. *Flying Missionaries*. Nashville: Broadman Press, 1954.

IX. GENERAL

Abundant Life in Changing Africa. New York: Africa Committee, Foreign Missions Conference of North America, 1946.

Bavinck, Johan Herman. *The Impact of Christianity on the Non-Christian World*. Grand Rapids: Wm. B. Eerdmans Publishing Co., 1949.

Brown, Arthur Judson. *The Foreign Missionary*. New York: Fleming H. Revell Co., 1950.

Carver, William Owen. *Christian Missions in Today's World*. New York: Harper & Bros., 1942.

Dillon, William Simon. *God's Work in God's Way*. River Grove: Voice of Melody Publishers, 1957.

Fleming, Daniel Johnson. *Ethical Issues Confronting World Christians*. New York: International Missionary Council, 1935.

Freytag, Walter. *Spiritual Revolution in the East*. London: Lutterworth Press, 1940.

Goodall, Norman, ed. *Missions under the Cross*. London: Edinburgh House Press, 1953.

Hay, Alexander Rattray. *The New Testament Order for Church and Missionary*. Temperley: New Testament Missionary Union, 1947.

Kraemer, Hendrik. *The Christian Message in a Non-Christian World*. Grand Rapids: Kregel Publications, 1956.

Lamott, Willis Church. *Revolution in Missions*. New York: Macmillan, 1954.

Latourette, Kenneth Scott. *Challenge and Conformity*. New York: Harper & Bros., 1955.

———. *Missions Tomorrow*. New York: Harper & Bros., 1936.

Lindsell, Harold. *A Christian Philosophy of Missions.* Wheaton: Van Kampen Press, 1949.

——. *Missionary Principles and Practice.* New York: Fleming H. Revell Co., 1955.

McAfee, Cleland Boyd. *The Missionary Enterprise and Its Sincere Critics.* New York: Fleming H. Revell Co., 1935.

Manikam, Rajah B., ed. *Christianity and the Asian Revolution.* Madras: Diocesan Press, 1955.

Northcott, Cecil. *Voice out of Africa.* London: Edinburgh House Press, 1952.

Paton, David M. *Christian Missions and the Judgment of God.* London: Student Christian Movement, 1953.

Pulleng, A. *Go Ye Therefore . . .* London: The Paternoster Press, 1958.

Soltau, Theodore Stanley. *Missions at the Crossroads.* Grand Rapids: Baker Book House.

Vine, William Edwyn. *The Divine Plan of Missions.* London: Pickering & Inglis, n.d.

——. *A Guide to Missionary Service.* London: Pickering & Inglis, 1946.

Warren, Max A. C. *The Christian Imperative.* New York: Charles Scribner's Sons, 1955.

Westermann, Diedrich. *Africa and Christianity.* London: Oxford University Press, 1937.

Zwemer, Samuel Marinus. *Thinking Missions with Christ.* Grand Rapids: Zondervan Publishing House, 1935.

INDEX

375